Marcel Proust

A N D

D E L I V E R A N C E   F R O M   T I M E

Marcel Proust

AND

DELIVERANCE FROM TIME

By

Germaine Brée

Translated from the French
by C. J. RICHARDS *and* A. D. TRUITT

RUTGERS UNIVERSITY PRESS

NEW BRUNSWICK, N. J.

Translated from:
Germaine Brée, DU TEMPS PERDU AU TEMPS RETROUVÉ
Paris: *Société d'Edition "Les Belles Lettres,"* 1950

To Marguerite Lehr

TWENTY YEARS have elapsed since this book was first published in France. During that time there have been many additions to the materials available for Proustian studies. Of these the most important are certainly the three trunk-loads of manuscripts that Proust's niece turned over to the Bibliothèque Nationale in 1962: exercise books, notebooks, typescripts, proofs, a seemingly inexhaustible accumulation of documents, a kind of subsoil from which Proust's published work drew its substance. From these, two now well-known unfinished early works have been extracted and somewhat hastily published, a novel, *Jean Santeuil* (1952), and a collection of critical essays, *Contre Sainte-Beuve* (1954). As the chaotic mass of materials begins to yield to some order, the processes of trial and error out of which little by little *A la Recherche du Temps perdu* emerged can be more clearly discerned. No knowledgeable reader will ever again take up Proust's novel and read it as a fully constituted whole in quite the same way as before. It seems likely that in the next few years major attention will be devoted to those manuscripts and what they tell us about the genesis of the novel.

With the passage of time, critical methods too have been changing and Proust's book has proved rich and complex enough to support many diverse approaches. Our understanding of the work has thereby gained steadily in depth and diversity. As I reread this volume, I was reminded that I had written it, twenty years ago, from a coherent though quite particular point of view. I was at the time intent on solving certain problems of structure, concerned primarily to give a description of the form Proust had chosen for his novel because that form disclosed, it seemed to me, what Proust rather vaguely called his "vision." It was his purpose to communicate it through his novel. There are a great many things about Proust and about his novel that I know now and did not know then. But this study, based on many others that preceded it, was an initial effort to grasp *A la Recherche du Temps perdu* as a structured whole, an exhilarating experience. Therefore, I decided that a revision of any consequence in my study would tend to destroy its inner logic.

GERMAINE BRÉE

Madison, Wisconsin
October 4, 1968

CONTENTS

Marcel Proust

AND

DELIVERANCE FROM TIME

1

THE PROUSTIAN WORLD

I HAVE long had the habit of going to bed early." From this first sentence of Proust's novel the reader is carried along in search of he knows not what, bewitched by the voice of the "I," which lures him along the strange meanders of an inner Lethe. The whole of *A la Recherche du Temps perdu* is projected through the long, monotonous, almost muffled soliloquy of the "I." The narrator first presents himself in his secluded bedroom, shrouded in obscurity, an "amphibious man" emerging from the wavering borderland which lies between sleep and wakefulness. The brilliant, brittle society which his tale evokes will always be bathed in that obscurity. Occasionally, out of the depths of sleep, the narrator summons up an image or a feeling which seems to come from the distant past. From this nocturnal birth on the borderland of sleep, the Proustian world retains the unreal atmosphere, vaguely disquieting and menacing, of those magic gardens and palaces which in fairy tales spring up from the heart of darkness or from some strange forest. It is an atmosphere which accentuates that world's incurable frivolity, and suffuses it with poetry. The theme of the bedroom reappears like a leitmotiv; each décor is built up before our eyes and then disappears to make room for the next, as we go from that first night in Combray to the Champs Elysées, Mme Swann's drawing room, the Allée des Acacias, Balbec, Rivebelle, Doncières, the drawing rooms of the Faubourg St. Germain, Venice, Tansonville, to return finally to Paris. The theme of the bedroom, which precedes and often creates the décor, remains bound, as in the opening pages, to the world of inner and outer night. It is a vast immemorial domain where time no longer exists. There the Proustian world will disappear, carried away into a dual death, the oblivion of the past and the void of the future, an obliteration foreshadowed by the ludicrous and tragic puppets of the Guermantes reception at the end of the novel.

The presence of these successive rooms, and, with them, of the night, gives unity to the intermittent memories which the narrator records. But the deeper unity of the book, formed as it is of heterogeneous elements, lies in the arresting continuity of the solitary and persistent voice which out of that night creates a world. The initial coincidence of a solitary human voice and of the night poses the enigma which is at the heart of *A la Recherche du Temps perdu:* What is the value of the short span of a man's life as it emerges from the void of past and future? After a long search which is more an aimless wandering than a search, Proust's narrator experiences a sudden insight into the nature of human existence. He becomes aware of the marvelous reality of life, his own life, unique, irreplaceable, and nearly at an end. It is the quality of this life which Proust tries to recapture in his novel.

The book which he conceived for this purpose, and which he was unable to realize completely, is intentionally complex. It would not have been easy to grasp its broad outlines even if they had not been partially obscured by the accumulation of pages which he continuously added. The work begins to take shape only at the end of a slow and lengthy development which does not seem to be moving according to any pre-existing plan. Each fragment is at first read for itself alone, for example the episode of the madeleine, which conjures up the luminous world of Combray, a fragment often singled out for lengthy comment. The perspective, which clarifies not only the story of the narrator and the world into which he is plunged but also the very manner in which Proust constructed that story, becomes apparent only at the end of the whole voluminous work.

The Proustian world is so rich and abundant in material that the reader picks his way with difficulty through the myriad paths that crisscross the story. The fact that he is often in danger of becoming sidetracked by the fantasies and meditations which the various themes may evoke, no doubt explains why so many writers extract one of these isolated themes—semi-philosophical, metaphysical, psychological, or esthetic—and treat it as an entity exactly as though it had not originally been conceived by Proust as simply one among the many elements of a fictitious literary world. In *A la Recherche du Temps perdu* Proust created: three great artists—Vinteuil, Bergotte, Elstir; a future artist, the narrator; several semi-artists—Swann, Charlus, Bloch, Ski, Andrée's husband, and others; but no philosopher. When, once only, a philosopher appears (the Norwegian at the Verdurins' table at the Raspelière), he appears as an incidental and amusing character, not as a philosopher. In all his writings Proust indicated clearly and abundantly what he considered to be the essential rôle of any work of art: the direct apprehension and communication of an experience, the quality of which escapes analysis. This quality is translated into the work of art, from whence it emerges in the new relationships which the artist establishes among the elements which compose his work. A work of art, then, is for the artist a testimonial, for the public a revelation; it has no equivalent. In the domain of esthetics, its structure is intellectual, but its meaning is immediately communicable in that it transmits the sum total of an experience which logical thought could only succeed in formulating in part.

This conception of art is not peculiar to Proust. It links him to Baudelaire, for example, and in this respect he can also be compared with Bergson. But Proust gives it more generality. He applies it to all the arts: the humblest, such as the art of cooking, which is Françoise's special talent; the more frivolous, such as the art of elegance, in which the Duchesse de Guermantes excels; and the more ephemeral, such as the art of the great actress la Berma. Works of art, he also thinks, prove that there is in the life of every human being a level on which the essential process of living in contact with the world is itself a creation. On that level, we lead "unimaginable lives," "poetic lives" in "enchanted realms." Our contact with the world brings us knowledge, but a knowledge which remains inaccessible to the intelligence and so evades us; the "enchanted realms" remain invisible, lost, unexpressed. Since all life on this level is a creation, we can find no image, no mental concept ready-made to express it, the ready-made being the very opposite of the "unimaginable." While obscurely living this "unimaginable life," which is the essence of any individual existence, we acquire little by little "the habit of giving to what we feel an expression which differs greatly from our real experience and which within a short time we take for reality itself." [1] Thus, according to Proust, we are drawn away from our own particular experience of life by our intellectual sloth and by the inaccuracy of the verbal equivalents we use. We so thoroughly corrupt the nature of personal experience that in the long run "our thoughts and our lives are constituted by the chain of all our inaccurate expressions so that nothing remains of what we have really felt." [2]

Each individual substitutes for the reality of his experience a verbal mythology, and his understanding of life is further and further removed from what he actually feels. There is a complete separation between his life as he thinks about it and his life as he lives it. Only a work of art can expose the false and schematic nature of the substitution. The work is not an evasion, nor an embellishment, nor an aspiration toward something else, but simply precision of language, the expression of the real quality of an individual's contact with the world in which he lives. Since this contact is different in quality for each of us, it gives to each a unique value. There are as many potential works of art—as many potential expressions of the real quality of human beings—as there are human lives. In this restitution of life through art, Proust allots an important rôle to intellect, granted a genuine will to escape ready-made patterns. The intellect must observe the basic and unpredictable facts of individual experience, grasp their meaning, and strip them of the worn-out words—and hence worn-out ideas—that mask them. And the intellect must preside at the transmutation of the artist's experience into a work of art: it selects the means of expression, the forms through which this experience can be communicated.

When Proust amuses himself in his pastiches by reproducing a particular style, he shows how intellect traces a path back to the original experience underlying a work of art. Intellect can define the relations which determine the arrangement of a work of art because it is intellect which established these relations. Thus the narrator, meditating upon one of Elstir's canvases, understands that when Elstir painted the earth in terms of the sea, and the sea in terms of the earth, he was expressing something specific: his vision of the unity which, on the Norman coast, binds two elements—water-earth—habitually separated in our thoughts. From his analysis of Elstir's canvas, the narrator in turn gains access to Elstir's vision, which otherwise would have remained incomprehensible to him. He understands that its creative value lies in its exactness. The work of art, by virtue of its very arrangement a conscious act of intelligence, is the means by which one can gain access to the knowledge of what Proust calls a life that is "really lived," a "real life," not an exceptional or extraordinary life but an ordinary, daily life. This ordinary life we lead remains unknown to us because on the whole our habitual mental approach and our everyday words are inadequate to express it.

This is why the complex structure of *A la Recherche du Temps perdu* is, in itself, of prime importance, for it is by means of this structure, even more than by the analysis which accompanies it and which explains it only in part, that the nature of the Proustian vision can be grasped. And it is the

Proustian vision which explains why Proust found himself obliged to modify greatly the form of the novel.

The very first line of the novel raises the question of the identity of the "I," of the narrator to whom Proust only twice, as though inadvertently, gives his own name, Marcel. *A la Recherche du Temps perdu* is so closely linked to the life of its author that almost all the incidents it records have as their point of departure some actual incident in Proust's life. It is not unnatural that to many readers Proust and his narrator are one and the same person; few authors have become characters in their own fictional worlds to so great an extent. That confusion between author and character exists, is apparent from the many essays devoted either to the real man or to the fictional character. All too often Proust is wholly identified with the "I" of the novel as though his purpose had been to write an autobiography as such. Unquestionably Proust is present in the person of the narrator, both in Marcel's personality and in the story he literally "lends" him, borrowing abundantly from his own life. The incessant analysis in which the narrator indulges is also obviously inherited from Proust. But it is nonetheless true that a great part of Proust's experience goes beyond that of his narrator, and is embodied in numerous other characters. The presence of Proust transcends the "I" and permeates just as intimately the rest of the novel. Furthermore, Proust dominates his world from a far greater height than does the narrator in his introspections. The "I" is only one individual among others, but it is Proust who creates the force which moves the narrator's world. The "I" can only observe it, submit to it, and try to understand it.

At one time Proust considered telling the entire story objectively, employing the third person as in *Un Amour de Swann*. His use of the first person then, was the result of a conscious esthetic choice and not proof that he considered his work as a confession or an autobiography. "You may tell all," we are told Proust once said to Gide, "but on condition that you never say 'I.' " [3] Since Proust's novel is projected entirely through the "I," this would seem on the surface to be paradoxical, but Gide was speaking to Proust at that time about his autobiography, *Si le Grain ne meurt*, and Proust's comment bears not only upon the uranism particularly in question but upon the autobiographical genre itself.

Although in *A la Recherche du Temps perdu* Proust does not directly attribute the passions of Sodom and Gomorrha to the "I," the narrator is nonetheless very closely bound to these two worlds; but it is through him as an autonomous character in a novel that we discover them, not through Proust as the author of his autobiography. It is risky, then, to substitute the name of Proust for the pronoun "I" and thus explain Proust's character by borrowing freely from the narrator. There are certain passages, written toward the end of Proust's life and inserted into his text, in particular a whole section of *Le Temps retrouvé*, in which, harried by a sense of impending death, Proust seems to abandon fiction and speak directly in his own name. It is not easy, however, to separate what, under cover of the "I," comes straight from Proust and what comes only indirectly from him to his narrator, just as it does to Swann, Elstir, or some other character. This confusion is present in the text itself, for sometimes Proust speaks through the narrator but sometimes the narrator speaks for himself. If both Proust's novel and his life are first carefully examined as separate entities, they eventually throw more light one upon the other, and each is better understood.

Though it is true that the Proustian vision and the nature of the world it created can best be understood through an analysis of the structure of *A la Recherche du Temps perdu*, it is also true that the novel has a history which throws considerable light on some of its disconcerting aspects. Its story is unique and poses textual problems rare in contemporary work. The reader who is unfamiliar with the facts runs the risk of misunderstanding the novel, Proust's particular methods of composition, the very meaning of his world, and what he has tried to express.

It should be remembered first of all that this novel was

never really finished even though Proust wrote "Finis" at the end of his manuscript. When he died in 1922, he was still correcting the proofs of *La Prisonnière*, rewriting *Albertine disparue,* and working incessantly on some notebooks, written in longhand and almost illegible. A third of his monumental novel was published posthumously. What, one speculates, would have been the text of this last third of the book had Proust lived? Among the notebooks there is one, for example, which contains a whole episode of the narrator's stay in Venice not included in the novel. At the very beginning of his tale it is mentioned and, toward the end of the book, an episode does take place in Venice, but in relation to the importance given the city in the rest of the novel it seems very briefly considered. The episode in its present form seems to be a draft, a fairly advanced but not definitive draft of what Proust had in mind. Would Proust, had he lived, have given this passage greater importance? In any event, this entire section of the novel gains clarification from his notebooks, fragments of which appear from time to time in various literary magazines.*

But would Proust ever have actually finished his novel? In 1913 Grasset published *Du Côté de chez Swann,* the first of three volumes which were together to total fifteen hundred pages. But from 1914 to 1922, to the second and third volumes, which he had considered finished in 1913, Proust added about twenty-five hundred pages; the novel had almost tripled in size. During these years he added to his original plan a whole episode, concerning the narrator's love for Albertine, one of the *"jeunes filles en fleurs,"* which starts in the second part of *A l'Ombre des Jeunes Filles en fleurs.* This episode is worked into the text of *Le Côté de Guermantes* and appears suddenly, in sharp perspective, at the end of *Sodome et Gomorrhe;* in *La Prisonnière* and *Albertine disparue,* it dominates all the other themes. In order to incorporate it into his novel, Proust made many alterations in his text.[4] From a

---

* It was only in 1954 that the text of the notebooks was published.

careful reading of *Du Côté de chez Swann,* it can be seen that Proust was already in the habit of reworking and expanding his text, although he did not modify this first volume after publication. Though he added to the text of the other volumes after 1913, there seems to have been no significant change in his habits of working.

One of his notebooks, published in April, 1945, by *La Table Ronde,*[5] gives precise data on how Proust worked on his manuscript long before 1913. The notebook contains in a few admirably written pages a first sketch of the section of *Du Côté de chez Swann* which describes the two alternate directions taken by the narrator's family on their Sunday walks toward Guermantes and toward Méséglise. With this basic geographical theme the narrator already associates a whole series of other themes such as the rhythms of his emotional life and the rôle of literature in his discovery of the "poetry of landscape." These successive revelations slowly educate the narrator spiritually, and his inner discoveries remain linked in his memory to one or the other of the two places. He recalls the inner succession of almost physiological "seasons," the anguish of the evening, the joy of the afternoon, then the death of his Tante Léonie and the solitary, exhilarating walks in the country in the autumn.

The great Proustian themes are all here, gathered within a few pages and developed according to a plan which was not rejected or even basically modified in *Du Côté de chez Swann.* Each incident has simply flourished naturally in the novel, developing according to its inner necessity. Into the novel Proust also inserts new elements either by an association of ideas or in order to prepare for future developments. But in the notebook the passage is already oriented toward a specific goal, not presented merely according to the rhythm of reminiscence. It is already fiction. The whole development relating to the countryside around Méséglise and Guermantes, with the lessons which the narrator learns there, is carefully composed in order to lead to an important discovery.

"It is from these solitary walks that I took in the autumn

toward Méséglise that one of the fixed laws of my spiritual life dates." The "fixed law" which the hero discovers is that certain among the images he recalls have specific meaning for him. He recognizes them because of the pleasure they bring him. Then comes an experience well known to any reader of Proust: the railroad trip, workmen hammering on the rails, and later, in a moment of despair and boredom, the revelation. "It was tea time, my teacher had brought plates for our tarts . . . I had clumsily laid down my fork which rattled noisily on the plate . . . the sound of the fork hitting the plate had suddenly given me an impression of heat, thirst, summer, river . . . of a trip which intoxicated me."

Frightened, I walked as though I were carrying something precious, charged with a mission more important than I and that I had to perform. Afterwards I could die. I felt that I was living above myself, in a poetic truth which was born of the meeting of a moment present and a moment past, which was in some way beyond time and the individual, and that what might happen to me in time mattered little provided that the extra-temporal truth for which I had at that moment become the ecstatic repository were safely put into pages that would last.[6]

The happiness aroused by this sensation evokes Querqueville, the future Balbec of his novel. There, breathing "the fragrance of new soap," of the sun, of the trunk . . . "of the rumpled bed with its fine sheets," he realizes that the various mornings which this fragrance recalls have "a kind of common existence, permanent, more real than they, extra-temporal . . . which arouses in us, in order that we may enjoy it, a being who escapes from time, who lives above the present and the past, a poet." The passage ends by describing the joy these fragrances bring to poets:

They accomplish even more than that faith which gave hope of possessing an eternal soul, for they give us the sensation of the relativity of time, the immediate conviction of it; being eternal essences, they instantly arouse in us an eternal soul which can savor them and be exquisitely gratified by them. And these moments, during which our souls are superior to time and to the course of events, are the only ones in which we are happy.[7]

This is the theme around which *A la Recherche du Temps perdu* is built, the theme which develops in its full power only at the end of *Le Temps retrouvé* when the narrator discovers his vocation by means of a revelation. This revelation, experienced with joy, springs from the unconscious memory of the narrator, and assures his triumph over time and over death because it reveals to him the world of the "eternal essences" of which he is the repository.

The changes which Proust made in his text between 1914 and 1922, important as they are, remain in the normal line of the novel's development from its initial conception, which seems to go far back in Proust's life, to its final state at his death. However, already in *Du Côté de chez Swann*— but later more obtrusively—these modifications introduce contradictions into the text, variations in chronology, and unconscious repetitions. They explain the grammatical vagueness of certain passages in which Proust, introducing an episode by association, leaves a gap between the new paragraphs he is adding and the earlier sentence. In this respect *Le Temps retrouvé* is especially chaotic, for Proust did not have time to correlate the different elements of his text. Thus, at the end of chapter I of *Le Temps retrouvé*, the narrator resolves to break with society in order to retire to a sanatorium from which, in chapter III, he returns to Paris "sixteen years later." In chapter II the narrator tells of a stay in Paris in 1916, and we find sketchy allusions to 1914, 1918, and 1919. Chapter III begins: "My new sanatorium, to which I then retired, did not help me any more than did the first one, and a long time elapsed before I left it." The world to which the narrator returns is directly linked with the world of Tansonville in the first chapter, despite at the end some allusions to the war. The war years of chapter II were inserted in that "long time," in those sixteen years; no connection is made, and they disrupt the previous chronology of the book.

Other incompatibilities of all sorts, of more or less importance but clearly errors, can be found throughout the text. The history of the composition and publication of the novel explain how such errors occurred, and it is a mistake to try to justify them esthetically. Their importance is limited, and overestimated only if they are misconstrued. Proust himself, who insisted on the value of great unfinished works which remained, like his, partly in the workshop, never felt he had altered the fundamental structure of his novel, even though he was unable to finish it. On the contrary, in his correspondence he emphasizes the unity and precision which characterized the overall composition of the work. Given Proust's esthetic theories, it would have been strange had it been otherwise.

A la Recherche du Temps perdu is the story of the narrator's life, told in retrospect. Though it seems almost an apologia, his life is, in fact, a veritable triumph. As a child he dreams of certain very definite future accomplishments: he wants to go to Balbec, to Venice; to know the Swanns, the Guermantes; to be loved by a woman, several women, in some romantic setting; and, finally, he cherishes the vague but ambitious dream of becoming a great writer. His life is like a game of solitaire in which the cards, falling one by one, end by forming the one combination that makes the game come out successfully. As the years pass, one by one all these childhood dreams come true. He becomes intimate with the Swanns; at Balbec he meets a group of young girls all of whom later grant him passing favors in this exceedingly romantic setting. He enters the world of the Guermantes, and possesses one of the Balbec girls to the point of keeping her a virtual prisoner for a certain length of time in his apartment. Eventually, he goes to Venice. Then, as his last card and final triumph, he even attains his most problematical goal: he discovers he has a real vocation as a writer.

And all around him other successes accumulate: the

social successes of Odette, of Gilberte, of Mme Verdurin, of Legrandin, of Bloch and many others; the professional successes of Brichot, Cottard, Rachel; the artistic successes of Vinteuil, Bergotte, Elstir. In this respect *A la Recherche du Temps perdu* differs markedly from Flaubert's *L'Education Sentimentale.* The world of *A la Recherche du Temps perdu* is not ostensibly peopled with failures, mediocrities, or disabled characters; quite the contrary. Nor does the narrator belong to the rebellious line of the Werthers, Renés, Childe Harolds and other misfits in a life which they denounce as inadequate.

The narrator recounts the life of a wealthy and sensitive young man who, with a great deal of curiosity and, at first, pleasure, moves in the social circles of Paris—that particularly brilliant and elegant Paris which flourished during the quarter of a century preceding the First World War. He tells of his occupations, the visits he makes, the teas, dinners, receptions, and plays he attends. His only journeys are the seasonal trips which take him from Paris in the winter to Combray in the spring, and short social outings. When he does not go to Combray in the spring, he settles down in the Grand Hotel in Balbec, on the Normandy coast, in the vicinity of the châteaux country. He makes only one somewhat longer trip, a comfortable journey to Venice, a classic in his world.

Loved and coddled at home, the narrator is the focus of the attentions of two women, his mother and his grandmother; they are utterly devoted to him and their unfailing affection is mingled with anxiety about his delicate health. He lives in a hot-house atmosphere, waited upon day and night by an indefatigable old maid servant, Françoise, slave to all his whims. Except for an avalanche of social successes, very little happens to him: the death of his grandmother; a period of intense jealousy aroused by a woman, Albertine, who also dies; his ever-present illness which finally forces him to retire to a sanatorium. He leaves this sanatorium three times: in 1914, then in 1916, and finally for good sixteen years after having entered it. It is then, during a last social gathering, that he discovers his vocation as a writer. His story, though hardly a story at all, nevertheless contains within it, as he tells it, a whole world. It comprises not one but several "novels," parallel or successive, which pale and appear insignificant before the most exciting adventure of all: the life of this man as it belongs to him in its entirety when, by chance, he rediscovers it preserved intact in his memory.

The narrator distinguishes two stages in the life he has lived. The first is a long one during which all his dreams, except one, come true, but without bringing him any satisfaction, for the real world never fulfills his desires. The exception is his failure to become a writer. His life becomes more and more arid as we follow him from the world of Combray to his final return to Paris after the war. This long first period is followed by a second stage, contained in its entirety in the third chapter of *Le Temps retrouvé*, which lasts only a few hours to end in a sudden revelation, brief and awesome, a revelation which completely alters everything that has preceded it. Without this revelation the ground covered in the first stage of his life leads nowhere. Though extremely brief in comparison with the first period, it nevertheless imparts meaning to the road already travelled, the road which, at that moment, leads him to his destination. Yet the long first part of the novel is told by the man for whom the road as yet has no destination, the man without a recognized destiny, who does not know what awaits him. The further he goes, the more he despairs. Between this and the second stage stretches a long period of silence, those "sixteen years" of which the narrator speaks. Then, in a few brief moments the discovery of the meaning of his long journey totally transforms his point of view and forces him to re-evaluate everything that went on during its progress.

Thus it cannot be said that *A la Recherche du Temps perdu* is constructed "in a circle." When the story begins, a man who is no longer in his first youth is describing his awakening in the dark. At the end of a certain number of pages he has become a person, a nameless, featureless being, but one already identified by certain allusions, certain images, which come naturally to his mind and could only have been formulated by this particular individual. Among these images are those of rooms, the very rooms which are going to re-appear in the novel. His memory lingers particularly upon one of these, the room of his childhood, of his springs and summers in Combray. Then he tells us how one day in Paris this same man, aged, weary, sad, raises to his lips a madeleine soaked in tea. His sadness and weariness disappear, a feeling of joy pervades him, and from the depths of his mind, re-called by the taste of the madeleine, a memory slowly emerges. He concentrates upon it, recognizes it: it is Com-bray, the Combray of his childhood where in the morning he used to soak a madeleine in his aunt's lime-blossom tea.

It is only by chance that out of all the years he "holds in a circle around him," [8] he describes, lying in the dark, only those spent at Combray; he could well have described other moments which he mentions fleetingly. It is also only by chance that one day when he feels depressed, the savour of a madeleine again recalls Combray. So at the beginning of the book, twice, by chance, Combray is evoked for the narrator. But it is certainly not by chance that Proust, in order to re-create a life, takes us so conveniently back to Combray where the narrator's life began. Actually there is no real chronologi-cal confusion in *A la Recherche du Temps perdu*. The tale once started, the narrator on the whole follows quite faithfully a chronological line of development for each block of memo-ries he recalls. We move from his childhood in Combray to his adolescence in *A l'Ombre des Jeunes Filles en fleurs*. After *Le Côté de Guermantes* we pass without interruption to *Sodome et Gomorrhe, La Prisonnière*, and *Albertine dispa-rue*, as the narrator relates the events of his adolescence and of his life as a young man. He reappears as an older man in *Le Temps retrouvé*.

Combray evokes the life of the narrator from childhood

to the end of his adolescence, but without following any special chronological order. The "time" remains vague, and sometimes the narrator seems to juxtapose memories of quite different periods. On the whole, however, the narrator follows the normal time sequence, he grows older as the tale develops. The end of "Combray," which deals with the death of Tante Léonie, overlaps the beginning of *A l'Ombre des Jeunes Filles en fleurs*, although there is no merging of the two stories. In *A l'Ombre des Jeunes Filles en fleurs*, however, the indefinite nature of the recollections changes. The narrator's love for Gilberte lasts through one autumn, a winter marked by a New Year's day, another autumn, a second New Year's day, and ends the following spring. Between the end of this love and the first summer at Balbec, the narrator makes it clear that two years have elapsed. So *A l'Ombre des Jeunes Filles en fleurs* is the story of discontinuous events which take up about four years of the narrator's life.

Between the summer at Balbec and the beginning of *Le Côté de Guermantes* there is a chronological gap. But from Doncières to the death of the narrator's grandmother, to Albertine's second entrance upon the scene ("about one year" [9] after Doncières), to the Guermantes dinner, to the reception at the Princesse de Guermantes, which opens *Sodome et Gomorrhe* "about two months later," [10] time flows very evenly. It is actually "more than a year after" [11] the death of his grandmother, that is, the summer after his first winter in the society of the Faubourg St. Germain, that the narrator experiences the "intermittence of the heart" and so at last knows the reality of that death. From that second summer in Balbec we go straight to the autumn when Albertine comes to live with the narrator. Exactly three years have elapsed since the beginning of *Le Côté de Guermantes*. The narrator's great romance seems to elude chronology, although it unfolds in one continuous sequence in time until it ends in the oblivion of Venice. Nevertheless, the narrator states explicitly that Albertine's stay with him lasted one year, [12] and the whole episode only a little more than a year. There is another gap in time between the end of *Albertine disparue* and the beginning of *Le Temps retrouvé,* then the mention of successive dates, 1914, 1916, and the final return to Paris, "sixteen years after" the Venice episode. The main portion of the novel, from "Guermantes" to the Venice episode, therefore forms a continuous whole which unfolds chronologically, although only certain moments of it are high-lighted against the background of the seasons and the years.

The narrator evokes a continuous sequence of discontinuous memories which are grouped in homogeneous blocks; each of these blocks has a clear internal development, and they succeed one another as the narrator lived them. This construction by blocks of discontinuous memories made it possible for Proust to add continually to his novel. Until he finally returns to Paris, the narrator is talking of the past. Proust could insert new "blocks" of the past into the ones already evoked simply by juxtaposition. He had only to spin innumerable threads between them, cross references which bind them into a closely woven unity. When Proust modified his novel in 1914 by adding the Albertine episode, he could insert the entire incident after one of the other blocks without changing the fundamental structure of the story. He simply did what he had done before; he loosely related this new episode with the rest of the novel. But the Albertine episode necessarily comes before the "revelation" at the end. It, too, is told by the man who does not yet understand the meaning of his life, the man without a destiny. It is only in the first part of his novel, however, that Proust could make use of this method of construction.

The point at which the narrator arrives at the end of the novel cannot possibly be superimposed upon the point of his departure, for this would bring the esthetic validity of the novel's composition into question. The title of the book indicates a quest in which the narrator is engaged. How could he tell of his hopeless "search" if he already knew its successful outcome? The "revelation" at the end would then be faked; the climax of the novel would lose all its value. Only at that point are the narrator's eyes opened, and only then does he reach the end of his long despair. If the narrator had known at the very outset of his story what the end was going to be and had capriciously held in reserve the "revelation" as a surprise for the reader alone, his experience and the emotions it entails would take on the appearance of a cheap mystification for the reader. As a matter of fact, at no point before the last chapter of *Le Temps retrouvé* does the narrator expect, or even suspect, the end of his story which, as it proceeds, appears to him to be leading nowhere.

But at one point in the tale the narrator's position changes. During the long first section of the novel he is turned towards the past; at some unspecified moment in his life, a moment which comes after the period described in the introductory pages in which he recalls his awakenings and tells of the episode of the madeleine, the narrator, who, as we know, is already old, unhappy, dead to life, begins to evoke the past, to record the progressive frittering away of his life. In this whole section of the novel, Proust uses the imperfect tense, the tense of retrospection. In the very first lines of chapter III of *Le Temps retrouvé*, the predominant tense changes. We move into a dramatic tale launched by a series of verbs in the past tense, the characteristic tense for the literary narration of present events. This marks a sudden change in the narrator's orientation in time, a change which is dramatic, and absolutely essential in the structure of the novel. Just as he is about to enter the drawing room of the Guermantes, he has a "revelation" of what his work will be. He enters the drawing room, and his eyes are now turned toward the future, the future in which this work will be written. As he enters he finally sees "the future" before him, but it leads to another void, death, which is very close and the mark of which is already upon all the guests. It is in relation to this change in orientation that the novel is constructed, not in a circle but in a planned asymmetry.

The very nature of the narrator's revelation posed an almost insoluble technical problem for Proust. The narrator returns from his sanatorium having abandoned all hope of becoming a writer, persuaded of the futility of a life which has no value. What he suddenly grasps is precisely the value of that life, his own life as he has lived it blindly. Throughout the story, Proust had to solve a difficult problem: he had to present in its multiplicity the particular quality of a life, a quality which the narrator who tells the story would come to recognize only at the end, but which had actually always been present. Proust could have described his narrator's life objectively and brought the protagonist to an awareness of its value only at the end of the novel. But for Proust the value of the revelation is that it brings about a change in the relation between the narrator and his life as he lived it. It is not his life which changes; it is the narrator's own evaluation of it which is so dramatically altered. This is necessarily a subjective experience which could not be effectively recounted by a third person.

When he decided to have the story told in the first person, Proust had to have the protagonist create a reality which he does not perceive and which he will discover only at the end of the book, but which in fact exists throughout his story. The overture to *A la Recherche du Temps perdu* is Proust's solution to this technical problem. The man who in the introductory pages lies in bed in the dark carries within himself a forgotten world, lost to his consciousness, from which sleep salvages a few chaotic fragments. What has become of this world? This question starts the narrator off on his search. But since it is a lost world, a world submerged, how can the narrator describe it? He can reach it only by accidentally stumbling into it. The discovery that this inner world exists makes it possible for the narrator to become a writer. This is the essence of the whole story: the discovery can be made only because of this inner world and yet the narrator is out of touch with it when the story begins. How can he conjure up a world which he can only recapture at the end of the book? Proust solves this problem by means of the madeleine episode. Thanks to the madeleine, the narrator—and the reader

with him—experiences as an aged and weary man an enigmatic and extraordinary joy which is linked to the existence
within him of this world. The two facets of the enigma are
clearly discernible: how can two such contradictory worlds,
one sad and empty, the other rich and joyful, co-exist simultaneously in the same man? The reader is ready to set out
with the narrator "in search" of this inner world, and Proust
is able to create simultaneously for both reader and narrator
the world which the latter will much later "find again." The
episode of the madeleine foreshadows the revelation of the
end, but for the narrator it is only a "sign"; for Proust it is
a means of presenting his world in the double perspective
which is so fundamental to his design.

The world which the narrator brings to life is present for
us; but for him, perhaps, it is gone forever; this explains the
remarkable stability of this world. By means of a psychological analysis based upon the play of involuntary memory,
Proust can introduce into his story the perspective he needs.
His narrator can recall his past in all its richness while at the
same time he examines and judges it with the disillusioned
mind of the mature man who has seen his life deteriorate and
has forgotten what was significant. Proust had thus to construct his world on three superimposed levels: first as the
narrator thought he was living it at the time (an experience he can describe in detail through the device of the
madeleine); second as he judges it when he recalls it a long
time later; and third as he discovers it at the end. On the
first level the child, adolescent, or young man advances toward the future and his conception of life slowly changes. As
he grows older his point of view gradually comes to coincide
with that of the elderly narrator who looks backward at events
and sees them only in the light of what he has become. The
movement which carries the child toward the future is
stopped, immobilized, neutralized by the retrospective meditation of the man. The narrator meditates upon the disillu-
sioning changes in his life, not on that life itself. The child's
progress toward the future is thwarted, destroyed by the very

fact that the narrator's thought is oriented so entirely toward the past, for this past was the future the child so eagerly anticipated. This delicate equilibrium is shattered at the end when the narrator's revelation totally reverses his values. It is only then that the Proustian world takes on its real dimensions. Between the void of the past and that of the future the narrator catches a glimpse of the edifice of his own life, fashioned by time. This life is a joyous denial of that double void; it exists, it asserts its own existence, it is itself beautiful.

Proust's world is deliberately ambivalent. His narrator's life has two facets: it is totally without value when he examines it before the revelation of the Guermantes reception; it is infinitely precious yet exactly the same when he considers it after the revelation. The whole Proustian world reflects the same ambivalence. The lives of Swann, Odette, Charlus, which first appear to be wasted, become infinitely precious and valuable when the narrator sees them in their full mystery as Proust created them. For from the start Proust had to introduce into his universe that value which the narrator would eventually discover. He had to give it a quality which would contradict the increasingly pessimistic conclusions of the "I." As the narrator sees his life according to the perspective of "time lost" or of "time regained" its whole significance changes for him. The same holds true for the reader who, spellbound by the use of the first person, embraces the narrator's point of view to the end; but the journey is long, and the reader does not always take the last step which qualifies—without transforming—the vision inherent in the lengthy "time lost" section of the novel. The very existence of Combray, of Balbec, of the Verdurins, or of the Baron de Charlus is enough to counterbalance all the pessimistic judgments of the world formed by the narrator—perhaps also by the reader and by Marcel Proust himself. The overall architecture of *A la Recherche du Temps perdu* enables Proust to describe both the joyous reality of life and the manner in which it eludes the narrator. He then goes on to show that once the narrator has grasped the nature of reality it immediately transforms those things it touches, placing upon them the magic stamp of beauty and happiness.

A la Recherche du Temps perdu is a success story, but it is not concerned with ordinary, tangible success. The narrator attains his goal and his life becomes a success in Proust's sense when he passes from the inner perspective of "time lost" to the inner perspective of "time regained." The entire novel is constructed with this revelatory passage in view. The two great stages of his narrator's life are necessarily assymetrical, for the very essence of the second stage is that it is a revelation about the first. A short transition in the introductory passages of *Le Temps retrouvé* marks the passage from one to the other. It is a "return" to life by a quick succession of steps recalling in a few pages the slow movement of the narrator's life as it has gradually lost all meaning. In brief, what Proust has done is to describe the narrator's long, slow progress toward a goal which he perceives only intermittently, and often forgets altogether. Failure to reach this goal would destroy all the significance of his life; its attainment gives meaning to the very discouragements which have marked his road. The narrator passes from failure to success, but a success made possible only by his failure: the "time lost" during the first long stage of his journey becomes "time regained."

There is no question in *A la Recherche du Temps perdu* of a return to the past, nor is the novel composed "in a circle," that is with no beginning or end. It is concerned with the problems of destination, of attainment. The narrator's last long meditation upon his past allows him to sum up all the various stages of his journey. But it is itself a stage, the next to the last one that the narrator must cover before reaching his destination, a stage at which he almost stops. He draws up the balance sheet of his life, a balance sheet which life itself will undertake to rectify. But it has to be drawn up before it can be rectified. In the process the narrator evaluates life as he never has before. This evaluation makes of his meditation something more than a long and pointless journey into the past, even though he finally passes a judgment of sterility upon that past. For because of this judgment, the narrator takes one more step toward his goal. Even this step would be useless, however, were it not followed by another more important one. Proust, who constructed his work with the dual possibility of success or failure in mind, was well aware of this. A great many commentaries on *A la Recherche du Temps perdu* forget that, in the long run, it is not this lengthy meditation that contains the significance of the novel; it is contained in the real joy of the revelation of *Le Temps retrouvé*, a joy which encompasses the whole of Proust's work and illuminates it. This joy alone assigns their true value to the themes of the narrator's meditation because it makes clear that they are limited, that they refer only to a partial vision of life. When the narrator judges his life, his judgment must be subordinated to the fact that he is alive, a fact without which such an evaluation could never exist. The narrator's meditations can only inadequately translate his actual experience. They almost succeed in stopping him on the road to realization because they leave in shadow what is essential: the very joy of being alive.

2

FROM TIME LOST TO TIME REGAINED

THE world through which the narrator takes his long journey 'from "time lost" to "time regained" is strictly circumscribed geographically, but it is continuously being
modified by time. The entire novel takes place in Paris, in
Combray, an imaginary small provincial town near Paris, in
Balbec on the Norman coast, in Doncières on the railway line
from Paris to Balbec, and in Venice. But within these geographical limits Proust creates a constantly changing historical setting, and describes it with minute precision. For instance, let us take a detail which at first seems insignificant.
While still an adolescent, the narrator, riding in a carriage
with Mme de Villeparisis, is dazzled by Albertine's bicycle.
Later, with Albertine, he discovers from the automobile in
which they are driving, a Balbec which is entirely new to him;
later still, he pauses to look up at a lone plane flying over the
English Channel. The plane, like the bicycle and car, plays a
rôle in the affair of the young couple in Paris—the Paris
which the First World War canopies with planes. Each time
the narrator draws our attention to the new "accessory" which
accompanies the couple, carefully introducing first the bicycle, then the car, then the plane. He comments at some length
upon each of these inventions, emphasizing their novelty;
each of the three makes, like the telephone, its "debut," and,
at a given moment, becomes part of the narrator's world. If
we group these descriptions together, we see that they give
us a picture of change. From the Marquise's carriage to the
planes above Paris, time has passed; they locate the narrator
in a definite historical period.

Despite a few intercalations of dates, the novel as a whole moves slowly forward chronologically. The period of Swann's love for Odette can be set with some accuracy: Alexandre Dumas' *Françillon* has just opened; Jules Grévy is president of the Republic; Gambetta's funeral takes place; and in the avant-garde salons Wagner is the fashion until Beethoven in his turn gains favor with the snobs. We are unmistakably in the decade of the 1880's. Then Odette, who had been the "incarnation of the World Exposition of 1878," becomes in 1892 "the incarnation of the Allée des Acacias" of the Bois de Boulogne.[1] We move from the beginning of the Dreyfus affair to its heroic period. The Prince of Wales, a friend of Swann's, becomes King of England; the Boer War comes to an end. At the same time we progress through various fashions in dress, music, and literature to World War I and finally, as the novel draws to a close, we are projected into the postwar world. Minutely, and with infinite patience, Proust describes the apparently trivial changes which are typical of the era: descriptions of the salons, of men's and women's fashions, of the theatre; names of *couturiers*, caterers, restaurants, clubs; fabrics, furniture; mannerisms of speech and modes of entertaining. The abundance and precision of these details constitute a veritable March of Time. Proust plainly wishes to give us a direct awareness of time passing. He treats the people who inhabit his world in the same way. The most important ones make their appearance in *Du Côté de chez Swann* and remain throughout the novel: the Swanns, Charlus, the Guermantes, the Verdurins, to say nothing of the little family group of Combray, which includes Françoise. They too present a succession of physical changes, a physical history which reaches a climax at the end of the novel with the Guermantes reception.

It is within the framework of this world, at once permanent and changing, that Proust sets up the patterns of his hero's experience, and it is the very nature of this world which gives his experience significance. The narrator's life is bound up in every way with this constant change; it furnishes the very substance of his experience and guarantees its authenticity, since every human being must of necessity have a continuous physical existence from birth to death, an "historic" existence. The narrator's life is made up of uninterrupted physical contact with people and objects which are always changing. In addition, his life and his quest are conceived as a journey toward a knowledge of the world, a journey "toward truth that no one can make for us" because "truth is a point of view about things." [2] His story is the story of his successive "points of view." As he progresses, each new point of view imperceptibly replaces an old one, though he himself does not realize until much later that he has changed.

The starting point of the journey is the child's conception of things as he sees them at Combray. If the narrator is led, often without his being aware of it, toward an unknown destination, it is under the impulsion of this childhood vision. The world of Combray is simple and harmonious. It is centered around the family group, the "inviolate people of Combray," [3] from whom the child draws his unshakable convictions. He believes in the existence of an absolute good and an absolute beauty, which are manifest on this earth and which art unveils. These absolutes exist outside himself and are accessible, though only under extraordinary circumstances. He has only the vaguest idea of the nature of this world of absolutes, but to it he attributes all that seems to him real or mysterious in his experience, in his conversations, in his reading, in the pictures he sees, and so he affixes the realm of the absolute to existing places as yet unknown to him. Two paths lead from Combray toward the unknown, an unknown which physically exists: the road to Méséglise leading past Tansonville and Swann's château, which his family never enters; and the road to Guermantes which in their walks they never reach. The child has a constant, almost violent, sense of the exciting mystery and beauty of these two places. Tansonville and the Swanns, Guermantes with its traditions and its inhabitants come to symbolize for him the vague and glorious world of absolute values—moral, aesthetic and intellectual—in which he believes with such "passionate conviction." Everything relating even remotely to the names of Swann and Guermantes becomes magical for him, the substance of his desires and dreams.

The names of "Swann" and "Guermantes" draw to themselves whole sets of images, real or from the world of art, as do names of places like Venice and Balbec which the child dreams of visiting. Images and names are impregnated with all sorts of vague emotions, often suggested by books. Out of this chance conglomeration of ideas, images, and feelings a world evolves which is tied to real people and real places—a world which benefits greatly because the child associates it with the ideas he absorbed in Combray, particularly the idea of perfection and beauty. All the child's aspirations are fervently directed toward this world which alone comprises all the values in which he believes. He is convinced that if he can reach it he will know truth and beauty, and finally possess them. "Even my most carnal desires," the narrator states much later, "were always turned in one direction, oriented toward one dream; I could have recognized as their primum mobile an idea for which I would have sacrificed my life, an idea which at its centermost point, as in my daydreams during my afternoon readings in the garden of Combray, conveyed the concept of perfection." [4] With this perfection he always associates the idea of art: for him art is a sign that perfection exists. He thinks that by becoming a writer he can gain access to this dream world, since literature, like all the arts, is imbued with truth, beauty, and mystery. His dream world becomes a real object of "his stubborn and active desire." [5] If any name or image belonging to it touches him ever so slightly, he feels that life has suddenly become intensely real. Just as the fairy princess awakens when her prince appears, so the narrator awakens to life at the name of Swann or Guermantes, Balbec or Venice, and the "dust of reality is mixed with magic sand." [6]

The narrator eagerly starts along the path that leads to romance and, step by step, he becomes disenchanted. He wants reality to correspond exactly with his imaginary world;

Balbec, Venice, Gilberte, Swann, the Duchesse de Guermantes
must coincide with the vague images he has drawn from
books, pictures, and dreams. He wants his images to come to
life, to live up to his expectations, and to act according to the
standards which prevail in his dream world, which remains
nebulous but is harmonious and noble. Only one of his aspirations, the vaguest, is never put to the test of experience: his
desire to be a writer. The Swanns, the Guermantes, Balbec,
all lose their glory as he approaches them, and his magic
world is shattered. Everything that the "golden gate of imagination" has opened to him loses its value when he reaches
it through the "low and shameful gate of experience." [7] His
desire to attain the world of his childhood beliefs is so powerful that he tries to reach, one by one, all the people and the
places from which he expects the revelation of mystery and
beauty. He is led along strange roads, "roads which meander
nowhere or crisscross meaninglessly" or lead to "dead ends." [8]
But his belief drives him forward and prevents him from
being bogged down in routine. He gradually becomes familiar
with the world of objective reality. And beyond its superficial
aspects he discovers another reality which is not at all beautiful, mysterious, and precious, and which for a long time he
refuses to accept.

He discovers that everything within himself as well as
everything outside himself is subject to the inexorable law
of change and falls more or less rapidly into oblivion. Nothing seems able to check this ebb; it deprives the present of
all significance. Imagination, desire, memory, or to a greater
degree, love and jealousy, may occasionally create worlds that
appear to be more stable; their reality may even seem temporarily unquestionable. Actually, however, they are no more
real than the dream world in which he moves when he has had
a little too much to drink, or during his sleep. His emotions
always project upon reality the same monotonous patterns.
But the world of these patterns is rapidly destroyed by his
inability to remember the past and so give them form. Life
is a series of interrupted moments in which the human being,

like Sisyphus, repeats unendingly the same meaningless gestures. The constant movement of life itself is monotony. Beneath it the narrator gradually discerns a kind of permanence; he distinguishes certain laws which regulate change itself. The world then appears to him as though viewed through a kaleidoscope. The innumerable elements of the kaleidoscope are always identical; they merely combine to form different patterns. Each new pattern presupposes a former one which it has replaced and thereby destroyed. But the patterns of life differ in one fundamental way from those of a kaleidoscope: the changes are irreversible, for the elements themselves are continually being altered by time. No combination can appear twice.

In people this alteration is invariably degradation. Every natural impulse, like love for example, which at first gives an illusion of freedom, soon becomes trapped in mechanical and automatic routines. All the characters who surround the narrator undergo this degradation; all that at first seems unexpected in them becomes banal. The narrator struggles, more or less conscientiously, against the stifling bonds of habit, but its mechanisms are as automatically released in him as in others. They function in a vacuum, and as often as not are set in motion by mere circumstance; they subtly destroy all possibility of development. The situations may change but the mechanical responses to them are always the same, and show that any apparent development in personality is a sham: the sameness of Swann's loves before and after his love for Odette, of the narrator's loves after he has forgotten Albertine; the sameness of all the salons despite their minor variations. Certain people, like the narrator's grandmother, may seem for a long time to escape degradation, but only to be subjected to it later even more brutally and dramatically. Nothing illustrates this more mercilessly than the narrator's account of his grandmother's illness. He gives us a pitiless description of a human being who rapidly becomes physically and morally exhausted, and dies. Pitiless also is the picture of her degradation in her grandson's dreams, which record his progressively dimmer remembrances of her until at last she vanishes completely even from his memory. The narrator notices, first in others then more slowly in himself, that individuals whose initial response to life seems entirely new are in fact rigidly confined within the spatial and temporal limits of their families, their period, their ancestors. These responses are a veritable mosaic of separately inherited characteristics which manifest themselves successively or simultaneously in combinations which appear to be new but which have virtually long been present in them. They really have no future. The narrator himself ends up by reproducing one by one all the little quirks of the group of adults who surrounded him at Combray, from his father's preoccupation with the weather to Tante Léonie's neurasthenia which keeps him, as it kept her, shut up in one room. The same holds true for the "social organisms" which the narrator observes with such passionate interest in the salons of the Faubourg St. Germain, and follows from their beginning to their end. He describes at length the salons of the Verdurins, of Odette, Mme de Villeparisis, the Duchesse de Guermantes, and many others, cataloguing the thousand phases of their disintegration.

Instead of the splendid world of his childhood dream, the narrator now sees only a rather ludicrous, senselessly whirling universe controlled by a system of abstract laws. After living through a series of varied experiences, social, emotional and intellectual, he finds himself enclosed within rigid mechanical patterns of repetition. At first he had thought he was moving toward the magic kingdom projected at Combray, but once he has discerned the laws that determine his actions all he can do is helplessly observe them at work as they infallibly determine his own behavior—his and that of the many people with whom he associates who all together constitute his historical milieu, the world in which his own history must unfold. There is nothing unknown toward which he can progress, either inside himself or outside.

But deep within him there still remains a trace of his

childhood faith. It now takes the form of permanent dissatisfaction because it is repeatedly betrayed by his experience. Each time he attains one of his goals, the Swann's salon or the world of the Guermantes, Albertine's presence then her departure, his unsatisfied desire for perfection prevents him from accepting it, and urges him to exact something more from life. On another level he is affected by a set of experiences which move him deeply but unconsciously. He is never able to explain them to himself lucidly, but they inject into his life sensations of joy or pain so intense that he is freed from the mechanical routine of his life and becomes sensitive once again to its challenging mystery. An exultant and inexplicable joy sometimes takes possession of him even while he is still a small child, and quite often later, at moments when he comes into contact with certain aspects of the sensory universe—a hedge of hawthorn, for example, or three church spires seen from a buggy in motion, or, much later, an apple orchard, or a solitary pear tree in bloom in a Paris suburb. Later, when he has acquired "a past," an unexpected joy surges up in him when some sensation, like the taste of the madeleine, stimulates his involuntary memory to recreate some forgotten moment of the past. Elstir's canvases or Vinteuil's "Septet" transport him into a state of deep and serene concentration, as though he were surely approaching a mystery implicit in their very existence and which they alone could elucidate. He does not connect these experiences, which are stored away deep in his memory, but they are always accompanied by an intense sensation of mystery and joy which he recognizes as belonging to his childhood days in Combray.

In sharp contrast to such moments of delight, he is at times, and particularly when he is involved with human beings, stricken by a sharp anxiety. Because he cannot control the pain they cause, he feels how real people are and how inaccessible. The Combray child, securely protected as he was by the family, knew that anxiety. It would well up within him at bedtime, and he thought that what he urgently needed was his mother's presence reinforced by her kiss. The same anxiety seizes him when the memory of Montjouvain casts its shadow upon Albertine, and the woman whom he believes he knows so well suddenly becomes enigmatic. It is then that he is brought face to face with the "unimaginable" reality of suffering. Later, after the death of his grandmother and of Albertine, a chance sensation suddenly awakens the love which he had felt for them, a love which he believes to be dead; it surges forth in all its stark reality. His very grief is evidence that these people had had an existence independent of his own, and were now annihilated. Their absence is the source of his suffering; their "real" deaths create his "real" suffering, which is an inescapable reality.

These experiences of joy and anguish are "intermittent." They remain isolated and unproductive because for a long time they seem unrelated to each other, and the narrator gives them little thought. Only once does he seize upon one of them and, instead of letting it dissolve in reverie, tries to give it some clear expression in words. As he sits in Dr. Percepied's buggy, he tries to express verbally the exact impression produced by the three spires of Martinville and Vieuxvicq. This simple act intensifies the delight he feels, and induces in him an almost physical gaiety. He does not repeat the experiment. In the face of M. de Norpois' disapproval, the narrator, then an adolescent, decides that he must find his literary inspiration elsewhere. In the narrator's mind the association between these "joyful sensations" and his vague desire to become a writer remains to the end alive but unconscious. Only Vinteuil's "Septet" seems enigmatically to offer him, in its joy and its sadness, something like an equivalent of his own recurrent impressions, a denial of the futility and insignificance of life.

Little by little, the narrator's hope that life holds for him some enigmatic truth is crushed beneath his experience of life as it appears in the "sterile logic" of intelligence. He reaches the last stage of despair at the beginning of *Le*

Temps retrouvé; all his literary hopes are swept away along with his belief that there is a mysterious significance in life. The last surviving hopes of the Combray days succumb, and with them goes the delight that the "joyful sensations" have always brought him.

After a long period of conflict between grief and forgetfulness, the narrator's love for Albertine vanishes, like everything else, into the oblivion of the past. In Venice old fantasies are reborn; the narrator dreams of seducing the Baronne de Putbus' chambermaid, for example. The obsessive world of jealousy in which he had lived with Albertine is dissolved; his great drama becomes an insignificant episode, and seems no different from other such episodes. A visit to Tansonville follows, and there the narrator is faced with a problem of value bearing upon his whole life. The Combray of his childhood, every recollection of which has hitherto retained its power to make life desirable, has now lost its potency. "It made me sad that last evening as I went up to my room to think that I had not once gone back to see the church at Combray." [9] To this grief is added another. Only one of his Combray dreams has remained intact, simply because it has remained a dream, that is the desire to become a writer. The narrator has slowly come to believe that he has no talent and has gradually given up his vague plans to write, but he holds on to one last belief that through art, including literature, it is possible to grasp a form of truth which has escaped him. The works of Bergotte, Elstir, and Vinteuil have taught him that such truth can come only if the artist has a direct and personal contact with the world in its full reality. He now begins to question this last article of faith:

When, before blowing out my candle, I read the passage transcribed below, my lack of aptitude for writing, about which I had had misgivings on the way to Guermantes, misgivings which had been confirmed during this last evening of my visit . . . appeared to me less regrettable, as though literature did not reveal a profound truth; and at the same time it seemed to me sad that literature was not what I had thought it to be.[10]

The passage which the narrator reads at that point is a skillful pastiche of the *Goncourt Journals*. It describes a salon the narrator knows all too well, the salon of the Verdurins. But the description in no way corresponds to his own recollections, either because he has not known how to appreciate the value of what he saw, or—and this is a more shattering hypothesis—because literature is nothing but falsehood and merely cloaks life with an "illusory magic." The question he now asks marks the pivotal point of the whole novel. If literature deceives us as to the value of life, covering it with an "illusory magic," then the narrator's life is entirely lost, lost because what he has sought is precisely that value which literature, like all the arts, seemed to guarantee. The question remains unanswered until the time when, "sixteen years later," the narrator returns to Paris. Then, as in a classical tragedy, the drama of his life is resolved in twenty-four hours, passing through a crisis and two possible solutions, one bringing disaster, the other achievement:

During the trip back to Paris by train, my thoughts turned to my lack of literary talent, a talent which I had once, on the road to Guermantes, believed I possessed and the lack of which I had admitted with so much sadness in my daily walks with Gilberte before coming home to a late dinner at Tansonville; the talent which, while I was reading a few pages of the *Goncourt Journals* on the eve of my departure from Tansonville, I had more or less identified with the vanity, the falsehood of literature. My thoughts were less painful perhaps, yet drearier, when I dwelt not upon my own weakness, peculiar to me only, but upon the *non-existence of the ideal in which I had believed*. For a long time I had not thought of this disillusionment, and it struck me with a force more distressing than ever.[11]

Then only does the narrator experience the last stages of disenchantment:

It was, I recall, when the train stopped in open country. The sun shone halfway down the trunks of a row of trees which bordered the roadbed. "Trees," I thought, "you have nothing more to tell me, my cold heart no longer hears you. Here I am in the midst of nature's beauty, yet it is with indifference, with boredom, that my eyes note the line that separates your luminous foliage from your shadowy trunk. If I had ever thought myself a poet, I know now that I am not." A little later I had noted, with the same indifference, the gold and orange light with which the same setting sun was speckling the windows of a house that seemed to be built of a strange rosy-colored substance. *But I had made these various observations with the same absolute indifference* as if, strolling in a garden with a lady, I had noticed a piece of glass, and a little further on an object similar to alabaster, the unfamiliar color of which did not rouse me from my overpowering lassitude and as if, out of politeness for the lady, I had said something to show her that I had noticed the color and pointed out in passing the tinted glass and the piece of stucco. In the same way, and only to clear my conscience, I had pointed out to myself, as though to someone who might be accompanying me and who might have derived more pleasure from it than I, the flame-like reflection in the windowpanes and the rosy transparency of the house. But the companion to whom I pointed out these curious effects was doubtless of a nature less enthusiastic than many well-disposed people whom a beautiful view delights, for he had noticed these colors *without any shadow of joy.*[12]

Even the "joyful sensations" have lost their power. The peculiar beauty of certain images in nature no longer holds any appeal. Beauty is nothing but a frivolous object, a bit of glass or stucco which can be used to fill the emptiness of a conversation. All this while, therefore, the narrator has been in quest of something which was at the very start illusory. His life has been wasted; it has been a sort of meaningless digression. Now he may as well return to the pettiness and boredom of daily life. He has, in fact, let life pass him by without grasping it, doubtless because there is nothing to grasp. " 'It was hardly worth depriving myself of worldly pleasures,' I said to myself, 'since I am not, or am no longer, equipped to do the precious work which I hoped every day that I would start on the morrow. I am not suited, or am no longer suited, to the task and perhaps it no longer even corresponds to any reality.' " [13]

Just as the narrator has reached this dead end the novel pivots completely. He has given up of his own free will any attempt to direct his own life. The magic world of Combray has been destroyed, section by section. The narrator abandons it, and with it goes the faith that gave it its vitality. Stripped of all preconceptions and preoccupations, he enters the real, the present world, the world which he left a long time ago, and which he has forgotten. He is a man without a past and without a future, without memory and without aim. Rapidly, but by successive stages, he then undergoes a series of experiences which contradict all his pessimistic conclusions and bring him finally to the end of his journey.

He sees before him an invitation which bears the name of Guermantes. Guermantes—the name means nothing to him now; it merely serves to designate a group of uninteresting society people among others no different from themselves. He decides to go to the concert to which he is invited. "But," he notes, "it was only because of the name of Guermantes, a name which I had not thought of for so long a time that, as I read it on the invitation, it caught my attention, stirred the depths of my memory and brought to light a portion of the Guermantes' past, and with it all the images of ancestral forests and long-stemmed flowers that I used to associate with the name in Combray." [14] Slowly the mystery of life emerges again. The narrator continues "to reread the invitation until the moment when, in revolt, the letters composing a name as familiar and as mysterious as that of Combray, asserted their independence and traced before my tired eyes a name which seemed unknown to me." [15] From this moment, as in a dream, the narrator is plunged into a strange atmosphere. He becomes physically conscious that he is moving in the midst of a reality which is different from the one which his senses perceive. Just as the name of Guermantes comes to life again clothed in all its former prestige, a place, the Champs-Elysées, now introduces him into a realm the magic of which is not "illusory." His carriage travels through the streets that lead to the Champs-Elysées:

They were very badly paved at that time, but from the moment I entered them I was recalled from my rêverie by a sensation of extreme smoothness; the carriage seemed to roll along more easily, quietly, as when the gates of an estate are opened and the carriage glides over a driveway covered with fine sand or dead leaves. Actually it was nothing of the sort, but I suddenly felt that the road before me had been cleared of all obstructions, as though it were no longer necessary for me to make any effort of adaptation or attention such as we unconsciously make in new situations. The streets through which I was now traveling were the long-forgotten ones I used to take with Françoise when we went to the Champs Elysées. The very soil seemed to flatten itself in my path. And like an aviator who after clumsily taxiing on the runaway suddenly "takes off," I rose slowly toward the silent heights of remembrance.[16]

His detachment is complete, detachment from the Combray world of belief and aspiration, detachment from the world of logic, detachment from the real scene before his eyes, which is physically present in the jolts of the carriage but which he neither sees nor feels:

When I arrived at the corner of the Rue Royale where the street vendor used to set up the stall showing the photographs Françoise loved, it seemed to me that the carriage, drawn by the hundreds of times I had turned there, could not help but turn of its own accord. I was not crossing the same streets as those trod by the strollers who were out that day; I was traveling through a sad sweet past that glided by me.[17]

The past is still enclosed in this sensation, the equivalent, in its empty uniformity, of the imaginary world of magic lanterns into which the Combray child projected his dreams. It is at that moment that M. de Charlus, half paralyzed, terrifying and grandiose, appears before his eyes. Like the world of Combray, M. de Charlus is stripped of everything that had once seemed to define his personality. Of his aristocrat's pride, as well as of his inimitable conversation, there remain only studied gestures and a quavering stammer. Yet, grandiose and indomitable, he looms up before the narrator at the entrance of the Guermantes house:

It was with an almost triumphant harshness that he repeated in a level tone, stammering slightly and booming sepulchrally: "Hannibal de Bréauté, dead! Antoine de Mouchy, dead! Charles Swann, dead! Adalbert de Montmorency, dead! Baron de Talleyrand, dead! Sosthène de Doudeauville, dead!" And each time the word "dead" seemed to fling upon the deceased a great spadeful of earth, hurled by a grave digger who was anxious to rivet them more firmly in the grave.[18]

The narrator approaches the Guermantes' house to the refrain of this leit-motiv, dead, dead, dead, to which he pays no attention; he is again a living being, but a divided one. The pleasure born of his ride through Paris has no echo in his intelligence, which has remained far behind and has not caught up with the new feeling which now nevertheless orients the narrator away from the present toward the past:

I now tried to bring out other snapshots from my memory— especially snapshots of Venice, but the very word "snapshot" was enough to make it all seem as boring to me as an album of photographs; I felt no more taste, no more talent, for describing now what I had seen in the past than I had felt yesterday for describing what I had so minutely and drearily observed. In a minute or two I should be besieged by friends whom I had not seen for years, who were doubtless going to ask me not to isolate myself again, to spend my days with them. I should have no reason to refuse them, since I now had the proof that I no longer was good for anything, that literature could no longer give me any pleasure, either through my own fault, since I was too little gifted, or because literature itself really was not so imbued with reality as I had thought.[19]

It is at this point that all the narrator's previous conclusions are instantly and totally refuted, in a moment of emotional conviction which owes nothing to his intellect. He suddenly finds himself emerging in the dimension of those "joyful sensations" which he had tended to neglect. A streetcar passes, forcing him to step aside, and he places his foot on a paving stone which is a "little less high than the one next it," a discrepancy in level exactly like that once felt by his foot as he entered a bapistry of St. Mark in Venice:

All my discouragement vanished before the sense of happiness which I had already experienced at different moments in my life, at the sight of trees I had thought I had recognized when driving around Balbec, at the sight of the spires of Martinville, in the savor of a madeleine dipped in herb tea, in so many other sensations I have mentioned and which the last works of Vinteuil seemed to me to synthesize. Just as they had been dispelled when I tasted the madeleine, all my worry about the future, all my intellectual doubt again disappeared. The misgivings which had assailed me a short while ago as to the reality of my literary gifts, and even as to the reality of literature itself, were banished as if by magic. This time I firmly resolved not to remain in ignorance (as I had done on the day that I tasted the madeleine) as to the reason why, without my having worked out any new line of reasoning or found any decisive argument, the difficulties that only a short while ago had seemed insoluble, now had lost all significance.[20]

At last, and it is clear that the episode of the madeleine is long past, the narrator's intelligence and attention are going to turn inward. The long quest which started in Combray and which the narrator has recalled, beginning with the experience of the madeleine, has been fruitless because the seeker has followed the wrong road. His error is one he has observed as common to all human beings, for "during the whole course of our lives, our ego consistently envisions the goals which the self deems precious, but it fails to observe that very self which never ceases to examine these aims . . ." [21] It is only when he has rejected all the aspirations which in his childhood he designated as "precious" that the narrator finally turns toward the "I" which is himself. This marked change in orientation, which coincides with a change in his orientation in relation to time, prepares the transition from "time past" to "time regained," the transition which the experience of the madeleine had failed to set in motion. It is essentially an intellectual conversion, but not a sudden one; it had already started with the reappearance of the word "Guermantes," and had become progressively more pressing during the trip through the Champs-Elysées. But at that time it had not reached his consciousness. In his conscious thought, he was still in the grip of despair and ready to give up all hope. Life now overtakes thought, which is obliged to turn towards it, though the process is not immediate. There are no abrupt mutations in the Proustian world.

Entirely by chance as far as the narrator is concerned, but clearly because Proust decreed it deliberately, the narrator now joyfully "regains" his life in an orderly progression, beginning with Venice which a moment before meant nothing but boredom and which now, thanks to the uneven paving stone beneath his foot, is dazzling and luminous. Later, at the reception, a spoon clatters upon a plate and he "regains" the row of trees which, twenty-four hours before, he had contemplated from the train without the slightest interest. In orderly retrogression in time, Balbec takes its place beside Venice, and the sight of a volume on the bookshelves of the library, *François le Champi*, brings back to life the painful bedtime drama at Combray. His whole world of "joyful sensations" comes surging back with its ecstasy and its anguish, and fills him with delight, a delight which is an end in itself, unique and self-contained, and independent of any intellectual concept.

Until this moment the narrator has never reached any equilibrium in his relation to time. As he lived his daily life, he continually projected himself into an anticipation of the future. As he re-lived his life in his long meditations, beginning with the episode of the madeleine, he lived it in retrospect. He now focuses upon the present and takes stock of what exists within him. He had thought of the external world as spatially changeless and of time as forever passing. What he finds within himself is the exact opposite: a timeless world whose spatial dimensions perpetually change. It is an ordered world structured on natural laws of coherence, quite independent of the fragile human creature who is the receptacle of it.

Within the world of universal change, of universal relativity to which he belongs, an absolute world has coalesced; formed by the hazards of an individual's life, discovered by chance in an individual's sensation, it is doubly gratuitous. There is no logical explanation for its existence, yet because it exists, all the narrator's doubts are banished. It brings him the proof that there has been a real continuity in his life and that all his evasions were evasions in relation to a self which is permanent. Because this self is permanent, it eludes our intelligence since our intelligence allows "the chain of days to slip by and in our journey through time recognizes as real only the place where we are at a given moment." [22] It is because he has never taken into account the existence of this inner being that the narrator could observe in himself only incoherence and chaos.

Simultaneously, he discovers his literary vocation: he must give this world an expression worthy of it; he must find its literary equivalent. Now he "regains" time in a twofold guise.

In the first place, the world within him is not abstract; it contains in its entirety the rich substance of what was a moment in time as it was actually lived. That is why only involuntary memory can adequately restore the past: any moment in time which does not totally disappear from the narrator's conscious memory is lost because it always undergoes immediate change, the multiple transformations born of dreams, imagination, memory, and emotions. It is caught in the general evolution of human beings in time. That is also why the narrator's sixteen years' absence, during which the name of Guermantes and of the Champs Elysées stop evolving in his consciousness, prepares the resurrection of what they really were for him in the past. Absence, like involuntary memory, makes possible a direct synthesis between two separate moments, one present and one past, both free from the disintegrating process of time.

In the second place, as he realizes this extra-temporal being which is within him, he also realizes that his own life is measured out in absolute time. He sees that there will be an end to the monotonous succession of phenomena which life brings, and that even the unchanging reality he perceives will cease to exist for him. Each part of the inner world which he now perceives defines a duration which tends toward an end, the span of a man's life, which for each man is an absolute. Only the spirit can transcend time; the human body is rigorously subject to its passing. Death, as proclaimed by M. de Charlus, is a stark reality. The narrator grasps this fact at the Guermantes matinée, which is suddenly transformed into a sort of Last Judgment with the baron in the rôle of the Angel of Doom. That which binds together all these people who are already on the threshold of death, that which gives them form and substance, the narrator sees, is time, their time, the meeting place common to them all, the medium which holds them in suspension and which will vanish with them. He had dimly perceived this truth once before. One day, after a long absence, he caught sight of his grandmother's face; in that instant he saw her objectively, without the blindness of love and habit, saw that she was aged and ravaged, and "suddenly . . . in our drawing room she belonged to a new world, the world of time." [23]

It is only within this span of a lifetime, rigorously ticked out by the clock—as the narrator immediately understands —that the world of which he is the repository can exist. He is in full possession of himself, and observes the faces around him objectively, with the detachment born of many years' absence. Time has clearly marked all these people who were once "known" to him. All are in more or less advanced stages of immobility, of death. The Baron de Charlus is at the very brink of death; no stimulus awakens in him the life that has indeed "passed," though occasionally a visual impression releases in his body a meaningless, automatic gesture. The narrator now takes the last step on the road to revelation. He finally sees himself objectively, moving toward death, like all the people around him, along the trajectory of time, and he realizes that the clock imposes its peremptory conditions on his work. If he is to produce a work of art, he must do so in the short space of time that is allotted to him; he will literally have to work in "time regained." He is now at the end of his quest, and his point of view is decisively changed. Instead of seeking outside for a world he had built up within himself, he accepts this world which has come from outside. And thus he discovers that within himself there is a reality which is at once external and subjective. He takes possession of this world, and in so doing he realizes the objective limits of his existence, for at the same time this world in turn possesses him. He is already close to death.

It is not merely by chance that death looms so large in the narrator's tale. There are no fewer than seven deaths, of which four are important and consume many pages: Swann's slow death, the grandmother's brutal death, Bergotte's serene death, and Albertine's violent death followed by a second slow death in the narrator's memory. Aside from the deaths of the characters, death is one of the fundamental themes of the novel: the death of memory, of feeling, of hope, of society. All human life gradually disintegrates, inexorably moving toward final oblivion. Now, instead of trying to stop that movement, the narrator, in his novel, will bring together life and death—those two contradictory and inseparable facets of experience, long foreshadowed in the ecstasy aroused by his "joyful sensations" in Combray and in the anxiety which at night held him in its clutches. The narrator relives the anguish of bedtime in Combray when he reads on the cover of a book the words *François le Champi*, but his pain is encompassed by a greater joy; so, in a work of art, life triumphs over death, which it encompasses. For in art, life is present in all its immediate brilliance; it has been rescued from the twofold oblivion which threatens it, and yet it preserves intact the transitory substance of time. Through art the narrator can rise above his own death. Ephemeral though he be, he can leave proof of his own existence in a world which he makes immortal by translating it into objective and communicable form. This world will refute the oblivion of death which will inevitably envelop him.

The narrator has reached the end of his journey; not by an intellectual process but by direct experience he has discovered the answer to his question. Behind him stretches a road on which no step has been futile, which no longer seems to have meandered along aimlessly for it has led him to a definite destination. As for Proust, his novel is finished. Not content to allow his narrator merely to give us an account of his psychological evolution, he deliberately created both a particular world, occupying a definite place in the course of history, and a human being who in his journey through this world comes to understand it. He had to depict the physical characteristics of that perpetually changing world in order to show how it coexisted with the closed world of the individual, a world which reaches its conclusion in death. Since the narrator must discover all these elements for himself, Proust's universe had to contain them: the physical reality of change, the strict determination of the narrator's development, the climate of his inner life and its fluctuations. At the same time Proust had to fashion the stable and rich world which slowly emerges in a coherence of its own from the apparent discontinuity of the narrator's experience. He had to make sure that the whole complex background was present in his novel in full detail. For it is from this background that the various stages of the narrator's quest develop, each putting into relief one aspect of his total world without eliminating its other potentialities.

Stage by stage, the narrator must advance in his discovery of that world until he grasps it in its totality; but the possibility of that total discovery had to be implicit in each of the successive stages through which he passes and which he describes without recognizing their significance. No element of complexity, nothing which was not present in some form in the preceding stages could be contained in each of the successive stages. Everything must be there for its potential development. Proust carefully set up his narrator's world so that from the beginning it has all the elements which he eventually discovers. It contains all the unique and rich substance of life to which the narrator's sensory perceptions give him access, to which he owes the glorious moments which his memory later salvages: the sea at Balbec, Odette's walks in the Bois, the hawthorn and the apple trees, so steeped in poetic beauty. His world also includes all the ordinary stages, with the appropriate motivations and reactions, through which men pass from birth to death, and through which the narrator also must pass; all these, particularly the psychological reactions, are the elements of human experience in time. What Proust succeeds in bringing about is an authentic adventure in the two kinds of time which he created. Time sweeps the narrator along in a continual flow, but it is also creating for him an inner structure; and this structure, formed from the accumulated impressions which define his real lifetime, is completed only with death. For Proust, unquestionably, a work of art is the projection of a continuing experience of which time is the essence.

In order to enter the world of reality, the narrator necessarily starts from those facts of reality which penetrate his consciousness through "the golden gate of imagination" during his childhood. When we read Proust's novel, we advance with the narrator into his world and we see its mystery as he sees it, with the fresh eyes of childhood. The reader must start, like the narrator, from Combray; it is an esthetic necessity for him as it is a psychological necessity for the narrator. The first glimpse we get of Swann in the light of Combray, of Mme de Guermantes in the chapel of Gilbert the Bad, is a poetic impression which stimulates our imagination: we enter easily into their fictional domain. In order to introduce us into his world, Proust opened wide the "golden gate of imagination."

Though all the elements of the novel must necessarily

be present in the early Combray passages if the famous
"laws" of evolution discovered later by the narrator are to
appear valid, one of these elements at least cannot be present
in the child's world: an adult and fully experienced love. Only
certain emotional patterns appear in the child, yet that form
of love plays the most important rôle in the narrator's journey
toward a knowledge of what reality means to him. But that
form of love also is part of the child's world through the intermediary of Swann. The story of Swann's love for Odette,
enriched by all the glamour Swann has for the child, belongs
to the world of Combray, the only world upon which Proust
could base his novel, for it is the sole object of the narrator's
quest. "No doubt," the narrator tells us, speaking of his love
for Albertine, "it was *because of the power that Swann's example had so long exercised over my imagination and my
emotions* that I was prepared to accept as true what I feared
rather than what I might have wished." [24]

The novel, as Proust conceived it, obliged him to set up
a complex structure of relations which would be permanent
and yet would be subject to an evolution which was equally
complex, though at times scarcely discernible. And at the
same time he had to portray the narrator's progress toward
an awareness of this dual complexity. We can see why Proust
continually went back to re-work his story as he developed
it in an attempt to make its fabric consistent. But the novel
as a whole is conceived and consciously organized with great
precision: the two evocations of Combray, marked by the
narrator's two "chance" recollections of Combray; the exact
correspondence of the two sets of "joyful sensations" he experiences by "chance" at the Guermantes reception, and
around which the novel pivots when, in *Le Temps retrouvé*,
the narrator passes out of the dead world he observes from
the train into the world which exists within him. However, as
the book increased immoderately in size, its equilibrium
could not be maintained. The world of the "joyful sensations," so rich in color and form, immediately accessible to
the senses and impregnated with what had been a complete

instant of life, recedes more and more. It gives way to a set of abstract laws which determine the evolution of a world which is disintegrating. The transcendental order of life which persists through all the vicissitudes of time temporarily disappears; what remains are the mechanical laws which regulate its destruction. Through his narrator, Proust seems intent on ruining his world, relentlessly and mercilessly, so grimly does he emphasize in his incidents and his characters all the proofs of moral decay.

At the end, his world seems governed by a clearly deterministic and pessimistic concept of both man and society. Proust sees both as variable expressions of social relations, also fluctuating, at the mercy of physical laws which condemn all things to degradation. As a result, his world can no longer contain the essential substance of time which, according to Proust, the artist can grasp and which the work of art reveals to us all. Despite this, Proust leads his narrator to the revelation of "time regained" and to the affirmation that a work of art is a "sign of happiness," though all logic deny it. Although the narrator in his journey toward knowledge of the "real life" seems to progress only by deletion, all the necessary elements of his experience are found at Combray, and in the story of Swann's love—*Du Côté de chez Swann*. Here, assembled in a complex structure, are all the elements of a childhood world, a world whose changing form, slowly discovered, will be to him evidence of his own growth as time passes. *Du Côté de chez Swann* reveals the character of Proust's creative vision; the entire novel, in fact the very possibility of the novel and its structure, grows out of this vision.

3

THE WORLD REGAINED

THE narrator is in complete possession of himself by the
end of his journey. Henceforth he is like an architect
who, having assembled the materials necessary for his work,
has drawn up the final plan for the projected building. Now
all he need do is concentrate on this plan in order to achieve
his end. His project has remained dormant throughout the
years because he himself, as a man, had not yet come to that
point of view about life which would give vitality to his
literary efforts. For had he not undergone the experience of
the Guermantes reception, he would not have known what to
express in his book. Artistic creation becomes possible for
him only when it is based upon a direct experience of life,
profoundly felt, and then thought out, "intellectualized." To
be authentic his work must be a direct rendering of that
experience and reflection. Proust's relation to *A la Recherche
du Temps perdu* must also be subject to this criterion if we
are not to question its authenticity. In the last pages of *Le
Temps retrouvé*, which are often hurried, even harassed,
Proust seems to have been afraid that he would be misunderstood, and in the guise of the "I" is careful to explain the
task which he himself has already accomplished and which
the narrator describes only in anticipation. It was possible
for Proust to make this double use of the "I" only because
he conceived of his own work as having sprung from personal experience, and as completely determined by it. The narrator makes it his future task to "depict reality" and to do it

by "transcribing a universe which would be completely 're-designed.' " [1]

For Proust the novel cannot be a simple objective description or a straight narration. The most painful moment in the narrator's life occurs when, on his return to Paris, he thinks that reality is reduced to what he sees of it objectively. He then no longer understands what literature is. In terms of the narrator's later discovery, a literary work is constructed out of the subjective world, which in turn exists only in response to the specific experiences of life. In his novel Proust used material which was drawn almost solely from his own life, simply because that was the only valid material he could use. That is the first criterion by which his universe is limited; it is linked, by definition, to his own life, to the milieu in which he lived, to his experience. He could not omit, *a priori* and arbitrarily, certain of its aspects such as, for example, the frivolities which he enjoyed or the homosexual drama which he lived. His novel is not a gratuitous product of his imagination; it is firmly rooted in his own experience.

But the narrator's experience is not all of the same ultimate importance. His problem is that for a long time he is unable to distinguish those aspects of his life which will become part of his inner reality, and thus material for his novel. His life is full of vicissitudes precisely because he is continually drifting and dreaming. Out of the physical universe which he sees, in which he lives, to which he belongs, and about which he thinks, he picks certain elements and spins romantic tales about himself. At one point, for example, he builds up around the Duchesse de Guermantes "a whole romantic adventure story, quite unprofitable and without a grain of truth." [2] However, as he passes from one of his stories to another, he learns the "limits and constraints of reality." [3]

The great adventure which he does live is to progress from the realms of fantasy to a genuine knowledge of reality; the great danger he runs is that he may be content, like

Ulysses and his companions, with some Circe's island which he has created himself. He gains genuine knowledge in a moment of sudden illumination followed by patient meditation. He has discovered that his world, though a reality within him, is unknown to others; as a writer, then, his task is to make it known. This is the task which Proust, too, set for himself. Instead of presenting a fiction which appears to be real, *A la Recherche du Temps perdu* presents a reality which at first seems to be a fiction because it destroys the make-believe world in which we habitually live. It destroys this fiction as, at the Ste. Euverte soirée, the motif of the Vinteuil sonata destroys the false, smothering, sterile world in which Swann lives. According to Proust, all great novels, in fact all great works of art, are the opposite of fiction. The writer or artist has therefore a heavy burden and a tremendous responsibility, for his work must continually call us back to reality from our habitual falsifications. Even though it is only by ricochet, the artist is also necessarily a moralist.

The reality which the narrator discovers in himself is a "redesigned" universe, for only certain aspects of the outer world have survived within him to be transformed into a new spiritual substance. The narrator ultimately recognizes that the only reality for him is what has endured within him, what has acquired a permanent value after having withstood the myriad fictions he has woven about objective reality. He notices that, unconsciously, in some dark inner recess of himself, he has been continually screening the various aspects of his experience. Apparently arbitrary, these choices have really been inevitable and in no way self-determined. When he discovers within himself those "hieroglyphs," the meaning of which he seeks, the narrator says: "their primary characteristic was that I was not free to choose them for they had been given to me as they were. And I felt that this must be the mark of their authenticity." [4] It is this unconscious selectivity which leads the narrator towards art, towards the miracle in art; it slowly creates within him a new, unpredictable, yet strictly ordered vision of the world.

Proust portrays this process as being quite normal; everyone is in this sense a "seer." It is neither extraordinary, intentional, nor inspired. It is simply the interaction between the individual and the world that surrounds him, a vital function like breathing. The narrator has been a "seer" for a long time, quite unconsciously; he will become a writer only at a further stage of development. In this sense, Proust really explores two problems: the problem of the distortions imposed upon the exterior world by the "self-perpetuating creation" [5] of an individual life and the problem of the individual's recognition of the creative power implicit in his own life. Two conditions assure the transfer of the narrator's creative power to the work of art linking these two problems: first, he must recognize his power, and second, he must utilize it to transcribe his vision. Both presuppose a considerable intellectual effort, reinforced by a strong will. The work of art, which is by definition the product of both a revelation and an "intellectualization" of this vital individual re-creation of the world, requires a similarly deliberate and sustained effort of intelligence and sincerity on the part of the reader. It is not a frivolous game for the author, nor a mere diversion for the reader. On the contrary, a work of art is one of the most important sources of knowledge available to human beings. Essentially an interrelationship with the world, its subjective character in no way detracts from its objective value. It is the only way to communicate, in its entirety, an experience of life which the intellect cannot manage to convey; it has an autonomous value, intellectual and moral in nature, as well as esthetic.

Even before discovering his own "redesigned universe," the narrator often recognizes the value of a work of art by analyzing his reactions to music, painting or literature. Reflecting upon Vinteuil's "Septet," he comes to think that "Every artist seems to have come from an unknown country which he has forgotten, a native country different from that of any other artist." His thoughts lingering in a rather Baudelairian fashion on the "clear sound, the loud colors which Vinteuil sent forth from the world in which he composed," the narrator explains to Albertine that

for the geranium-like fragrance of his music one would have to find, not a common-sense explanation, but the esoteric equivalent, the unknown, parti-colored festivity of which his works seem the disjointed fragments, the crimson-streaked shards; one would have to discover how he "heard" the universe, and how he projected it outside himself.[6]

In each work that he studies, in Barbey d'Aurevilly, Stendhal, and Hardy, he sees just as in Vermeer, ". . . fragments of the same world; however great the artist he recreates always the same table, the same rug, the same new and unique beauty, enigma. . . ."[7] Dostoevski's works present exactly the same enigma, this creation of a new and autonomous form of beauty. "This new beauty remains the same in all Dostoevski's works," he says to Albertine, ". . . As I already said the same scene reappears in one novel after the other and, what is more, it is from the heart of the novel itself that the same scenes, the same characters reappear if the novel is very long."[8] He ends by concluding that every work of art is a harmonization, even a kind of metaphor. It can be understood only in relation to something else, for it is always in harmony with something of a quite different nature which exists only in the author's mind. A work of art is not an aspiration, a fulfillment of desire, an expression of faith, or a means to any end whatsoever; nor is it a discovery of something new since it only reveals a discovery which necessarily precedes it. It is the concrete equivalent of a reality belonging to another order, an order perceived because it confers upon things this "enigma" of new and autonomous beauty. The "artistic sense" is, for Proust, inseparable from "submission to that inner reality"[9] without which there can be no esthetic beauty, for it is itself the source of beauty.

At a very early stage, thinking over some lines of poetry, the narrator understands that one of the elements of their beauty is rhyme. "Is this not already," he thinks, "a primary element of formal complexity, of beauty, that upon hearing a rhyme, i.e., something that is at the same time similar to and yet different from the preceding rhyme which inspired it, but introduces into it the variation of a new idea, one feels two systems which are superimposed one upon the other, one of thought, the other of meter." [10] The beauty of a work of art is of the same order. It "rhymes" doubly: with the world, and with the inner order to which the artist refers. In it one senses, on a scale more complex than that of rhyme, the "superimposition of two systems" which generates the work. Hence, according to Proust, the novel itself is not the "creation of a world," but the creation through language of a work of art, replica of a world which existed before it reached artistic expression. Therefore, the book that the author, Proust, writes is composed with the utmost care, the material it presents is doubly "redesigned," for it is analogous to an inner world which also has been redrawn. It cannot be read as a straightforward account directly expressing the experience of its author, any more than it can be looked upon as a simple story. In the sense that it is an analogy, it is fiction.

This conception of art gives us a key to Proust's work. First, it explains why over a period of years Proust actually wrote only one book, to which he continually added hundreds of pages. In his opinion, this is exactly what all novelists do, even when they begin what they think is another novel. Proust did not wish his novel to be divided into separate parts. It was only much against his will and for practical reasons that he finally agreed to divide his novel into separate volumes. For Proust the story of Swann cannot be detached from the novel, any more than can the story of the narrator's love for Albertine, because these stories are always the same story, emerging from a universe which is always the same. *A la Recherche du Temps perdu* also presents both the "disjointed fragments," the "crimson-streaked shards" and, in the course of the story, the reiteration of repeated scenes which, according to the narrator, identifies any work of art. It is, therefore, not surprising that the same characters reappear over and over again. They repeat themselves, reverberate from one to the other in a thousand echoes, forming and reforming identical patterns which are recognizable despite their apparent diversity. The "disjointed fragments" correspond to the discontinuous blocks of memories which bear the weight of the whole novel; Combray, the Champs Elysées, the Allée des Acacias, Balbec, Rivebelle, or Venice are evoked each with its own characteristic substance "distinct, unique, of a special ambience and resonance." They are characterized by that "monotone" of genius which Proust mentions and which merges them into a unity so real that the reader easily forgets that the world "projected outside himself" by Proust differs from the everyday world in that it comprises and elaborates only certain fragments of experience. These are the fragments of the narrator's life "coinciding" with his "inner" world; they are at the same time fragments of Proust's own inner and "unknown native country." The narrator reports on a world formed in him which coincides with his "native country." Every element of that world has meaning; this sets it apart from that which remains insignificant in his life. Proust excludes from his novel all those elements in the narrator's life which remain without meaning. A work of art cannot tolerate the meaningless. This is the second criterion which sets the limits of Proust's literary world, and distinguishes his novel from a direct account of the narrator's life or an autobiography of Proust.

Both in its construction and substance, *A la Recherche du Temps perdu* reveals Proust's esthetic conception, which is sharp and clear. This conception is determined by another, no less clear and no less linked to personal experience: a conception of the factor which relates the work of art to the world through the medium of individual experience. This relationship is necessarily special, since it can only be established by the individual who is himself the sole point of contact. Proust's narrator is inextricably bound to his own world; both he and his world are in turn closely bound to Proust in a quite complex manner and that in itself is a "visible transcription" of Proust's conception, and a very accurate one. It holds his answer to any question one might put as to the meaning of such vague terms as "reality," "the universe," "the world," which the artist must "paint," "transcribe," "translate," or "redesign."

Proust develops the narrator's entire story from the persistent images of certain people and certain places in his life; they live in his memory and escape oblivion. Whether it be in the fixed patterns of the conscious memory or in vital resurrections from the unconscious memory, it is always Combray, the Champs Elysées, Balbec flanked by Rivebelle and la Raspelière, Doncières and Venice which he remembers. Everything outside his unconscious memory is dead. What did the narrator do during the two years which separate his love for Gilberte, so closely linked with the Champs-Elysées, and his departure for Balbec where he was to meet Albertine? How was he living in Paris during those years when at Easter he visits Combray? And the sixteen years he spent in the sanatorium? At one point the narrator mentions vaguely a trip to Germany; Germany has no place either in his "native country" or in his story. At the end of the Guermantes matinée he sees before him the "masks" of a whole assembly of people; among them is Mlle de Saint-Loup:

Like most human beings, was she not a kind of crossroads in a forest where paths leading from the most diverse points converge, just as they do in our lives? Many were the paths of my life which met in Mlle de Saint-Loup and radiated outward from her. First of all, in her converged the two principal directions along which I had taken so many walks and dreamed so many dreams: through her father Robert de Saint-Loup, the Guermantes; through her mother Gilberte, Méséglise, which was Swann's. One of the directions, through her mother, led me back to Swann, to my evenings in Combray near Méséglise; the other, through her father, to my afternoons in Balbec, where I saw him again beside the sunlit sea. Already between those two roads there were many crosspaths.[11]

Gradually a group of people are placed on the geographic chart of his inner world. These people are linked together by a rich network of relations. Each moves freely and is himself the center of a complex communication system. One need only follow any one of these people to see all the others inevitably spring up in the same place.

The places and the people, that are always the same, although observed under various circumstances, begin to exist for the narrator in Combray. They are connected because they are held in a common matrix, the narrator's life. Just as at Balbec the young man's love eventually focuses upon one of all the possible girls in the group of the "jeunes filles en fleurs," so in his childhood, out of as many possible worlds, only one takes form; that one will ultimately become "real" for him, a permanent core of life. Combray is the story of the creation of that world, which is composed of elements the child unconsciously sorts out from the reality at his disposal. At Combray the narrator's formless world begins to take shape; this world will last, and the rest of the novel tells us what form the narrator imposes upon it. So it is esthetically necessary for the narrator, by a "chance" play of memory, to evoke Combray twice in the opening pages of the novel.

One can apply to all of Combray what the narrator says of Swann: he was one of those friends who by "a chance that in retrospect seems a fatality determined the future course of our life, thereby excluding all the other lives which we might have led"; and "because of this, the outer pattern of our lives and the very substance of our work derives from him."[12] The outer pattern of the narrator's life and the substance of his work are indeed determined by Combray. The inner substance of his life and the outer pattern of his work derive from his own temperament, which at Combray begins to shape his personality.

"Think not that fate is more than gathered impressions of childhood," says Rilke in the "Seventh Elegy." *A la Recherche du Temps perdu* delineates the concrete and complex universe these words suggest; they express the idea which guided Proust in ordering the world of his novel, an idea rooted in his own experience.

Combray is a real place for the narrator. As a child, he and his parents arrived there with the spring, at Easter, and with the fall they left. Proust shows us first what the child considers to be its center, the closed world of the family, gathered in the house of his great-aunt and his Tante Léonie, with its garden facing on a village street. From the windows of that house, one could see the center of the town, the church with its spire, apparent everywhere, regulating the life of the inhabitants to the rhythm of the centuries by marking off the hours of the days, of Sundays and holidays. It is a curious family in which the child lives. Gathered about him are two generations of grownups: his parents, grandparents, three great-aunts, one aunt and, at one time, a great-uncle. The household revolves around one person, Tante Léonie, who from her room, which she never leaves, maintains its established order. Her realm has its own laws, its own rhythms. The symmetry of her days is interrupted once a week by the asymmetry of market day, and Sunday has its special character, bestowed upon it by the weekly ceremony of mass. Upon arriving at Combray, the narrator's family settles down to a life in which even the variations are repetitive, an ageless pattern of existence. The child is completely a part of this world, participating in its rhythms, belonging to it entirely. It is an absolute for him, and everything which is a part of this world is imbued with the same absolute quality, fully and unquestioningly accepted.

The narrator describes a bourgeois childhood in a well-to-do household. Everything is respectable, substantial, and plentiful; it is a world of leisure, one of whose chief characteristics is the enjoyment of succulent meals. The child is watched over, cherished. He is extremely sensitive, delicate, with keen senses; his imagination and intelligence are continually on the alert. He is often immersed in books, and lives in an atmosphere of happiness and wonder. This world is not an earthly paradise; it has its crises and its cruelties. But it is a friendly world, with a temperate kindness and a wit that is jovial rather than biting. Anything even remotely connected with culture and art is revered. The family life goes on in the midst of an average small town with its population of aristocrats who are seldom in residence, of a middle class made up of snobs like Legrandin or shy creatures like Vinteuil, and of the working people who include Tante Léonie's servants and, in particular, Françoise, who is an authority on the whys and wherefores of the relations between the various levels of the social hierarchy. Combray is a perfectly ordinary town where virtues and vices flourish undramatically, where there is a concern about basic values such as stability, dignity, honesty, a sense of "what is fitting" and where there are vices such as envy, jealousy, cruelty, and others more subtle and singular, such as Legrandin's snobbery and Mlle de Vinteuil's sapphism.

From the Combray house, center of the child's world, two roads lead to unfamiliar country: the road to the Swanns and the road to Guermantes, two "worlds" which are "unknown" to the child. This is also the world which Tante Léonie pursues feverishly when it appears even briefly in the streets of Combray in the form of a person who is "not known." These two worlds, the world of Combray and the world situated beyond it, are kept in equilibrium and separated from one another by the force with which Combray resists any threat of intrusion. The hierarchies and values of life in Combray split the child's universe in two: socially, it is split into the people one knows and those whom one "does not know," that is, the social group of the substantial middle class to which the narrator and his family belong, and the people who do not belong to it; morally, it is split into feelings that are noble and permissible and those that are blame-worthy; ethically, into absolute virtues and vices; intellectually, into truth and falsehood; esthetically, into the beautiful and the ugly. The "people one knows," the proper feelings, the virtues which one acquires by discipline, the truth one respects, the beauty found in nature and art—these are the fit preoccupations of respectable people. On a geographical, social, ethical, intellectual, and esthetic level, the world of Combray is well charted; when an individual, like the narrator's grandmother, introduces a few variations, they change only the order of the hierarchies by placing, for example, the beauty of a piece of furniture above its solidity, or by classifying a person according to the virtuous nature of his sentiments rather than by his social label. Each person is assigned a definite place in this system and relationships derive their meaning from it.

The child lives in this environment and accepts it, but his curiosity is nonetheless stimulated by the world which seems to him to lie beyond the everyday limits of Combray. His mind continually escapes into reveries about it which are not yet conscious thoughts. Fostered first by images, magic lantern slides, and stained glass windows, then by reading, his phantasies project him out of that family world. These images have the authority of an absolute reality which he believes they reflect. They seem to him to exist, like Combray, in the absolute, but to be quite different in essence. The child's reveries are elaborated from these images; his belief in their reality is reenforced. Just as the ancients used to locate on the map of the world the Garden of the Hesperides, the entrance to Hades, and the dwelling of the Gods, so the child sets up around the known center of Combray a mythical map of the unknown, affirming his belief in its tangible existence. His instinctive élan toward a mysterious world manifests itself in the unceasing activity of his imagination. Unlike his Tante Léonie, he is always giving substance to his unknown world by putting into it any unusual element which his imagination seizes.

This unknown world is created from elements actually present in his daily life, but which seem exceptional and unconnected with Combray; he abstracts the exceptional from the actual. These juxtaposed elements merge to form a picture of the unknown. They are so imbued with the child's sense of mystery that, like an ingenuous spectator who confuses the actor with the character he is portraying, he attributes as intrinsic to them the attraction that they exert over him. To the name of Balbec, which designates a real town, he adds, for example, an image created from a few words of Legrandin and touched up by Swann; the Balbec of the narrator's dream emerges, "storm-tossed and lost in the mists" where, on a cliff, a Persian-style church is eternally glistening with the spray of a wild sea. In the same way the stranger, Gilberte Swann, emerges as a result of the mention of her name with that of another stranger, Bergotte, the author most admired by the child, and from the juxtaposition of the two images attached to these names. These elements are fused into a single picture: the "bard" Bergotte, gentle, aged, and profoundly wise visits a church portal with Gilberte, in some world forever inaccessible to the narrator.

By such associations of images, the unknown world begins to take shape; assimilating chance fragments from the outer world, it becomes polarized and localized in relation to the known world. Thus the child's dream world becomes accessible, a desirable actuality. Two of its centers, Balbec and Venice, are geographically accessible because they have a location on the map; accessible to him because his mother has mentioned them as probable destinations for a trip, or even a visit. Two others are situated very near to Combray. They are both unknown and very real: Guermantes, although situated at the end of a familiar road, is too far to be reached according to the time-hallowed traditions of Combray; and Tansonville, the Swanns' château, is forbidden by Combray's ethical code. Balbec and Venice remain solely "places" without inhabitants, in the narrator's imagination, but Guermantes and Tansonville are near enough so that he comes into some contact with the people who live there.

So the "fabulous characters" make their appearance in the child's mythological world. His imagination is irresistibly drawn toward these "fabulous" people rather than toward the ones he knows, like Vinteuil's daughter; and they lend themselves far better to the demands of his sensitive imagination than do the "places." He invents a series of vague stories about them, all of which he develops along the same lines: in an imaginary landscape, imbued with an atmosphere of harmony, gentleness, and kindness, he is loved by one of these inaccessible women. This love, he feels, will introduce him to some "superhuman and ambiguous" joy, the nature of which he cannot even conceive.

To satisfy both his compulsion toward the unknown and the demands of his sensitivity, the child constructs, parallel to the "real world" of Combray, of Françoise, the grocer Camus, Eulalie, and Madame Sazerat, characters to "supplement" that world. They alone interest him and he "lends" them the names of people whom he knows to be real but who seem to him completely beyond his reach. So he is able to pass through the "golden gates of the imagination" into an inner world of his own making, and it is these places and these people alone who will continue to enrich the life of the narrator. But their latent power is revealed only when their actual counterparts appear. This occurs one day in Paris at the end of a winter. As he is playing in the Champs Elysées, oblivious to his environment and still living in his imagination in Venice or Balbec, the child overhears the name "Gilberte." Instantly the Champs Elysées springs to life for him, transformed from a dreary, insignificant playground into the one indispensable and enthralling focus of his life.

The forbidden world of the Swanns and the inaccessible world of the Guermantes become part of the child. His images, which have no substance other than their tantalizing mystery, mold themselves to the dictates of his imagination, just as Golo, wandering off the screen during the magic lantern sessions, borrowed the shape of the door knob. They live on within him, side by side, shrouded in a dream, apparently innocuous. Their latent strength, revealed whenever a place or person whose name the narrator has "borrowed" enters his everyday life, lies in their power to awaken his curiosity. The "prolonged sojourn" of certain names in his imagination directs his attention towards the real places and people they designate and to these he transfers the mystery which their names had contained. But the narrator's world is dislocated when he faces the real person outside the realm of dreams, when he actually sees, for example, the Duchesse de Guermantes in the Combray church. People and places then emerge from his harmonious inner world; for a while they retain an ambiguous character, and only finally become integrated into the "known." Their integration requires of the narrator a profound scrutiny, an individualization of each person and place. They become objects of rational contemplation and thereby sources of experience. But, in the process, the world of dreams in which the narrator has believed so implicitly reveals its illusory character. He has confused the actors with the rôles he allotted to them; now the discrepancy between the characters and their actual counterparts forces him to deny the existence of his world "beyond the real." He does not realize that it existed before he placed them in it.

From the child's first selections among the strange and unusual fragments of his life, Proust develops all that is significant in the narrator's story; they constitute his unknown and longed-for world. The child places himself outside this world. He always sees himself going toward it, entering it— all this in the future, that vague, vast space of time which stretches before him like a blank screen; his dream is inscribed upon the future. That is why these places and people and only these, except for Combray, resist the vicissitudes of time; only these can be resurrected by involuntary memory. The vague images which the child projects before him are, in fact, pale adumbrations of the future. The outer course of his life will pass through all of them, people and places; they are its way-stations, but that is because the inner course of his life has been so prescribed. They are the focal points common to his two worlds; precisely for this reason they are also subject to bewildering transformations.

Because of their origin they alone have the power to enhance reality: they are the only source of experience for the narrator. In his eyes their equivocal "double lives" stamp them with an enigmatic and disturbing beauty, and the mystery he unconsciously sees in them keeps him on the path of his vocation. Because of them he experiences the resistance that reality opposes to his dreams and to his desires; his dreams and desires in turn resist reality, and this opposition brings him deep disappointment. The significant course of his life simultaneously includes the realization of his dreams and a profound disillusionment. He will not accept a dual world. The unity which his own singleness of soul confers upon his "elect" gives these chosen people and places their continual attraction; but because they continually shatter this unity, they have both creative and destructive power.

In Combray their latent power is only suggested; they remain harmonious and innocent images. Only twice are they confronted with reality; the narrator sees Gilberte on the lawn at Tansonville and the Duchesse de Guermantes in the church of Combray. Their presence shakes the narrator, temporarily dislocating the landmarks of his invented world, and initiates in him great waves of emotion and tentative analysis. But these events are transient and do not recur; the child's imagination soon absorbs these "doorknobs" and fuses them with the shadowy images of the unknown which he continues to project into the future. They serve rather to kindle his interest than to shake his convictions.

In the Combray later resurrected, the child lives through his imagination in felicitous domains which he has nonetheless abstracted from Combray. Actually his life is solidly anchored in the family routine and the events of the small town.

This life is evoked by the narrator in an extraordinary set of pictures, always the same, which he recalls when he describes the bed-time drama at Combray. And it is a set of even richer memories that the taste of the madeleine brings back to life. These images are actually reborn, imbued with their own emotional atmosphere. They are no longer fashioned at will and merged by phantasy; they are shaped by a real emotion which gives them unity. The world they recall is not an arbitrary one. The child occupies his designated place in it; it is, in fact, his given world. The narrator recalls it as the child experienced it, through the medium of two emotional states which are interposed between the world and himself, isolating certain moments of his life. When these feelings become sufficiently intense, the child is forced to act and to establish a new relationship with the world around him.

The first of these intense emotions is anxiety; it detaches one moment of the day, isolates it, appropriates it completely, and wipes out all the rest. This anxiety is born of evening, the solitude of evening. In an attempt to cope with it, the child attributes his torment to one specific factor: the absence of the person he loves most, his mother. This is the only way in which he actually shows his love for his mother, whom he scarcely distinguishes from himself. His evening torment is accentuated when Swann's visit modifies the rites and customary exorcisms of bedtime. It charges Swann's arrival and "the deep yet silvery tinkling of the visitors' bell" with an importance commensurate with itself. To escape this torment, the child puts on a great act one evening, changes the usual order of events, and subjects the will of his parents to his own desires. Though he gets what he wants, he experiences a feeling of failure and guilt, and altogether the whole evening leaves an indelible impression on him. The picture of the garden, of the stairs, of his room, of the different phases of his act, are vividly preserved in his memory, together with the development of his anguish.

Balancing this suffering, is the happiness of daytime Combray, which sometimes culminates in moments of ecstasy.

This ecstasy is always accompanied by a particularly intense sensation which occurs in the presence of quite natural phenomena: a hedge of hawthorn, the scent of lilac, a church steeple. The joy which he experiences also compels him to act, to make some exclamation or gesture. One day, without making any particular effort, the narrator finds another outlet for his joy. The spires of Martinville and Vieuxvicq stamp so brilliant an image upon his mind that it seems to call out to him a joyful message; words surge up within him in response and he writes down a description of the spires so that their image is translated into a conscious literary expression, objective and autonomous. By this act the narrator creates a new combination of words; he also creates a new relationship with his own emotions and with their cause. The relationship is twofold for he has now experienced an emotion and expressed it.

These two acts, the act that starts the family drama and the act of writing, spring directly from his own sensibilities; they are definitive and mutually opposed. The first reveals the child's tremendous capacity for suffering, and so intense a need to escape pain that he will sacrifice his mother's wishes and peace of mind to appease it. He discovers that people, especially those who love him, can be molded to his will, at least to a certain degree. It is the first sign of the child's penchant toward a form of tyranny in which he sacrifices what is best in him to his weaknesses, the beginning of a conflict between his avowed aims and his will power. By this act he opens the road to evasion. His second act is of a different kind; an inner submission to an outer stimulation. It is accompanied by joy, and is the road to accomplishment. In both cases, the child's ego is asserted; he frees himself from his environment and attempts his first step forward, establishing with the world a relationship no longer patterned after the responses of his family. However, theoretically at least, he continues to accept their mode of life. The first road, the road of evasion, is the one which the narrator will follow almost to the end; it is the psychological source of a long "error" which will be finally rejected only when he takes the second road.

The child's anxiety condenses, unifies, and defines its own period of time; it merges a whole series of evenings into one, organizing the events remembered as they might be organized in a play; the child's joy extends time and space indefinitely, and comprises in all their diversity the myriad varied tableaux of daily existence. When the taste of the madeleine resurrects Combray in the narrator's mind, the village rises before his eyes in an aura of poetry, still, fixed in a miraculously clear light, brilliantly colored and enamelled with flowers. This tranquil world, set in an eternal spring, outside of time, is the embodiment of happiness. Combray comes to life again in this way because, recalled by a sensation, it is restored as a whole, with all the emotions that were once attached to it. And the emotion which dominates all the others is that of wonder, of simple awe before the world as it is apprehended directly by all the senses. This wonder is scarcely marred as yet by the need to understand, to evaluate, to relate the images one to another. It creates the inner happiness that is inseparable from a sense of mystery, of newness. The Combray thus recalled—its landscape and the two symmetrical "côtés" with their flowers, their scents, and their perfect beauty—is an embodiment of the child's state of mind.

The child is deeply impressed by the mystery implicit in the existence of people and things; his "other" world, peopled with "other" beings and "other" places, is merely his way of expressing that mystery. His imaginary world is only the pale expression of the strong tie which binds him to life itself, of the consciousness of a mystery so close to him that it springs from the very flowers at his feet. In his happy reveries he feels himself to be a part of this harmony, and it is only through an error that he always places the reality of happiness outside the known world, unwittingly symbolizing that "distance" which mystery implies. Because of this error he goes on the long journey which he records. It can only take him far from his Ithaca because the poetic atmosphere which makes his imaginary world enthralling has its actual source in the child's Combray.

Within the enchanted circle of life at Combray, there is an infinitely varied world of ideas, pleasures, and emotions which are continually being created, destroyed, or modified by the changes in the narrator's relation with what he notices around him. A word of Bloch's, for example, is sufficient to alter completely his idea of literature, presenting him with an unexpected and all-absorbing problem; Swann's image is modified by the various opinions and attitudes held by the different members of the narrator's family; and the beautiful image of the "lady in pink" is connected with the family quarrel of which she is the disconcerting cause. The child's mind constantly grapples with the problem of the collisions and contradictions which he observes around him. They disconcert him because they are shifting and their relation subtly undermines the harmonious and well-ordered enchantment of Combray.

The child's future life is already implicit in the orientation of his imagination and desires, in his sensitivity and in the direction of his thought. He tends to destroy the order and hierarchies of life in Combray. During his childhood this tendancy is still part of a game, and does not disturb the firm foundation of his convictions; but it is nonetheless effective. The rest of the novel simply traces that development of his life which starts with his rejection of Combray's established hierarchy and continues with his exploration of the devious paths which finally converge at the Guermantes matinee.

It is clear that Proust created the world of Combray with the utmost precision so that it might fulfill a certain specific function in his novel. In those few pages he intended to enclose the narrator's whole future, already determined by the interplay of chance and of necessity. Seen in retrospect this interplay, carrying the narrator from sequel to sequel, creates his individual destiny. Proust himself at the beginning of the novel did the work that time will accomplish for his character.

He describes the first contacts between an individual, the narrator, and a specific milieu. These contacts determine the particular quality of the narrator's experience and define his vocation—emotional, intellectual, and artistic—within the limits of his individual personality and character. The two-dimensional images, real or imaginary, with which the child in Combray is concerned, his emotional and intellectual moods, are the background against which everything in his life will be projected. Sometimes an image, an emotion, or a thought remains dormant for a long time as his life develops, but it finally surges up with all its cumulative force. Mlle Vinteuil's image in Montjouvain, for example, comes into focus only when it gives Albertine's life a troubling ambiguity. Every tiny fact which the narrator apparently evokes spontaneously is the first term of a future relationship; it often initiates a whole set of new relationships which in time mark the course of its development. In retrospect, Combray comprises the sum total of the narrator's possibilities as well as the psychological principle that determines which among these possibilities he will realize, and how. Thus Combray contains all the factors which are decisive in the narrator's life. All the roads he follows throughout his life start from Combray; he follows them sometimes simultaneously, sometimes successively, just as he followed the inner paths he found when walking along "Swann's way" or the "Guermantes way."

The course of the narrator's life is determined by very complex factors. Though his life is in constant motion, these factors never change; it is their relative importance which varies. The narrator does not move ahead in a straight line. His progress is erratic and fluctuating. He goes through periods of relative calm, crises, and transformations which are not immediately perceptible. Never until the end of the novel are all these factors successfully organized in a harmony comparable to the one reigning over Combray.

Proust's creation of the world of Combray is far from being a simple reconstruction of the past based on the play of unconscious memory, the psychological and esthetic device which sustains his fiction. Combray is the world "given" to the narrator, the world out of which his life must of necessity grow. Even the most insignificant incidents in Combray, those which appear to be related merely by chance, the landscapes, the conversations, and the characters are conceived in terms of the future which will evolve from them. Proust also introduced into his world of Combray the inner momentum which was to carry all these apparently fragmentary elements through time to a conclusion in which they would converge to form a pattern. At its climax—the Guermantes reception— the narrator's life at last seems to him to have had a definite direction. Because the world of Combray is by now so far behind us, the conclusion of the story confers upon the gestures, images and people of Combray a symbolic character. They no longer seem arbitrary, picked at random by the author. The end of the story is reached only with the "revelation" at the Guermantes reception. Until then all the narrator's attempts to give his life some coherence have failed because he has overlooked a factor which continually intruded and destroyed the order he was always attempting to establish. This factor is time, which flows along heedlessly, bearing with it change and oblivion.

When the narrator tastes the madeleine, Combray returns to his consciousness in its entirety, unmarred by the transformations and oblivion of the intervening years. He recognizes the very substance of Combray and recaptures through memory what made Combray what it was, his own sheer joy at being alive. Beyond thought, emotion, and disillusionment, the narrator has finally come back to his "native country," defined by a joyous contact with reality. Proust, therefore, had also consciously to create this magic contact with reality. He achieved this by depicting a world rendered marvelous by the child's direct apperception of it. Combray proves that beyond the fluctuations of emotion, the conclusions of the intellect, and the disintegration of the body, there is a level on which individual existence is happiness, a har-

mony established between the individual and the world.
Beauty is born of this harmony; it is neither in the individual,
who is variable, nor in objects themselves, whether they are
water lillies or lilacs, but it comes when they are mutually
present. In this harmony the world of Combray flourishes,
and it is in search of this harmony that the narrator goes.
Without it, the world cannot be reconstructed, lifted above
time, and set within the closed sphere of art.

Sensory harmony with the universe is at the core of the
narrator's happiness in Combray. When he thinks about his
life, he fails to take this into account because it does not belong to the realms of emotion and intelligence, though it pervades them like a powerful musical accompaniment. A
chance sensation, evoked intact from the past, revives in his
consciousness first a feeling of joy at being alive, and then
an entire part of his life of which this sensation is the over-
tone. It is only by chance, and intermittently, that he can
thus recapture the joy intrinsic to life and which is actually
the most permanent quality in him. It is for this reason that
Proust composed the narrator's story by describing his successive "plunges" into the past. He could do this only by
placing the narrator at a certain vantage point with regard
to the entire course of his life, which must stretch behind him
at a certain "inner distance" in time. When he "plunges"
into the past, what first reappears is the general atmosphere
of the "period of time" he has recaptured, and which Proust
always creates—at Combray, Balbec, Guermantes, or in the
room shared with Albertine—before he moves on to particular events.

Proust's novel is constructed in relation to this basic
conception. The significant moments in the life of his narrator
are those in which he has most fully this sense of existence.
After Combray these moments are always placed at the "intersection" of reality and the dreams of Combray. These are
the moments which Proust has the narrator recall by the
"chance" recollection of involuntary memory.

Proust's overall conception allowed him to imbue his

novel with a poetic atmosphere, which occasionally even becomes "precious" and which certainly is not characteristic of
the traditional French psychological novel. He does not describe an evolution which follows a straight line, isolating
certain psychological reactions which justify the plot. He sets
down large discontinuous blocks in which he recreates, or attempts to fix in all its complexity, the subjective and variable
content of the narrator's life. The events in each block are
permeated by a certain "color" of existence. People, feelings,
memories, meet and play their hazardous games against a
magic background of imagery which endows them with an
aura of poetry. Each block is clearly individualized. Altogether they form a continuous fresco, the basic decorative
elements of which are identical: urban landscapes in harmony with the human figure moving in them, and characterized by a certain human luxury and art.

Combray is an ancient town surrounded by a cultivated
countryside sprinkled with churches; it is a vast garden, a
place where a medieval human order still reigns, as inseparable from the church as it is from the land. The sea and
paths around Balbec circle the Grand Hotel and its inhabitants. The Adriatic Sea makes of Venice and its palaces a
semi-marine, semi-architectural city from which rises the
song of the gondolier; and the Bois de Boulogne draws its
disturbing beauty from being an "artificial place" where
the trees "forced for so many years by a sort of grafting, to
live in common with woman" evoke "the dryad, the beautiful
wordly woman, above whose fleet and colorful passage they
spread their branches." [13]

Elstir's canvases of Balbec derive their character from the
metaphor by which the painter links the earth to the sea. One
of the characteristics of the Proustian vision is that it always
establishes a fusion between two elements which appear to be
quite distinct from each other; "nature" and the "artificial"
creations of man—the cathedrals, paintings, hotels, villages,
or, even more transitory, vehicles of transportation and wom-
en's clothes. The human being is indispensable to this fusion

and is never absent from the scene. The hawthorn in the Tansonville garden, the sculptured hawthorn of the church, flowers, acacias, closely associated with all worldly elegance, chrysanthemums in Odette's salon—women-flowers, and flower-women constantly call to one another in nature, art and the world of human beings. But in this décor only "marvelous beasts" flourish—the race of Guermantes, a race of birds, the glittering "pack" of valets. Behind the panes of the Grand Hotel or in their theatre boxes move the dandies, like tropical fish in their aquariums, subaquatic fauna, marine demi-gods. Except for Françoise's chicken and an occasional horse, the animal has disappeared from the Proustian earth except in culinary form—*boeuf en daube* or turbot, skillfully prepared.

This terrestrial marriage between "two superimposed systems," nature and art, produces a semi-animal, semi-divine fauna corresponding to the semi-natural, semi-artificial flora so characteristic of Proust's world. Both are ambiguous, poised, like the Proustian landscape itself, at the intersection of a dream—a cultivated dream, nourished upon literature, history, art, and the classics—and of the scintillating ceremony of an idle and elegant society luxuriously set up in its fashionable gardens, apparently immune from any threat save from within. The background and the characters of his novel delineate the exact limits and special quality of Proust's own "inner world," the product of his intimate experience. They correspond to the peculiar harmony which Proust, perceptive, hypersensitive, and literate, established within the limits of his life as a member of the wealthy upper class in the aristocratic salons and châteaux of a world which the war of 1914 was to shake to its foundations.

4

THE INHUMAN WORLD OF PLEASURE

GEOGRAPHICALLY close to Combray, Tansonville and Guermantes are equally prominent on the narrator's map of his own "enchanted realms." Linking him to these two worlds are the people who live there, and whom he actually sees: Swann, Gilberte, and the Duchesse de Guermantes. They are for him at once real and imaginary. As an adolescent and a young man, they seem to him like magicians whose favor would assure his entry into the domain of his dreams. Anyone who belongs to these worlds becomes the object of his passionate curiosity, not because of themselves, as he would have it, but because they seem to him guardians of the keys of paradise. In this way the narrator takes his place in the social scheme, and gravitates toward these two different spheres, of which both, according to the social values of Combray, are outside his orbit; the "solid bourgeoisie" does not mix with the aristocracy to which the Guermantes belong; Swann has hopelessly lost caste in their eyes by his marriage. The narrator categorically reverses this unwritten social law; the people who are rejected by Combray have for him an irresistible attraction: they are inaccessible. In addition, they have a glamorous aura which seems to the adolescent the very essence of social superiority: wealth and elegance in the case of Swann, ancient lineage in the case of the Guermantes.

In spite of the convictions of his immediate milieu, and even in opposition to them, the narrator feels himself compelled toward a "worldly" life. In order to make his way into the society of the Swanns and the Guermantes, he breaks down the gentle, unspoken resistance of his mother and grandmother by using the emotional blackmail which he had discovered to be so effective one evening in Combray. And so he follows the path of flight from Combray, and embarks upon a course which impels him to sacrifice everything to the fulfillment of his phantasies and his desires. He is led to violate the social boundaries which the "virtues" of Combray have defined for him, and to lead a life which is in direct opposition to them. As he moves further and further away from Combray, the stable core of his life recedes. He leaves his home territory by degrees, venturing first into Swann's milieu. "Our Combray society couldn't have been less worldly. Association with Swann was a step in the direction of sophistication." [1] Taking advantage of the "social looseness" of life at a seaside resort where various social groups "mix," [2] he also begins to make his way, through Mme de Villeparisis, St. Loup and Charlus, whom he meets in Balbec, toward the world of the Guermantes. He comes into contact with various other groups of all types which are represented among the motley inhabitants of the Grand Hotel, such as the young bourgeoises of the "little set" or the Jewish colony to which the Blochs belong. He discovers an infinitely enlarged and quite new social universe which he explores with burning interest.

This social barrier breached, he penetrates, thanks to the Guermantes, into the heart of the Faubourg St. Germain. Then, during his second stay at Balbec, he runs into fantastic and innumerable imbroglios, myriad threads of which cross and re-cross from one social milieu to another in a veritable comedy of errors and fortuitous events, until the day when, as in a vaudeville show, a flurry of marriages sanctifies the real but disguised unity of Proust's social world. This only takes place after Proust has dragged all these worldly people who were excluded from the bourgeois society of Combray into a dizzying downfall. Like the narrator, we shall then have seen, in mirrors or through the half-open doors of houses of questionable repute like Jupien's, a dark region where on a strange footing of equality, princes, businessmen, and valets meet, avoid each other, or spy upon one another. The "virtues" of Combray have taken their revenge.

From its beginning in Combray, the narrator's world is limited to his own field of vision, that of the well-to-do middle classes and of the aristocracy with their respective satellites, their servants on the one hand, artists and intellectuals on the other. If through Françoise and her daughter, Jupien, or Morel, we catch a glimpse of other classes, it is only in passing. Proust concentrates his attention upon the "upper classes" of society and their social life. Except in its social aspects, he almost entirely ignores their professional life. In the Proustian world an individual can be both a Guermantes and a senator, a military officer or even an ambassador, just as he can be a bourgeois and a doctor, engineer, professor, civil servant, writer, or artist. The Proustian characters are not as idle as they are often said to be, but they interest Proust only in their social relationships because in the world of wealth and leisure "social relationships attain their purest form." [3]

As a whole, Proustian society is classified according to certain general principles which remain fixed. The peasant Françoise easily distinguishes between the social levels of the laboring class, the middle class, and the aristocracy, to each of which appertain certain privileges and obligations. Inside her own class she establishes an inflexible hierarchy and a well-defined code of manners which are the expression of certain definite values. The other two classes live according to rules which she does not understand very well, but about which she has certain simple and inflexible notions: the middle class "owes it to itself" to be rich, and to look it; the aristocracy to be royalist, and toward them Françoise owes it to herself to show her independence. She looks at them from a distance with a curiosity tinged with dislike, but without the slightest desire or the slightest aspiration to belong to their class. This attitude is roughly that of the great-aunt, of Tante Léonie, or of the Prince de Guermantes, each in his own sphere. For the narrator's great-aunt only one social milieu is worthy of consideration: that of the solid middle class which is characterized by the almost hereditary exercise of certain honorable, well-remunerated professions, administrative or intellectual, and by respect for solid values, both material and moral. The gradations of superiority within the middle class are a matter of occupation and fortune. To be, like Swann, the possessor of a substantial upper-middle-class fortune, and to spend a lifetime collecting bibelots and paintings and hobnobbing with the aristocracy is a disgrace. To be a worthy member of his class, Swann should have undertaken the respectable occupation of stockbroker. The narrator's great-aunt surveys the social scene with complacency: she receives from the inhabitants of Combray the respect due her, and regards the aristocracy with a rather vague irony, and with a certain scorn as well, because she confuses it with the demimonde which is frivolous, spendthrift, and immoral. For the Prince de Guermantes and his class, aristocracy is a matter of name. The name is the mark of the family's past, of its lineage and its rank in the feudal and monarchic order. People so "named" thus belong, each in his place, to high society. A hierarchy is established. At the top are individuals bearing the most illustrious heraldic name, such as Guermantes and families related to them, and the name itself confers an absolute superiority. In the eyes of the prince, all individuals who are not "named" are equal from the aristocratic point of view—they do not belong to "society."

Belief in a hierarchy creates within each group a veritable miniature Versailles. The shadow of Louis XIV and of the world of Saint-Simon is thrown across each echelon: Charlus, heaped with honors, receiving the eager homage of the Faubourg St. Germain; Tante Léonie, flanked by Eulalie and Françoise; Françoise lording it over the butler and the valet, or the manager of the Grand Hotel framed by the respectful crowd of bellboys, waiters and valets. The individuals at the top of their hierarchy enjoy a prestige which they do not question, and exercise over those inferior to them a certain capricious tyranny which confirms their rights: Françoise's tyranny over the scullery maid, Tante Léonie's over Françoise, Charlus' over the Faubourg St. Germain. Around these centers veritable court plots are hatched, intrigues of precedence and self-interest comprehensible only to those who know the tacit code which governs the group. However, like Françoise in relation to the two classes above her, like the great-aunt and the prince, the bourgeoisie and the aristocracy have certain vague conceptions and elementary impressions about one another which are prompted by total ignorance or outright hostility. Secure in their well-defined conception of their own rights and prerogatives, the individuals of one class look askance at those belonging to another. They fail to make any distinction between "degrees" and regard them with the sly, ironic complacency of the narrator's great-aunt, or with the vague kindliness of the Princesse de Luxembourg when Mme de Villeparisis introduces the narrator and his grandmother to her:

The Princesse de Luxembourg had given us her hand, and from time to time, as she conversed with the Marquise, she would bestow a kindly look upon my grandmother and myself, a look that contained that embryonic kiss which is put into a smile reserved for babies out for an airing with their nurse-maids. Indeed, in her anxiety not to appear to belong to a sphere higher than ours she seemed to have miscalculated the distance between us and by an error in adjustment, her eyes beamed with such benevolence that I could see the moment approach when she would stroke us with her hand as she would have stroked a couple of friendly animals which had stuck their heads between the bars of their cages at the zoo . . . But she said good-bye to Mme de Villeparisis and put out her hand to us with the intention of treating us in the same way she treated her friends, as intimates, and to put herself on our level. But this time she had doubtless promoted us in the hierarchy of creation, for her equality with us was indicated by the Princesse to my grandmother by that tender, maternal smile one gives a little boy when saying good-bye to him as to a grown-up. By a miraculous stride in evolution, my grandmother was no longer a duck or an antelope but what Mme Swann, a passionate anglophile, would have called a "baby." [4]

From its own sphere, each group views the others through a strangely distorted lens which gives rise to a body of errors: the middle-class group, for instance, thinks that the Marquise de Villeparisis and the Princesse de Luxembourg are "two hussies of the kind that it is difficult to avoid in spas." The principles according to which the people within each group classify themselves do not carry over from one group to another, nor does the knowledge of how these distinctions are made. Their mutual relations are a veritable "comedy of errors," full of the blunders, mistaken identities, and muddles of all kinds, from which Proust draws the material for his social comedy. So it is that when the flower of the aristocracy of the Faubourg St. Germain are invited by the Baron de Charlus to Mme Verdurin's, they behave with the most blatant crudeness—even though theoretically their social relationships are built upon a strict code of politeness:

Having come there partly out of friendship for M. de Charlus and partly out of curiosity to see a place of this kind, each duchess went straight to the baron, as though he were the host, and said within earshot of the Verdurins, who naturally missed nothing: "Where is the old girl? Must I really be introduced to her? I do hope that at least she won't have my name put in the papers tomorrow; my family would never speak to me again. What! It's that white-haired woman? Why, she looks quite presentable . . . " and each having found a number of friends, they gathered in little groups that watched with ironic curiosity the arrival of the "faithful," finding nothing to criticize but an occasional odd hairdo . . . and, in short, regretting that this salon was not very different from those they knew and feeling the disappointment of society people who, having gone to a dive to see Bruant in the hopes of being rudely greeted by the entertainer, find themselves welcomed by a courteous bow instead of the expected chorus: "Look at her! Look at her puss! My gawd, what a mug she has!" [5]

Social distances are thus based upon the premise that the people whom we do not know are different from us. This belief dehumanizes social reactions, creates a viewpoint which is distorted, sometimes to a preposterous degree, and introduces into society the comedy of incongruity in attitudes, opinions, and gossip. Charlus, for instance, whose easy insolence is nourished by his unquestioned belief in the superiority bestowed upon him by his noble birth, seems to the uninformed narrator a shady and somewhat alarming character; the Marquise de Villeparisis looks to Odette like a little old woman who might easily be a concierge, and Mme Verdurin states positively that the Duc and Duchesse de la Trémoille eat with their fingers.

Nothing is further removed from these rather spiteful deformations than the distortion, similar in origin but of a very different kind, manifest in the narrator's view of society during the period when a "social springtime" enraptures him. This vernal glamour of society is due to his "curiosity about all ways of life hitherto unknown," [6] a curiosity which is particularly piqued by anything related to the two sumptuous "realms" near Combray. The appearance of Gilberte Swann in the Champs-Elysées marks the narrator's point of departure toward that "society" which still seems mysterious to him. Irresistibly drawn by the prestige that glorifies the name of Swann in his eyes, it is toward the Swanns that he directs his avid curiosity. Everything that seems to him to have the slightest contact with them, to belong in their lives, be it merely by a simple proximity, or an association of ideas, becomes, like Mme Blatin, a focus of attention and attraction, a center around which gravitate all the various feelings which agitate him. "Plunged in a restless sleep," he says, "my adolescence enveloped in one long phantasy the whole section of the city where it first contained my dreams," [7] the section where the Swanns live. This vague restlessness becomes focused on Gilberte, and he names it love. The obsession which springs from this love is not enough to assure the narrator's entry into the Swann salon; that entry is brought about by chance, but it is because of his love that his introduction to the Swanns becomes a real social "migration." His love for Gilberte is the magic carpet by means of which he crosses the gap which he had mentally established between himself and the Swanns. But he does not lose his place in the Swann's milieu when his love for Gilberte dies; he remains in their world.

If originally he frequents the Swanns so that he can see Gilberte, that which keeps him there after he no longer wants to see her is a purely social element, the attraction of elegance, of social prestige, which, although he is unconscious of it, also plays a large part in his love. This attraction had already oriented his childish dreams toward a certain way of life, the opulence of which seems to him to reveal an inner wealth, an exquisite treasure reserved for an élite, inaccessible to ordinary mortals. It is through its atmosphere—that of a chatoyant, animated tapestry—that social life first exerts its charms upon the adolescent narrator. These charms are epitomized in the voluptuous and brilliant scene that unfolds "between quarter past twelve and one o'clock in the month of May" [8] in the Allées des Acacias in the Bois de Boulogne. There is the pure show of social life, an urbane, luxurious spectacle which is an end in itself and has no other spectators than the actors who take part in it. It is a gratuitous display of opulence, but of an opulence which utilizes life and the means gained by wealth for the sole purpose of extracting from them an ephemeral and perfect creation; woman is its focus and elegance its criterion. Elegance in itself creates momentarily an autonomous assembly of people set apart from the toil of everyday life, as well as from its cares, its suffering and solitude. The ritual develops merely to perpetuate its own existence. At least so it appears to the dazzled eyes of the narrator when he comes first to see and later to participate in that perfect flowering of affluence, Odette Swann's morning walk in the paths of the Bois de Boulogne. The Bois is the classless realm which belongs to a special social ilk: the women on the fringe of high society, or the demimondaines, both cultivated in the hothouses of Parisian elegance in "the era of the horse and carriage."

"But most often . . . as I had learned that Mme Swann took a walk almost daily in the Allée des Acacias, around the Grand Lac, and in the Allée de la Reine Marguerite, I guided Françoise toward the Bois de Boulogne." It is there that the pageant of worldly elegance unfolds, there that all social Paris meets, forming a retinue for the beauties then in vogue:

I thought that the beautiful—in the hierarchy of feminine elegance—was determined by occult practices into which they [the women] had been initiated, and that they had the power to create it; and I accepted beforehand, as a revelation, the aspect of their attire, their carriages, the thousand and one details which to me were like the agents of an inner force that gave the cohesion of a masterpiece to this ephemeral and moving pageant.[9]

It is, however, upon Mme Swann that the adolescent boy's "troubled" and "reverent" gaze rests:

Suddenly, on the gravelled path, late, unhurried, and luxuriant as the most beautiful flower that blooms only at midday, Mme Swann appeared, radiant in a costume always a bit different, but as I recall, usually mauve; then at the moment of her brightest radiance she raised and unfurled at the end of its long stem the silken banner of a large parasol that matched the shimmering petals of her gown. A retinue surrounded her: Swann, four or five clubmen who had come to call on her in the morning or whom she had met on the way; their dark mass attentive, performing the almost mechanical movements of a squad immobilized in a setting around Odette . . . made her stand out, frail, fearless . . . like the apparition of a creature of a different species, of an unknown race with an almost martial strength that made her seem a match for her multiple escort.[10]

So "Mme Swann, majestic, smiling, amiable, advancing down the avenue in the Bois," passed by in a veritable apotheosis, hailed universally. Each salutation "released . . . like clockwork the gesticulations of minor characters who were none other than Odette's entourage, with Swann the first to lift his topper lined with green leather, with the smiling graciousness he had learned in the Faubourg St. Germain." [11]

The world of elegance here, as in all its ceremonies, is focused to such an extent upon the woman that the men of her entourage, although distinguished, are reduced to little more than automatons. The extravagant ritual which takes place before the eyes of the narrator in the Allée des Acacias in May is peculiar to elegance. The ceremonial life of society in all its forms exerts upon him the same fascination: that of large hotels and restaurants, of salons, of dinners, of afternoon and evening receptions, as well as the ceremonial of the kitchen. These rituals seem to the adolescent the very essence of social life; they are apparent in fashions or liveries, in fixed and almost mechanical ceremonies such as Odette's outing, in the behavior of waiters at a fashionable restaurant. Each change of scene brings the young man into contact with a form of life which at first appears to him stylized, and in which people behave with the ordered and beguiling grace of dancers in a ballet.

These ceremonies, which he observes from the outside, appear to define a way of life in which everything is choice; they are, he thinks, signs of a mysterious life oriented toward some precious goal unknown to him. The social concept of his parents, content to belong to the solid middle class, gives way to an entirely different attitude which is essentially adolescent. Everything that belongs to his world is depreciated, everything that differs from it acquires value. He is ashamed of Françoise when he compares her with Gilberte's English governess, and his grandmother's familiar habits cover him with confusion before the personnel at the Grand Hotel in Balbec. He feels himself compelled to appropriate the new ceremonies, and participate in them, whether by using Odette's anglicisms, eating chocolate cakes which make him sick, or playing hunt-the-slipper with Albertine and her friends.

The social universe is split into two, the ordinary world,

his own, and the extraordinary world, which alone interests him. Any group which behaves self-confidently, and from which he is excluded, is society as far as he is concerned. The individuality of anyone belonging to any of these groups is enhanced for him because of the marvelous atmosphere which radiates from the coterie itself, and which transforms any member of it into a creature of a special species. Thus, "surrounded by monsters and gods," [12] the narrator observes the evolutions of these groups with wonder, timidity, and longing. In "the delightful anxiety of partaking in an unknown way of life," [13] he unconsciously experiences the feelings which initiate and maintain all social ceremony. He scorns his own social group, and creates fictitious social values based solely on his ignorance and on the attraction that emanates from an apparently self-contained and closed coterie. These feelings all amass around the worldly passion par excellence, complex and protean—snobbery. They also determine the continual gravitation of one group toward another, and of individuals toward the groups. Each time that a social gap is crossed, the group previously mysterious when viewed from afar falls into the depreciated domain of the known, and another group acquires prestige.

For the narrator a whole world of emotion revolves around these encounters. When young St. Loup, heralded by Mme de Villeparisis and already a legend of worldly success, appears in Balbec, the passionate curiosity with which the adolescent narrator observes him transforms him at first into a young sun god:

One afternoon of scorching heat I was in the hotel dining room which had been left in semi-darkness to keep out the sun, . . . when . . . I saw a young man with piercing eyes, tall and slender, his head held high on his long neck, his skin and hair so golden that they seemed to have absorbed all the sun's rays. Clothed in a plain white suit of a thin material that suggested, no less than the darkened dining room, the heat and glorious weather outside, he walked quickly by. His eyes, from one of

which a monocle kept falling, were the color of the sea. Everyone looked at him with curiosity, for the young Marquis de St.
Loup-en-Bray was noted for his elegance.[14]

The young sun-god, who is to become an intimate and devoted friend, is rapidly transformed into a monster of "innate
hardness" and "insolence" when he passes the narrator without greeting him, "his slender body just as inflexibly
straight" as when seen before, "his head just as high, his
glance indifferent." [15] The "monster" St. Loup is simply the
form taken by the narrator's frustration because he is not at
once able to make the acquaintance of the young Marquis.
Precisely at that moment, the adolescent experiences the
power of that unique motivation which activates the whole
social movement from the top to the bottom: to "become
acquainted" with a person or group, or to refuse to "become
acquainted." Everyone in the social game is looked upon as
a connection desirable or undesirable, established or virtual,
past, present or future.

The members of the middle class who engage in this
game are close enough to the aristocracy to be aware that it
exists; they recognize an aristocrat because he bears a name
preceded by the nobiliary particle "*de.*" It is essential for a
socially ambitious member of the middle class to close the
gap which separates his name from the "noble" name, and to
make the acquaintance of someone who has the coveted "*de.*"
The Faubourg St. Germain as a whole seems to the bourgeoisie a citadel which is defended by the aristocracy and can
only be taken by assault. In *A la Recherche du Temps perdu,*
a *sub-rosa* social "war" is carried on which Proust presents
at length, and most humourously. The Verdurin clique is a
war machine, scientifically armed; within it all the ruses and
strategies of assault are developed. In the center of the Faubourg St. Germain, grouped around the Duchesse, the aristocracy defends its positions. Its defenses, however, are weakened from the inside by psychological tendencies which are
common to all human beings: curiosity, the fear of boredom,
the need for diversion, and self-interest. The Verdurin phal-

ange assures its rise up the social ladder by cleverly playing upon these weaknesses.

Extremely rich, the Verdurins give sumptuous receptions. They counterattack worldly snobbery with an artistic or political snobbery which gradually attracts attention; they combat aristocratic exclusiveness with intellectual exclusiveness. The clique makes its appearance in the social world as a unit strongly organized around its "chief" and his lady, with an acknowledged code tyranically enforced. People who are not in the group are "bores." Its sole avowed aim is the creation of an agreeable and stimulating life for the "faithful." But its implacable progression in time reveals its true goal. As a social organism, it proceeds by successive assimilations and automatic expulsions. The appearance of a new element within it and the identical quality which marks each successive acquisition clearly show where the group is headed: Swann, Forcheville (whose *"de"* delights Dr. Cottard), Charlus, then, little by little, the whole Faubourg are absorbed until Mme Verdurin after her husband's death finally reaches the heart of the aristocratic citadel and marries the Prince de Guermantes. Everything is used in this assault: Swann's love for Odette, Charlus' passion for Morel, Elstir's genius, Vinteuil's sonata, the Dreyfus affair, the war, Morel's talent. As soon as they deviate from the invisible route that "Ma" Verdurin is following, Swann, Charlus and Elstir are coldly eliminated. The little clique is not concerned with human beings as much as with the rôle they play in the coterie's social strategy, a rôle to which they must entirely submit themselves; the Verdurins are never concerned with the real value of an individual.

For the Duchesse de Guermantes social art consists not only in forming a salon closed to all but the most exclusive aristocracy, but in arranging to bring into it, to a cleverly calculated degree, people of a different kind, like Swann. She gives the aristocracy the impression that what counts in Oriane's salon are spiritual values, and that her salon is not like the others. She enhances this impression by making herself inaccessible. To make Oriane's acquaintance, or to have her as a guest at a soirée, becomes an event in the Faubourg St. Germain. In Oriane's salon certain signs also appear which indicate where it is going. The need for novelty and diversion push the Duchesse further and further afield, away from the Faubourg until at the end of the novel, she has wandered far outside her own class. She now sees only artists and actresses on the fringes of society and only hesitates still a little between Balthy and Mistinguett through fear of the Duc. In both cases the social battle is waged around a group, a coterie which, because it has the reputation of being exclusive, creates around itself a zone of attraction and that climate of prestige in which snobbery flourishes.

Proust shows that the laws of society are always the same as he describes all the phases of worldly ascent and descent through countless salons. Behind the ritual of salon life, the game of human relationships—complicated and sharpened by the game of social relationships—continues to be played from individual to individual and from group to group. The narrator discovers it slowly, and he himself is subject to its laws: attractions and repulsions, invitations and refusals, intertwine in all directions, determining meetings, factions, friendships, evolutions and revolutions of individuals in relation to one another. Society forms a sort of biological culture in which individuals can try out all the means by which they can make contact with one another, a medium in which emotions are experimented with freely; it is essentially the sphere of relativity. Love is born there, friendship is cultivated, as well as the whole gamut of sentiments, running from generosity to cruelty, which accompany the desire to please and to dominate. But, more than anything else, what flourishes in all its forms is the need for "diversion" in the Pascalian sense of the word.

"Diversion" for society people is the art of using others for the sole purpose of satisfying one's needs and disguising one's boredom. Where affections are concerned, this exploitation can be admitted neither to oneself nor to others. That is why Proust's characters hide, dissemble, and betray one another. They lie to themselves and to each other under various pretexts, hiding their real motivations, which may vary from the needs created by a habit which has become automatic to the exacting demands of homosexuality. In the Proustian world the constant reshuffling of social sets becomes apparent when Proust juxtaposes characters whose presence side by side is in itself the sign of a social mutation: Swann seated next to Odette in the Verdurins' salon; Bloch at the Marquise de Villeparisis' tea; Charlus travelling with the "faithful" in the little Balbec train; the narrator chatting with Mme Swann under her parasol as "under the reflection of a wisteria arbor," or dining at the Duchesse de Guermantes'.

It is also conveyed by the variations, which can be infinitely sudden and numerous, that one person undergoes in his apparently stable relations with another person: Swann's relations with Odette, the narrator's with Albertine. Instead of being organized around a social hierarchy, society in this sense seems to the narrator a vast jungle where everyone ferociously pursues his own gratification. In so far as this is concerned, there is no distinction between the Verdurins and the Guermantes. Their social universe is the same, regulated by a strong generic need to be amused, to organize their lives with a view to immediate pleasures. This exigency is the Trojan horse by means of which all social citadels are taken and all class conventions foiled. The narrator, once he has entered the Swanns' milieu, remains there; in the same way, once someone has been introduced into society to satisfy its demand for amusement, he remains there despite displacements and disfavors, as do Bloch and Morel, participating only in the general gyrations of the social kaleidoscope.

Possessing both money and leisure, left entirely to its own devices, the social set has only one deep-rooted desire: to be protected from the emptiness of existence and to draw from the sterile and disquieting substance of life a mask which is reassuring and flattering to itself. Carried along in the toils of pleasures, all of them worldly, the members of society experience a violent aversion when confronted by the slightest unpleasantness. It is infinitely more important to avoid unpleasantness than to respect the values of a social, moral, or intellectual code, or to grapple with spiritual problems. It is for this reason that, even while these people make a point of cultivating the emotions, they cannot tolerate the blossoming of any deep feeling, any more than that of a real talent or a vigorous intellect. They want neither to understand nor to know, only to be adorned and amused. In society Brichot's knowledge becomes pedantry, Cottard's curiosity expresses itself in lumbering absurdities, and Swann turns into an amiable dilettante; no solid values are tolerated. Proust emphasizes this characteristic of society in his portrayal of the unconscious behavior of his characters, pointing out the disparity between their words and their acts, or the disparity between the truth and their distortion of it.

Among the numerous dinners, teas, and soirées described in the novel, there is one soirée that is particularly important both because of its position in the very center of the book and because of the space allotted to it. It is the ball at the Princesse de Guermantes' which consumes about two hundred pages between the moment when the narrator reads the invitation: "The Princesse de Guermantes, née Duchesse de Bavière, will be at home on . . . ." [16] to the moment when he leaves the Duc and Duchesse at the end of the ball to find Albertine.

Closely connected with the account of the ball is an episode which runs through an almost equal number of pages, and which concerns the Duc and Duchesse de Guermantes only:

The day on which the Princesse de Guermantes was to give her party I heard that the Duc and Duchesse had returned to Paris the day before. It was not the Princesse's ball that brought them back; one of their cousins was seriously ill and, besides, the Duc was most anxious to attend a fancy-dress ball that was to be held that same evening at which he was to appear as Louis XI and his wife as Isabeau of Bavaria.[17]

A ball, a fancy-dress party: these are social obligations, imperative pleasures—secondary, however, when compared with the important social obligations entailed by the death of a relative. The two obligations coincide, and a single act, the return to Paris, fulfills both. But it is not long before they are in direct conflict. As the Duc and Duchesse, after returning from the ball, prepare to dress for the fancy-dress party, M. de Guermantes is confronted by two cousins who are faithfully keeping guard on the stairs in front of his door:

"Basin, we felt we must warn you that you must not be seen at the ball: poor Amanian died just an hour ago." The duke felt a momentary alarm. He could see the delights of the ball snatched away from him . . . now that he had been told of the death of M. d'Osmond. But he quickly recovered and flung at his two cousins a retort in which he declared, along with his determination not to forego his pleasure, his inability to assimilate the niceties of the French language: "He is dead! Surely not, it's an exaggeration, an exaggeration!" [18]

And the fancy-dress party is not sacrificed.

This episode, from its introduction to its conclusion, is an intrinsic part of the account of the Princesse's soirée and its theme reappears intermittently. As the time of the fancy-dress party draws nearer, Osmond's death becomes more imminent and the attitude of the Duc, harassed by two opposing obligations, becomes more transparent. It becomes progressively clear, from the discreet beginning of the tale to its end, that in the Duc's mind a common standard prevails with respect to the two opposing events, and that as far as he is concerned pleasure definitely takes precedence over mourning. All the Duc's worldly acumen is brought into play so that the ill-timed death will not interfere with his own pleasure.

During the afternoon that precedes the ball, the Princesse de Silistrie comes to see the Guermantes, who are back in Paris chiefly, they claim, because of their cousin's illness:

She spoke sadly to the Duc of a cousin of his . . . whose health had been very bad for some time and who was suddenly much worse. But it was evident that the Duc, though full of pity for his cousin's lot, and who kept repeating "Poor Mama! He's such a nice boy," but it was clear he was still hopeful.[19]

A little later, the two cousins, Mme de Plassac and Mme de Tresme, "came to call upon Basin and declared Cousin Mama's state left no more hope." [20] The problem is posed:

The Duc called back the footman to ask whether the servant he had sent to enquire at his cousin d'Osmond's had returned. His plan was simple: as he had reason to believe that his cousin was dying, he was anxious to have news of him before his death, that is to say, before he was obliged to go into the customary mourning. Once protected by the formal assurance that Amanian was still alive, he would high-tail it to his dinner, to the party at the prince's, to the ball where he would appear as Louis XI and where he had a most promising and exciting rendezvous with a new mistress. And he would not send again to enquire about his cousin's health until the next day when all the fun would be over. Then, if the cousin had died during the night, he would go into mourning.[21]

In order to ensure the complete success of this little strategy of etiquette and propriety, M. de Guermantes orders his valet to disappear: "Go out, go wherever you want, paint the town red, sleep out, but I don't want to see you until tomorrow morning." If d'Osmond's death cannot be prevented, its announcement will at least be delayed; and the Guermantes make a brilliant entrance at the ball. "Some well-intentioned people threw themselves upon the Duc to prevent his entering: 'But don't you know that poor Mama is at death's door? He has just been given extreme unction.' 'I know it,' answered M. de Guermantes, pushing aside the importunate person in order to enter. 'The last sacrament produced the best effect.' " [22]

The final "You're exaggerating" of M. de Guermantes is thus only a stronger declaration of his persistence in preventing the social conventions which surround death from interfering with his pleasure. Proust dwells at some length upon this incident, and emphasizes it; he does not hesitate to exaggerate to the point of absurdity the Duc's reactions and retorts, and his complete complacency. The importance of the episode seems markedly greater when we note that the story reappears, in a more or less modified form, three times in the course of the novel.

On the evening of the famous fancy-dress ball, the Duchesse Oriane, as she is about to enter her carriage, learns from Swann that he has only a short time to live. " 'What are you saying,' said the Duchesse, stopping for a second on her way to the carriage and raising her beautiful blue eyes, which were grieved but full of doubt." [23] Startled by Swann's words, she hesitates, but is hustled along by the Duc. "Mme de Guermantes continued determinedly toward the carriage and repeated her previous farewell to Swann. 'We'll have to speak about that again, you know. I don't believe a word of what you're telling me, but we shall have to talk about it. You have been frightened by some silly fool.' [24] and the Duc, as he was leaving, bellowed from the door to Swann who was already in the courtyard: 'And don't let yourself be taken in by those idiot doctors. What the devil! They're nothing but silly asses. You're as healthy as the Pont-Neuf. You'll bury us all.' " [25] Although the same word is not repeated the conclusion is the same: Swann and the doctors are exaggerating. But when the Duc suddenly catches sight of Oriane's shoes his hurry to be off disappears; and Swann, the Duchesse's favorite friend, who is now close to death, sees, more clearly than the Guermantes' dying relative, that going to a ball in slippers of the right color is more important to them than a word of sympathy to a doomed friend.

These two episodes, so close to one another, are juxtaposed for a definite purpose. The second raises the question of the claims of friendship in the face of death, and reflects on

the attitude of the Duchesse as well as that of the Duc. Somewhat less automatic and brutal than the Duc's, Oriane's attitude and her words are, nevertheless, so exact a repetition
that one is tempted to see in them an expression of that philosophy which characterizes the "Guermantes species" and to
which they all conform, each in his individual manner. Yet
the trait does not belong solely to the Guermantes'; their reaction in the face of death reappears in an entirely different
milieu, that of the Verdurins.

The habitués of La Raspelière are arriving for the usual
Wednesday dinner: "But à propos of the young violinist,"
continues Brichot, "I was forgetting, Cottard, to tell you the
big news. Did you know that our poor friend Dechambre,
who used to be Mme Verdurin's favorite pianist, has just
died? Isn't it awful?" [26] The "faithful" exchange a few
words on the subject and then resume their own topics of
conversation until their arrival at La Raspelière, where the
question of mourning comes up. What will Mme Verdurin's
reaction be? Will the dinner be put off? M. Verdurin decrees
that it be ignored. " 'What, you're still talking about Dechambre?' said M. Verdurin, who had preceded us and who,
seeing that we were not following him, had come back. 'Look
here,' he said to Brichot, 'there must be no exaggeration in
anything.' " [27] Dechambre's death, the reaction of the Verdurins and their côterie to that death are described in ten
pages of the novel and culminate with the word already used
by the Guermantes. After this the evening flows on quite
peacefully.

And finally there is the soirée given by Mme Verdurin
in honor of Morel for the aristocratic guests of the Baron de
Charlus, the soirée which occurs just after the death of the
Princesse Sherbatoff, an inseparable friend of the Verdurins.
"Just as we were going to ring the doorbell we were overtaken
by Saniette, who told us that the Princesse Sherbatoff had
died at six o'clock." The guests enter, remove their overcoats
and are welcomed by M. Verdurin. "M. Verdurin, with whom

we condoled on the subject of the Princesse Sherbatoff, said to us, 'Yes, I know that she is very ill.' 'But she died at six o'clock,' exclaimed Saniette. 'You always exaggerate,' Saniette was told curtly by M. Verdurin who, since he had not called off the reception, preferred the hypothesis of illness." [28]

Obviously Proust is repeating the same anecdote deliberately. In each of the four cases he juxtaposes a social event and a death. In each he depicts a contradictory situation in which social convention demands that the conventional sentiments of either family or friendship be respected; and finally we have a barefaced evasion of convention, denoted by the same word "exaggeration," applied to the state least susceptible to that description, death. Could this repetition have been unconscious, merely vague reminiscence? Proust makes use of his anecdote in different ways, but perfectly symmetrically: twice with the Guermantes, twice with the Verdurins. This symmetrical repetition seems to indicate that Proust has some purpose in mind, and is not writing haphazardly. The repetition of the episode has a value in itself for because of it the anecdote acquires a meaning it would not possess had it appeared only once.

By repeating his anecdote, Proust relates the Verdurin group to the Guermantes group, and shows that their reactions are identical. It is a concrete yet subtle demonstration. Two different groups in identical circumstances might react once in the same way by mere chance; but when the reaction is repeated not only within the framework of each group but from group to group, it can scarcely be a chance reaction. Proust sets up this evidence to make us realize that despite all their individual differences, the Guermantes and the Verdurins are alike. The behavior described in the four successive and distinct incidents becomes progressively impersonal and automatic. The gestures seem to be isolated from the individuals, and to belong properly neither to the Duc nor to M. Verdurin; the words are not spoken reflectively, but mechanically. We come to think of these reactions as particular not to any individual but to a "group," a "species," of which the Duc and Duchesse are one specimen and the Verdurins another.

This species flourishes in society and unites Odette with Albertine, with the Duchesse, with the Verdurins, and with all the Guermantes. It is ferociously egotistical, anarchical even, and this explains the unproductivity of society, and its "prodigious aptitude for the disruption of class distinctions." The men accepted by the world of the Guermantes "had usually been brilliant men; but though gifted for a career in the arts, diplomacy, parliament or the army, they had preferred the life of the coterie." [29] Such a life does not tolerate a genuine talent which is not instantly employed to give pleasure. It is really the individual quest for pleasure which determines the apparently chaotic changes in the social kaleidoscope of Proust's world.

One pleasure is supreme above all others in this world. Before the narrator goes to the reception of the Prince and Princesse de Guermantes, he sees a meeting between Jupien and Charlus, and a whole aspect of Charlus' personality and relationships becomes clear to him. We are introduced first to the world of Sodom, and subsequently to the world in which Sodom and Gomorrha merge. The essential unifying factor of the Proustian social world is now revealed: the covert game of sex, especially in its forbidden form, homosexuality. In this respect Proust, possibly unconsciously, proves the force of his own esthetic theory; his own particular "inner" world tyrannically imposes its values upon his work. The narrator's view of life is now not unlike the one he entertained as an adolescent when he lived "completely surrounded by monsters and gods." For underneath the trappings and rites of society, underneath the worldly game which it pretends to play so solemnly, Proust gradually delineates another reality. Essentially neither bourgeois nor aristocrats, the inhabitants of the Proustian world are equivocal beings, man-like women and women-like men, androgynous, hermaphroditic. They bridge all social gaps in order to meet

each other in the hazardous game which they are always playing among themselves. They flout the laws and conventions
of society, laying themselves open to insult and misunderstanding. They live in a picaresque world; events are unforeseen, and everyone moves through a maze of disguise, im-
provisation, and mistaken identity.

Instead of leading him to a knowledge of the "occult
laws" of his "enchanted realms," the narrator's exploration
of society ultimately leads him to discover the cities of Sodom
and Gomorrha, reborn and surreptitiously allied. The inhabitants of these cities, dogged by the need for secrecy and
subterfuge, obsessed by their desire, cannot achieve any en-
during happiness. More than all the other Proustian figures,
they live in the "inhuman world" of an ever more demanding
sensuality which can only be satisfied by others as fugitive
as themselves. Vulnerable from every point of view, they
flourish in an atmosphere of blackmail and dissimulation
which leaves its mark upon them. And they in turn mark the
society which surrounds them: St. Loup marries Gilberte because he needs money to keep Morel, whom his uncle has
already pushed into society. Jupien's niece, having become
Mlle d'Oléron and a noblewoman, marries the young Marquis
de Cambremer, thus sanctioning Charlus' affair with Jupien.
Albertine through her "affairs" establishes a vast network of
"contacts" in which Morel and his friend the chauffeur are
involved in a rather shady way. And it is the Prince de Guermantes whom Charlus, spying upon Morel's movements, could
have discovered as a rival. The virtuoso Morel, son of the narrator's uncle's valet, loved by the Verdurins, adored by Charlus, associated in Albertine's pleasures, is the character
around whom the whole ambiguous network of homosexuality
develops.

The narrator's imagination had endowed the inhabitants
of the social world with a special aura; they were unknown,
mysterious. When he becomes intimate with these people and
thinks he knows them, he gets used to them and they lose their
aura. Homosexuality then gives them a disturbing, deeper

dimension, and a new and mysterious complexity, but this time it is the complexity of reality, less harmonious than that of imagination and infinitely more unruly.

The Princesse de Guermantes' soirée is the climax of the narrator's social ascension. It is also there that Swann makes his last appearance in society, and that the narrator first understands Charlus' personality. Swann disappears and Charlus embarks upon a Balzacian career which is more and more marked by his homosexuality. As a child peering through the gates of Swann's grounds in Tansonville, the narrator had seen Charlus at Odette's side. Odette, framed by Charlus and Swann, is already a sort of symbol of the society he will come to know. Swann, sensitive, cultured, talented, devotes his life first to social dilettantism, then to a love which combines the spice of artistic dilettantism with that of sensual dilettantism. Charlus is drawn outside his native milieu by homosexuality, which slowly usurps his personality and finally absorbs him completely. Always accompanied by his mother and by Françoise, the narrator crosses the territory of the Swanns and the Guermantes without permitting himself to be absorbed by them. Behind these two prodigious creatures, Swann and Charlus, emerges Proust's own countenance, surprisingly illuminated by this juxtaposition. Swann and Charlus, Charlus who develops when Swann disappears, could not these be the two great temptations that society offered to Proust, the two principal beings within himself to whom it appealed: the "little Proust" of the salons and the alarming Proust who for so long kept young men like Agostinelli, "imprisoned" in his apartment? Could not Swann and Charlus be personifications of the two forces which for a long time deflected Proust from his path, triumphing in him successively; Swann during the period of his "social spring," Charlus in the shadows at first but more and more triumphant? And could not the narrator's mother, pale reflection of the dead grandmother, and Françoise, constitute the symbols of those "virtues" of Combray, the concern for real values, the dogged industry, by which the "virtues" of Combray and the "vices" of society are finally synthesized in the work of art? Swann and Charlus are characters far more powerful in stature than the narrator. Their social career reflects a bitter experience; its tragic overtones are plain.

As he tells the story of the illusions and dreams of his narrator, Proust reconstructs the characteristic aspects of a whole era. Because of his love of imagery, reinforced by his theory of the image, he delights in describing lavishly the passing forms of fashions, of customs, of manners which are all part of the ceremony of social intercourse; his detailed evocations firmly locate his world in historical time. Precisely because it is not concerned with real values, the society which he depicts—fleeting mirror of images and opinions—lives for the moment. Consequently, it reflects the outer aspects of an era, transitory, quickly lost, yet aspects which were then more "present" than any other. It restores those elements of the tangible world which defy definition because they are constantly changing. Mme Swann's costumes are no more superfluous ornaments than the "joyful sensations" described at such length. Worldly ritual imposes its fragile mask upon the Proustian characters, placing them in their own time. Though they are not concerned with it, it nevertheless endows them, already so remote from us, with a compelling charm. This charm does not, however, prevent Proust from emphasizing the cruelty of the social comedy. He derives from it an austere moral code the meaning of which is made clear by the twin failures of Charles Swann and the Baron de Charlus.

5

THE HUMAN COMEDY

ALL human relationships in *A la Recherche du Temps perdu*, without exception and even including the narrator's relationship with his mother and grandmother, are in essence comedies. The characters act out with one another, either voluntarily or unwittingly, plays which, though sometimes gentle, sometimes brutal, are always marked by a certain unconscious humor. This humor pervades the novel, illuminating all the characters and the narrator as well; yet it does not emanate directly from any of them. No Proustian character is sufficiently detached from the spectacle of his own life to look at himself and the world around him with the perspective from which humor springs. There is a Guermantes "wit" which Swann shares with the Duchesse, for example, and a Charlus "wit"; but the former is a play on words and situations, and the latter a satirical verve sparked by a supreme insolence. On the whole the narrator appears, at least in matters that concern him directly, to be as totally devoid of wit as of humor—in this he differs completely from his creator. Implicitly, however, it is through what he sees, hears, and reports, apparently without reservation, that the human comedy staged by Proust is transmitted to us. The even tone of the narration seems often at first to mask the comedy, which later seems all the funnier. It is easy for the reader to overlook the reflective and ironic atmosphere in which so many scenes of the novel are bathed. Yet Proust's humor qualifies and humanizes the relationships of all the characters he creates; because of it, they are far from falling into the desperate patterns so many critics have set up for them.

It is perhaps because his attitude is one of affection that the narrator sees so clearly, in actions which are slightly absurd and therefore infinitely moving, the touching humanness of his grandmother's personality:

In all kinds of weather and even in the pouring rain, after Françoise had rushed out to save the precious wicker chairs, my grandmother could be seen in the deserted, rain-lashed garden pushing back the grey strands of her hair so that her forehead could better absorb the life-giving draughts of wind and rain. "At last we can breathe again!" she would say as she walked up and down the drenched paths, her lively, jerky little step in tune rather with the various moods brought about in her mind by the intoxication of the storm, the virtues of hygiene, the stupidity of my education, and the symmetry of the garden, than with the desire, of which she was totally innocent, to avoid the blobs of mud which gradually covered her plum-colored skirt, causing gloom and despair to her maid.[1]

The same affectionate humor envelops Swann when, carried away by his love, he speaks of the Verdurins to his friends:

"They are magnanimous, and magnanimity is after all the only thing that counts, the one thing that imparts distinction. You see, there are only two classes of beings: those who are magnanimous and the others; and I have reached the age when I must choose, decide once and for all whom I shall like and whom I shall despise, stick to those I like, and make up for the time wasted on the others, never again leave them until I die. . . ."[2]

and when a little later, crossed in his love, returning on foot through the Bois, alone and gesticulating, the same Swann speaks of these same Verdurins:

"What a fetid form of humor," he said, twisting his mouth into an expression of disgust so violent that he could feel the muscles of his throat tense against his collar. "How in God's name can a creature made in His image find anything to laugh at in those nauseous witticisms . . . I am too far above the gutters where these filthy vermin crawl and bawl their cheap obscenities to be spattered by the jests of the Verdurins," he exclaimed. He raised his head and proudly straightened his back . . . He could see the pianist sitting down to play the Moonlight Sonata and the grimaces of Mme Verdurin in frightened anticipation of the shattering effect of Beethoven's music on her nerves: "Idiot, liar!" he shouted, "and she thinks she appreciates art!" [3]

Swann's very suffering is brought back into perspective without being in any sense diminished.

Proust's humor rests almost always upon an incongruity between two aspects of a given situation, its aspect as felt subjectively, and as it appears objectively. This incongruity opens the door to all sorts of misunderstandings. The individual himself associates his actions and words with his feelings or intentions. Seen from the outside, and out of context, they appear to an observer simply as patterns or designs which do not in the least convey their real inner motivation. Swann, gesticulating and talking out loud in the avenues of the Bois in the middle of the night, could easily pass for a drunkard or a madman. It is the body which each person inhabits and through which he must approach others which imposes upon sentiments and emotions limitations that are both pathetic and absurd: a short staccato step in the pouring rain, a mud-spattered skirt, grimaces and gestures, and behind these a whirlwind of feelings and motives—such is the essence of the Proustian comedy.

The world of discourse lies somewhere between the individual's real intent and what his body expresses; "the oblique inner discourse" [4] and the no less oblique outer discourse. Each person sees others from the outside: they are first images, then categorized by words; but he never sees himself except from within, and in his behavior toward others refers to the whole gamut of his own invisible emotions. When he is indifferent to people, he merely observes their movements as he might those of an animal or insect. He registers a set of senseless and funny images. As soon, however, as a person is singled out and becomes an object of attention or desire both behavior and words cease to appear mechanical; they seem to fall away from the individual, and they become part of the inner world of the observer who endows them with his own meaning. They take their place on the inner stage of the observer's emotions.

The human comedy is then played out in a great confusion between the autonomous, physical reality of "others" and their "supplementary selves," that is, their imagined rôles in someone else's life—rôles to which they obstinately refuse to conform. The same discrepancy exists between the individual's subjective life and the coherent picture which he presents to society. Everything becomes comedy or drama, and conversations between individuals are almost always carried on in complete misunderstanding.

Despite this confusion and contradiction the characters in the Proustian world behave in ways that are idiosyncratic, peculiar to themselves. They are endowed with a certain basic naïveté which is intrinsic to them and differentiates them from others. The very unselfconsciousness of these individuals, contrasted with the intensity of their preoccupations, their essential ingenuousness as opposed to the Macchiavellian complexity of behavior in which they idly indulge, is a perennial source of Proustian humor. This form of humor has its source in the same double vision as that which produced, for example, La Fontaine's fables. Mme de Villeparisis, with her black woolen dress and her old-fashioned hat, advancing across the lounge of the Grand Hotel, preceded by her valet, followed by her chambermaid, completely immersed in her own microcosm and oblivious to the lorgnettes levelled on her; the Princesse de Parme seated at the Guermantes' table, dazzled, baffled, delighted and scandalized; the Olympian Duc de Guermantes "clad in his nightshirt shaving himself at his window in the morning," and many more such images, are the substance of Proust's comedy. Its origin is in an attitude seen and remembered, and not in psychological analysis. For analysis, according to Proust, destroys humor by pulling apart its mechanisms, disembodying the human being and depriving the initial image of its specific human flavor; whereas comedy depends upon a profusion of images, gestures, and words to animate a world which no amount of analysis ever succeeds in grasping entirely because life goes so far beyond it.

Tante Léonie's life in all its daily aspects is pure light comedy. Shut up in her room, having, she claims, renounced everything, she does not for an instant stop participating in a double drama: that of Combray and that which she provides for herself.

"Just think, Françoise, Mme Goupil went by more than a quarter of an hour late to fetch her sister; if she loses any more time on the way I shouldn't wonder if she arrived too late for the Elevation."

"Well, there would be nothing surprising in that." Françoise would answer. . . .

"Françoise, if you had come five minutes earlier, you could have seen Mme Imbert go by with asparagus twice the size of Ma Callot's; try to find out from her maid where she got them . . ."

"Françoise, you didn't hear those ear-splitting bells . . ."

"Françoise, for whom is the bell tolling? Oh dear, it must be for Mme Rousseau. To think that I had forgotten that she passed on the other night . . ." [5]

The show reaches its emotional climax when through the streets of Combray passes someone whom "she does not know."

"If, in the evening when I came back and went upstairs to tell my aunt about our walk, I was careless enough to say that by the Vieux-Pont we had passed a man that my grandfather didn't know . . ."

"A man that Grandfather doesn't know!" she exclaimed, "Go on!" Nonetheless slightly upset by this piece of information, she wanted to get to the bottom of the matter and my grandfather was sent for.

"Whom did you pass by the Vieux-Pont, Uncle? A man you didn't know!"

"Of course I knew him," my grandfather answered, "it was Prosper, Mme Bouilleboeuf's gardener's brother."

"Oh well," my aunt said, calm again but still slightly flushed, and shrugging her shoulders and smiling ironically, she added: "And he told me you had seen a man you didn't know!" [6]

The source of the comedy here is the passionate curiosity with which Tante Léonie follows the events which take place in Combray—events that hold no surprise for her and which she simply recounts to herself over and over again, like a child who repeats, without changing a single word, the same fairy tale. Between what she sees and the pleasure she derives from it are all the ties of familiarity. This pleasure is based upon an axiom which is never explicit: that nothing new can ever occur in Combray, that life there, in all its aspects, is unchangeable. This axiom confers upon Tante Léonie a kind of immortality. Her reliance upon this premise is exposed when the slightest alteration occurs in the daily drama, when, violating the limits of possibility, an unfamiliar person appears on the streets of Combray. The agitation, uneasiness, indignation, and relief through which Tante Léonie passes as she reduces to the absurd that shocking remark "someone we do not know" are emphasized by the increasingly ironic repetition of those ill-considered words. Yet it is an apparently reasonable and trite remark which acquires its real significance only when one connects it with the scene in which Swann appears in the garden—Swann, that obscure and problematical "personnage" whom the narrator's family believe they know so well, who consequently is treated cavalierly and with a slight superiority, and yet about whom they really know so little.

The complete absorption with which Tante Léonie, who has nothing to do, rivets her gaze upon Combray gives for the time being a universal significance to whatever she sees, and transforms everything that happens there into an event of cosmic importance. Her gaze is not intrinsically different

from that which each of Proust's characters directs upon his
own microcosm, introducing enormous disproportions into
the relative importance of things. Through the prodigious
magnifying lens of self interest, the Verdurins magnify all
their amusements, griefs, snubs, loves, and they reduce other
events, even the war, to the dimension of the importunate, of
"bores." The same lens imparts an immense importance to
the Sunday invitations the Cambremers extend to some of the
guests of the Grand Hotel at Balbec; and people who are
otherwise sensible enough go to lunch far from the hotel because they wish others to believe that they are at the château.
It is this same magnifying glass that the bourgeois of the
Grand Hotel direct upon Mme de Villeparisis or the Princesse
de Luxembourg, with the same excitement as Tante Léonie
confronted by the impertinent "stranger" in Combray:

Whenever Mme de Villeparisis passed through the hall the chief
magistrate's wife, who always thought the worst of any woman
she did not know, would look up from her embroidery and stare
at the intruder in a manner that convulsed her friends with
laughter.

"Oh, you know," she would say loftily, "I always start by
suspecting evil. I am willing to admit that a woman is married
only after I have seen her birth certificate and marriage license.
But don't worry; I shall start an investigation of my own."

And day after day these ladies would foregather and inquire
laughingly:

"Anything new?"

But on the evening of the Princesse de Luxembourg's call,
the chief magistrate's wife put a finger to her lips:

"There is something new."

"Isn't Mme Porcin wonderful! I never saw anyone . . .
but do tell us, what has happened?"

"Well, a blonde, with layers of paint on her face and a carriage like a . . . you could smell it a mile away—only a creature
of her kind would have come today to call on the so-called
marquise."

"No-o-o! Tut-tut-tut. Did you ever? . . ."[7]

Just as in the case of Tante Léonie, the unknown quantity is willy-nilly reduced to the known, but much less reasonably, for, with the malice introduced by social snobbery into the Balbec comedy, the Princesse becomes a cocotte; and then too at seaside resorts there are really people "whom one does not know."

Tante Léonie plays a comedy of a different sort when, at her game of solitaire, she is found "in a sweat, her false hair out of place, revealing her bald forehead." She conjures up in her imagination a fire in which her entire family is wiped out and she, the sole survivor, becomes the "sensation of the village, stunned, dying on her feet, courageously leading the procession of mourners." Or she makes up a story about Françoise, an imaginary Françoise, who has robbed her and whom she exposes. The latter theme is easier to project into reality and Tante Léonie's room becomes a stage on which she spies upon the real Françoise, and torments her mercilessly. The human comedy becomes drama in its most elementary form, and sets up the mechanisms of the comedy and the drama of love. Alone in her room, Tante Léonie seizes in her imagination upon the person nearest to her, Françoise. In order to amuse herself, without realizing what she is doing, she thrusts Françoise bodily into a commonplace novel, making her act as though she really were guilty. Swann and the narrator do the same when they seize upon the images of Odette and Albertine and force them to enter into their drama of love and jealousy. In her idleness, Tante Léonie, like Swann and the narrator, has discovered the diversion that other people provide when we force them in imagination to embody our own vague feelings. Emotions then take on a certain narrative power, and invent stories in which the chosen individual is cast in the rôle of protagonist; they enhance and dramatize life, giving it an outlet into the extraordinary and at the same time satisfying the demands of self-respect. Thus the spectacle which Tante Léonie enjoys from her bed at Françoise's expense, allows her, with no effort on her part, to fill the exciting and flattering rôle of detective and judge. This capacity to create an imaginary life which is emotionally entertaining and which includes specific aspects of real life, is the source of the pretense and the blackmail which people use with one another. It is chiefly this faculty of imagination which gives the grandiose life of the Baron de Charlus its extraordinary character.

And then there is the comedy of the sick woman who never sleeps. Her nephew finds her "lying on her side, sleeping" peacefully, snoring "lightly"; [8] but her insomnia is a fiction which the whole family, and even the village, respect to the point where the village vocabulary is marked by it, and hammering stops when Mme Octave, who never sleeps, is "resting." This fiction takes its place on a comic level with all the social fictions, no less amusing because more customary, by which people sublimely impose upon one another a wholly arbitrary way of life. The ritual of a reception or the life of the Verdurin "clique," and the conventions which order Tante Léonie's daily life have the same semi-poetic, semi-absurd character which marks, for example, the patterned Saturdays of Combray which the whole family recognize as mandatory. The unshakeable conviction with which Tante Léonie plays her rôle of a great invalid ends by making the game and the reality indistinguishable, and this is what in its turn creates Tante Léonie's singular and inscrutable character. The same can be said of the other characters. If the "social personality" of each individual is a "creation of other people's opinions," [9] it is also linked to certain basic and irreducible facts. Is it because her conduct is irreproachable that the Duchesse de Guermantes has the reputation of being so, or is it a legend "made up in reality of innumerable adventures artfully concealed?" [10] And does Mme Verdurin really like music?

Thus Tante Léonie's life is acted out on three comic levels. In reality, however, it is life itself which acts through her, just as it acts through all the Proustian characters, without their realizing it. Indeed, life often undoes their little comedies. It betrays them all too easily in that body which is visible to all except themselves, and which is less indomitable than the mind.

"Tall, handsome, a kind thoughtful face with long blond mustaches, disenchanted eyes, a refined politeness," simple in "his boyishly cut coat," [11] M. Legrandin, an engineer and a writer of some repute, holds forth on his horror of society and snobbery. But when, upon leaving mass, Legrandin is introduced to "the wife of a neighboring landowner," the narrator sees that:

Legrandin's face expressed an extraordinary zeal and animation; he made a deep bow followed by a brisk upward motion which brought him up so sharply that he leaned backward. . . . This rapid straightening out caused a sort of tense muscular wave to ripple over his buttocks which I had not supposed to be so fleshy. I don't know why this undulation of pure matter, this completely carnal fluency, totally nullifying the spiritual significance the bow was meant to convey, this eagerness of the basest sort lashed to fury, suddenly awoke my mind to the possibility of a Legrandin altogether different from the one we knew. [12]

This discordance between the body and the avowed personality betrays the comedy which the individual is playing: the real person is revealed beneath the artificial one. The unmasking is done with considerably more mercilessness in the Proustian world when there is a question of homosexuality. Nothing, from this point of view, surpasses the Baron de Charlus' entrance at the Verdurins':

"Oh! Here they are," said M. Verdurin with evident relief when he saw Morel at the door, followed by the Baron. The latter, who considered that dining at the Verdurins could hardly be termed going into polite society but more like going into a house of ill repute, was as shy as a schoolboy who, going into a bordello for the first time, shows an exaggerated deference toward the madam. And so M. de Charlus' usual desire to appear virile and aloof was lost in a fit of shyness which awoke his instinctive courtesy, so that it was with a simper and a flutter and with the same sweep that a wide skirt would have given to his waddle that he advanced upon Mme Verdurin with so flattered and honored a look that one would have said that being taken to her house was for him a supreme favor. He beamed affably. He could have been mistaken for Mme de Marsantes, so prominent in him was the woman that nature had placed in his body by mistake. To be sure, M. de Charlus had struggled hard to cover up this mistake and to assume a masculine appearance. But although he had achieved partial success, his tastes and his habit of seeing through a woman's eyes had given him a feminine appearance that was due not to heredity but to his way of life. And although he called upon his body to express . . . the courtesy of a great nobleman, this body which had fully understood what M. de Charlus had ceased to apprehend, displayed to such an extent all the attractions of a great lady, that the Baron would have deserved the epithet "lady-like." [13]

It is the face, the eyes particularly, which most often betrays the actor in the individual: Legrandin's expression when the name Guermantes is mentioned or when he is asked information about Balbec; Odette's "anguished look" when she is thinking up a lie, or her expression when Forcheville "executes" Saniette:

Odette had looked on, impassive, at this scene, but as soon as the door had closed behind Saniette, she had let her expression betray her base nature . . . a sly smile of congratulation sparkled through her eyes for his audacity, and a look of irony for the victim; she had darted at him a look of complicity in crime, [such that] Forcheville, when his eyes encountered hers, sobered in an instant . . . smiled and replied: "He could at least have tried to be pleasant. . . ." [14]

Almost all Proustian individuals are thus betrayed by their eyes: Jupien's eyes—Jupien of the "cold and jeering attitude, with fat cheeks and a florid complexion, . . ." but whose "eyes overflowing with a compassionate look, sad and dreamy, made one think that he was very ill or had just suffered a great loss," [15]—indicate the basic discord between his apparent personality as a man and his instincts as a homosexual; the "bright and roving look" of the Duchesse in

Combray, which is the "benevolent look of a suzeraine [16] . . . for her vassals"; the look of the Princesse de Luxembourg who, despite her desire for equality, transforms the narrator and his grandmother into beings of an inferior order, members of the middle class and remote from her sphere.

To study Proust's human comedy thoroughly the whole of *A la Recherche du Temps perdu* would have to be examined: the thanks of the two great-aunts for the Asti wine, thanks so complicated that Swann, to whom they are addressed and who understands not a word, remains speechless; the narrator's discomfiture when he speaks complacently of his meeting with the "lady in pink" and suffers the unexpected consequences of his naïve vanity; his timid adolescent attempts to impress the girls "within the budding grove" and the struggles which are quietly waged between him and his family, between him and the "others." Such comedy is invariably reinforced in the comedy of language itself, inimitable, guileful, yet at the same time revelatory. Each character uses his own specific form of speech which accompanies him like a musical leit-motiv: Odette's anglicisms, the Guermantes' mannerisms, or the Verdurins', so persistant that even when Mme Verdurin has "arrived" and has become the Princesse de Guermantes, she still repeats "with an exalted look and with the click that her false teeth made: 'Yes, that's it. We'll form a club! We'll form a clique! I like the young, so intelligent, so participating! Ah! What a muchishian you are!' " [17] Legrandin's flowery lyricism, Bloch's hellenisms, and the pompous, massive, solemn boredom which emanates from M. de Norpois' conversation, self-important even when it is only a matter of ordering a risotto.

But as soon as the Baron de Charlus appears it is around him that Proust's comedy finds its real dimension and significance in a succession of scenes which are at once dramatic, comic, and terrible in their truth. Proust traces the complete curve of the baron's life. We follow his progress from the time described by his nephew St. Loup, when as a young prince, insolent, rich, and admirably gifted, he belonged to the

Phoenix Club and was the arbiter of elegance, the cynosure of a dazzled Faubourg St. Germain, until the moment when he appears, "placed" rather than "seated" in the back of his carriage, "a forest of white hair" visible under his straw hat and with "a white beard like the one snow makes on statues in public gardens." [18] Half-paralyzed, half-blind, stripped of every visible pride, "courtly and stricken," the once insolent young prince, at Jupien's injunction, docilely greets Mme de Sainte-Euverte whom he used to scorn.

From the succession of these scenes emerges what is not apparent in each one taken separately—the complete and unpredictable creation which time, working on an individual life, has fashioned out of the young prince. Behind all the comedies and all the dramas which accumulate around the baron, Proust gives through this one individual example the basic design of the whole cycle of human comedy. For Proust, the nature of the comedy does not change because the baron is a homosexual. His peculiarity simply accentuates and dramatizes the various misunderstandings and contradictions which compose life. Furthermore, because it stems from one of the most powerful motivating forces determining behavior, the sexual urge, homosexuality accentuates the discrepancy between what the individual thinks he is revealing to others and the hidden motivations which so implacably mark "a personality that it eventually becomes impossible to touch up the imprint of individual vices and the extents of individual virtues." [19]

Because of the social interdict placed upon homosexuality, as the introduction to *Sodome et Gomorrhe* clearly explains, the homosexual more than any other person projects between himself and the world an artificial character who provides him with an alibi. He is the protagonist of a great comedy of masquerades, disguises, mistakes, quarrels, and exposures. The human comedy in the homosexual's case is coupled with a comedy of situation, the hazard of life having assigned to the body of a man the disposition and desires of a woman, or vice versa. This inevitably creates a whole series of false situations, blunders and mistaken identities, which are the natural result of homosexuality, and which gradually come to compose the baron's entire existence.

The Baron de Charlus stands apart from the narrow-minded conformists of his milieu because of his personality and because of the legends which have sprung up about him. Nonetheless, he seems to embrace all the prejudices of his class. An aristocrat, he has pride of birth and ancestry, coupled with a devout mysticism and an insolent scorn for all unfounded claims to nobility or social position. He escapes, however, the humdrum spirit of his group because, artistically gifted and sensitive, he often behaves in a fantastic manner. Shaken by sudden anger, then by equally sudden compassion, he often seems arbitrary and incoherent. His chief weapon is a free-flowing speech that can be savage or suave, imperious, imaginative or insolent—a kind of inimitable "record," the very mark of his personality. His princely title, his prestige, and the apparent arbitrariness of his behavior make him a solitary being in his own social sphere, feared yet sought after, a social dictator, irascible and sure of himself.

And yet, seen from the outside, unknown and stripped of his background, this is how he appears to the narrator:

The day after Robert had told me all about his uncle while he was waiting for him, in vain as it turned out, as I was walking alone in front of the casino on my way to the hotel, I suddenly had a feeling that I was being stared at by someone nearby. I turned around and saw a man of forty or so, very tall and quite stout, with a dark moustache who, as he nervously tapped his trouser leg with a small cane, stared at me with wide eyes. His glance betrayed at intervals the intent look so often fixed on strangers by certain men in whom, for some reason, they inspire thoughts that would not occur to others—such as, for example, lunatics or spies. He gave me a last quick look, bold and wary, quick and deep, like a parting shot fired by someone before taking flight, and after having glanced all about him, suddenly assumed an absent, haughty look, made an abrupt about-face and became absorbed in reading a playbill, humming to himself and adjusting the moss-rose in his buttonhole . . . He threw back his shoulders with an air of bravado, bit his lip, twirled his moustache and assumed an indifferent, hard, almost insulting look.[20]

A little later the narrator sees him again in front of the hotel:

Swift as a flash of lightning his look shot through me as it had when I first caught sight of him, darted away and returned, as though he had not seen me, to hover at a lower angle. His eyes had the dull, blank look which pretends to see nothing, to register nothing, a look which expressed only the satisfaction of feeling lashes spread wide in round-eyed bliss, the sanctimonious, sirupy look of certain hypocrites, the fatuous look of certain fools. I saw that he had changed his clothes. The suit he wore was even darker . . . when one came near him one felt that the reason for the absence of color in his clothes was due not to a lack of taste for it on his part, but because for some reason or other he denied himself the enjoyment of it. And the restraint his clothes displayed seemed rather the result of following the rigid rules of a diet than a lack of appetite. A dark green line in the material of his trousers matched the stripe of his socks with a nicety which betrayed a taste for color elsewhere subdued and which had been allowed only in this instance, while a red spot on his necktie was as delicate as a liberty one dares not take.[21]

And so appears the outer image of the baron to the eyes of the narrator, an image stripped of the attributes with which the aristocratic world imbued him *a priori*. It is an image doubtless too sharply etched by Proust himself, given the naïveté that the narrator professes. This direct contact with a character first seen from the outside is one of the essential elements of the human comedy, since the intellect of the observer, coming into play later, never succeeds, in Proust's world, either in exhausting all of its possible meanings or in choosing among them.

In this meeting of two individuals who do not know each other, the first contact is made through a profound, sensuous perception, a look that is felt before being seen, which acts physically upon the narrator and obliges him to turn around. It is a force which emanates from the baron and which temporarily isolates him and the narrator on a plane other than that of daily exchanges. Aware of the attention he has aroused, the baron instantly conceals this force. His scrutiny is replaced by a feint, a succession of feints in looks, gestures, and even in emotions as revealed by the "insulting" attitude he takes. It is the beginning of a maneuver. Everything betrays the baron's feint, particularly two things: his costume which unsuccessfully tries to conceal an inner tendency, and his eyes which seem to indicate some secret design. Everything about the baron is discordant, so that the narrator conjures up in his mind two possible explanations, both of which would certainly have surprised the noble lord that Charlus actually was: the hypothesis that the individual is a spy, that is to say, a person who conceals his true self in order to obtain secret information; or a madman, that is, a person who, according to some wholly subjective concept, establishes between himself and the world relationships which from the outside appear incoherent.

When the baron's name throws a light upon his social identity, these two hypotheses collapse, but not the curious comedy in which the narrator finds himself cast in a rôle which he does not know how to play. Invitations are given, then ignored; these are accompanied by preposterous and incomprehensible gestures, nocturnal visits followed by exquisite presents. And always in the baron's powdered face, as in his behavior, there is a theatrical element, a "scrutinizing look" which focusses upon the narrator's face "with the same seriousness, the same air of preoccupation as if it had been a manuscript hard to decipher." [22] "And the circumspect and ever worried expression of those eyes circled by dark rings that extended to his cheeks gave a look of great exhaustion to his face, however carefully he might control his expression. They made one think of a disguise assumed by someone in danger, or by a dangerous but tragic individual," [23] a dangerous person who, however, pinches the neck of the young man on the beach and says to him with "a familiarity and a laugh that were frankly vulgar: 'But he doesn't really give a damn about his grandmother, eh, little fake?' " [24] Charlus at times behaves like a perfect boor.

Charlus' mask is apparent only because it is imperfect; it does not succeed in deceiving the world as to the character hidden behind it who, from behind the mask, makes sudden and disconcerting sorties and sallies. Nor does it differ from the masks worn by other Proustian characters, who all are masked and who under their "known" faces remain riddles. Their disguises are always inadequate. Almost all of them change masks and, from time to time, behind the one currently worn make one of those revealing sallies in which Charlus so often indulges. The face, like the body, is itself a mask fashioned by the mind of which it is the instrument, though an unwilling one. There are the successive masks of Swann: the pleasant one "with the hooked nose, the green eyes under the high forehead surrounded by reddish-blonde hair, worn in the style of Bressant"; [25] the grotesque mask of Swann as he is dying, with cheeks so completely hollowed out by disease that "they fell away like an inconsistent setting" and whose nose now "seemed enormous, and crimson." [26] Then there are the masks of other Proustian characters such as the Verdurins, pretending to be amused, he with his pipe in the corner of his mouth, coughing and laughing as though he had swallowed smoke, she, "closing her eyes before covering her face with her hands"; [27] Cottard's mask, cold and ironical, the masks of the Duc and Duchesse de Guermantes, calling upon relatives or receiving at home; the mask fashioned by love which hides from the narrator that other aspect of his grandmother which he suddenly discovers one day as she is sitting "on the sofa, under the lamp, red-faced, heavy and vulgar, raising from a book dreamy eyes that were a little mad"—a defeated old woman whom he "did not know." [28] And the same holds true for those people whose real natures are hidden inside a ridiculous body: Vinteuil, Bergotte with his snail-like nose, Elstir, and the narrator, mannered and insufferable, who discovers within himself a timeless and almost divine being.

The whole Proustian comedy is a masquerade in which no one knows what part he is playing in what play, and what the exact nature of his disguise is. Thus the disconcerting nature of many of the Proustian characters, which may make them appear incomprehensible to the reader, causes them to be even more incomprehensible to themselves. For at least the reader benefits from the narrator's thoughts about them, thoughts that the other characters never have about themselves.

This thoroughly human comedy is based upon the powerful attraction which human beings exert upon one another according to arbitrary and variable methods of selection—either, as in the case of Tante Léonie, because they are just simply there, or because human beings feel that curiosity about the unknown of which snobbery is an example, or, infinitely more powerful a motive, because of sexual attraction. This attraction can be totally absorbing, as when the baron meets the narrator. It can take a variety of forms against which the individual struggles. Mme Verdurin's hatred of the "bores" is another form of her passionate desire to assimilate them almost digestively; her ferocity against Swann springs from a failure in that direction. The more or less persistent attempt to possess people, and the resistance which it meets, is at the basis of most of the social comedies as well as of the dramas of love. Only the overtones are different. Thus the gratuitously insulting look which Charlus gives the narrator is only the expression of a desire which he fears will be disappointed or scorned; the same kind of fear prompts Legrandin's speeches about the aristocracy, or Mme Verdurin's rage about the La Trémoilles. The reflex in all three cases is to jeer at what cannot be attained. There is not a single Proustian character who under his mask is not seeking to establish with other masked characters a means of communication; they try to abandon an incognito which becomes unbearable to them as soon as a human being approaches whom they wish to know. Each one wears on his mask hieroglyphics which are often unnoticed, but the meaning of which he would

like to impose forcibly upon those around him. Vinteuil indulges in such a comedy when he spreads out on the piano
sheets of music paper covered with notes, so eager is he to
communicate to others what they reveal and what his awk-
ward and clumsy body conceals.

In all its forms, the human comedy in *A la Recherche
du Temps perdu* relates to a clumsy attempt at communication. It is closely connected with the central theme of the
book, which demonstrates that communication between human beings is possible only through the intermediary of art.
The comedy is always a matter of relationship, of language
and artifice; its failures, which are always imminent, move
us deeply at times, imperceptibly at others, according to the
level on which the comedy is played.

The baron's disguise is more elaborate than that of the
other characters because, as the narrator perceives at their
first meeting, he is trying to build up a fictitious character
and at the same time to communicate something more than
this character conveys. He makes a much more concentrated
and passionate effort than do most of the others. Somewhat
like Tante Léonie, he carries it on at the level of his own emotions. His attempts both to conceal and to reveal what he is,
constantly annul and contradict each other, and explain the
incongruities of his character. There is one Balzacian scene,
both grandiose and grotesque, in which Proust shows the
baron revolving about the center of a vast, complicated and
shaky structure built up entirely by his emotions. The un-
bridled romanticism of this scene exactly represents the atmosphere of drama and semi-madness in which this Byron of
homosexuality and salons lives—a Byron, however, who will
not die at Missolonghi.

Invited by M. de Charlus to drop in one evening after
a dinner at the Duchesse de Guermantes', the narrator waits
for over half an hour in an immense greenish drawing-room
before he is shown in to see the baron. When the door finally
opens, he sees Charlus "in a Chinese dressing-gown, his neck
bare, stretched out on a sofa," and next to him a high hat and

a fur-lined coat. A scene then takes place between them which plunges us abruptly into a fantastic world. "I thought that M. de Charlus was going to get up. He stared at me without making the slightest movement." The baron's anger, aggravated by all the gestures of the unfortunate narrator, is vented in a lengthy soliloquy in which the few words proffered by the guest, who has now become a defendant, are nullified by a flood of abuse.

The whole scene is played around one theme: "the interview which I consent to grant you . . . will mark the final point of our relations"; it is reiterated in different forms: "the last words which we shall exchange on earth," "now it is my turn to move away from you and we shall no longer know each other." This leit-motiv is all the more surprising because the narrator has scarcely seen the baron more than two or three times. The exact nature of the reproach aimed at the narrator is that the latter misunderstood the baron's gesture in offering him a book of Bergotte's, which had a binding encircled with forget-me-nots. In short, the narrator is accused of not having known how to interpret the baron's meaning, the cipher language of the flower. Compared to the violent anger it arouses, the grievance is slight.

On the basis of this triviality, M. de Charlus builds up a scene which ranges from lashing irony to violent anger, passing through a display of emotion that ends up in tears. He becomes crudely insulting when the narrator, taken aback, "bidden to sit in the Louis XIV chair" sits instead in a Directoire chair. The baron overwhelms him with sarcasms: " 'I can see that you don't know any more about periods of furniture than you do about flowers'; 'don't argue about style,' he screeched, 'you don't even know what you are sitting on. You are offering your bottom a Directoire footstool for a Louis XIV bergère. One of these days you will mistake Mme de Villeparisis' lap for a lavatory and heaven knows what you will do there. . . .' " Propelled by the sound of his own words, he becomes magnanimous, solemn, and moralizing: " 'As in Velasquez's *Lances*,' he continued, 'the victor

steps toward the humblest in rank, as is the duty of a man of
nobility. Since I am everything and you are nothing, I am
the one who took the first step toward you . . . I put you to
the test that the only truly great man of our world has so
ingeniously called the test of excessive friendliness and which
he quite rightly declares to be the most terrible of all, the only
one that can separate the wheat from the chaff. . . .' " Then,
still moved by the sound of his own words, he turns maudlin
and with "a sad gentleness" and "tears in his voice," pleads
his cause. "Only it seems to me that you might have . . . if
only out of consideration for my age, written to me." From
these successive emotions, M. de Charlus returns to fury,
"while his voice became in turn piercing and roaring, like a
deafening storm" he shrieks insults at the young man seated
before him. The scene reaches a climax of pointless and night-
marish absurdity. Exasperated, and in the throes of fury
himself, the young man dashes forward, grabs the baron's
new hat, tramples upon it and tears it to shreds, while the
baron continues to vociferate. Then suddenly, as the narrator
makes a dash for the door, comes the calm after the storm.
The baron's voice becomes "gentle, affectionate, melancholy"
and "invisible musicians" play the first chords of the third
movement of the Pastoral Symphony. The scene is terminated
with the unexpected proposal of a carriage ride through the
Bois in the moonlight.

From its beginning to its end, this scene and its setting
have been carefully and painstakingly planned by the baron,
as the narrator suspects when he sees two footmen behind the
door. Under cover of the pretended insult arising from the
narrator's obtuseness, an insult which obliges the baron to
break off relations, the baron is playing another game. The
anger and abuse are only a by-product. The imagined griev-
ances are a pretext which allow the baron to create out of
whole cloth the feverish atmosphere he needs in order to
throw the narrator into a state of emotion and confusion
which increases, from afar, the baron's desire for possession.
The gamut of simulated emotions masks his desire and at

the same time satisfies him, and the words arouse in the narrator reactions which are powerful stimulants for the baron's emotions. The game the baron is playing is the savage game played by all the characters, whether it be the Duchesse de Guermantes taking pleasure in inciting the admiration, envy or disappointment which is the very substance of her prestige, or Mme Verdurin satisfying a certain instinct of cruelty by tormenting Saniette.

In this scene the whole comedy of homosexual desire is dramatically condensed; but underlying it is the fundamental drama of the impossible human desire to possess someone, to force this someone into the mold of one's emotion. The baron's aim is not to possess the young man physically, but to satisfy his desire to dominate this individual who unconsciously has taken a certain hold over his imagination. In the eyes of the baron any contact between himself and the narrator is fraught with significance; the young man's slightest gestures, words and intonations are elements which Charlus effortlessly weaves into a fabric of subtle and perverse psychological complications which has but one purpose. To achieve this purpose he makes use of all the resources of his erudition, of his position, and of his prestige. Within a few moments, when he has transformed by the mere force of his words the naïve and detached young narrator into a monster of rage who reacts violently to each word, his goal has been reached. The narrator has played his part in the scene prepared by the baron for just such a climax. He reaches a peak of enjoyment, of vicarious and frenzied physical pleasure which the double outburst of temper and its subsequent appeasement actually creates.

With a studied dilettantism, Charlus makes use in this way of those young men who elude his physical domination. At the same time, he cultivates all the thrills of emotion, of confidences given and taken, of dramatic situations in order to obtain the physical and emotional satisfactions which he craves. In the end he is taken in by his own play-acting. The episode contains the seeds of masochism and sadism. The narrator is temporarily maneuvered blindly by an outside force, and without understanding anything in the scene he is playing, reacts to the provocation of the baron. Although Charlus is far more conscious of the rôle he is playing than the narrator, the baron is doing nothing more than the narrator himself when one day in the Champs Elysées he pretends to wrestle with Gilberte, and discovers through the contortions of the game the mechanism of sexual pleasure; wrestling then becomes a pretext for sexual play.

The scene with Charlus discloses another game in which Proustian characters indulge, the game of rationalization, which begins as soon as their emotions are involved. When M. de Charlus' desire is aroused, his lucidity disappears, as it does also when the question of aristocratic values arises. As the narrator listens to M. de Charlus' words and observes his convulsed face, he realizes to what lengths the violent egotism of his rationalizations might influence the baron, who seems ready to justify even a crime. To the comedy of emotions is added the equally marked comedy of rationalization. Nor is this trait peculiar to the baron; it extends to all the Proustian characters, who are constantly deluded by the justification which rationalization unerringly gives to the meanest of sentiments—pride, snobbery, vanity. They are able to feed openly the emotions on which they live because they rationalize them. In this respect, when Swann sits in judgement on the Verdurins he is no different from the baron. This power of rationalization makes the Proustian characters very changeable and, save for a few rare exceptions, quite unpredictable. Their reactions can never be relied upon, so skillful is their ability to find reasons to support the maddest suggestions of their imaginations. With respect to aristocratic values, the baron accepts as reasonable his faith in those beliefs which define his social existence; with respect to homosexuality, he rationalizes what is only a physiological fact. Consequently the two apparently most "theatrical" traits of his personality really define what is most authentic in Charlus, in spite of all the comic situations to which they give rise. The narrator, however, who is still a little naïve, discovers only much later the second key to Charlus' personality—his homosexuality—which, along with his aristocratic pride, explains the passionate logic of the baron's superficially illogical, somewhat mad actions.

The narrator makes this discovery when he (rather too conveniently) witnesses a comedy of another sort—the baron's meeting with Jupien, "face to face in the courtyard where they had certainly never met before." "The baron, his half-shut eyes suddenly opened wide, stared at the former tailor who stood on the threshold of his shop, while the latter, instantly rooted to the spot, gazed admiringly at the middle-aged baron's stout figure." [29] A ridiculous scene takes place between these two slightly grotesque characters. Yet in the narrator's eyes it is "stamped with a strangeness, or, if one prefers, with a naturalness the beauty of which increased steadily." [30] The mute scene between the two men finally reveals to the narrator the homosexuality which determines M. de Charlus' conduct. The "conjunction" of Jupien and Charlus follows its own pattern of ritual, apparent in their gestures and mannerisms; the superb unselfconsciousness of the two partners gives their movements a significance which raises them from the grotesque to the cosmic. It is not surprising that Proust did not understand Gide's reproach that he had made homosexuality appear vile and absurd. For Proust, homosexuality is only one of the forms taken by the universal gravitation of individuals, stars, plants, or animals toward each other, a form more fascinating only because of its complexity, and because of the curious social effects which it brings about. The dramas and comedies to which it gives rise in the Proustian world carry that world into the realm of the fantastic. Homosexuality, as Proust sees it, is a fertile source of the romanesque in life, of preposterous adventures. It is one of the great levellers of people who are superficially completely dissimilar, and it gives to their existence the unexpected, bitter, burlesque savor of a Mardi Gras.

M. de Charlus' great drama rapidly gains momentum

after his meeting with Jupien. It is both grandiose and grotesque, since it is based on the ever-increasing disparity between Charlus' concept of himself and the personality he is forced to assume as he becomes increasingly uninhibited in his homosexual behavior. This disparity is illustrated by the difference between the language he uses, which is always grandiloquent, and that which Jupien uses; for example, Jupien's "you've certainly got a fat fanny" [31] shows what social distances the baron will travel when his passion is concerned. And there are other disparities: the disparity between the position which the baron thinks he occupies in the Verdurins' little clique and the rather cruel comedy which every evening in the Balbec train evolves around this middle-aged man and his passion for Morel—the passion is obviously known to everyone, yet the baron believes it to be a secret; the disparity between the projects and honors which he dreams of bestowing upon Morel and those which, to a lesser degree, he actually does bestow upon him; the disparity between a Morel he thinks of as an upright agreeable young man and the latter's hostility to his benefactor, his actual unscrupulousness and orneriness—all these disparities end in disaster. We then see Charlus himself, so often mean and cruel, silent and defenseless, being "executed" by the Verdurins. It is as if he then discovers for the first time the depth of human meanness. The comedy goes on to include a simulated duel, a scandal, threats, and an outburst of religious zeal on the part of the baron who transforms Morel into an angel of goodness. It continues to unfold and becomes grotesque and pathetic as the irascible baron, who gradually degenerates, becomes a frequenter of houses of ill repute, a masochist who has himself chained and beaten, a fat old man who is followed in the streets of Paris by shady individuals, and who wanders about at night ogling men in uniform. In the end he becomes a social outcast, dubbed a "boche" because his opinions of the war, derived from feudal and homosexual origins, are highly unorthodox and deemed subversive.

But in the Proustian comedy this powerful and absurd

being towers above all the characters among whom he moves. Proust has placed Charlus' story on the strange yet natural level of vital necessity; in Proust's eyes the corpulent middle-aged man covered with makeup, who modestly lowers his eyes when Morel appears, is no more strange than an orchid, or the rare tree of the Guermantes, or some curious bird. Because he has in him this driving force, the baron demands a theatrical setting in which to parade; by means of it he escapes the insignificance of the Courvoisiers as well as the automatism of the Guermantes, and though he is often ridiculous, he becomes a character of a different stature. Through homosexuality life takes hold of him and the windmills of life become his giants. Because of his homosexuality the proud and fantastic visionary finds the will to break away from his world and to join a vaster humanity, playing to the end his rôle of the Don Quixote of homosexuality, accompanied by the enigmatic Jupien. Charlus and Jupien may be classed in literature alongside Pantagruel and Panurge, Don Quixote and Sancho Panza.

In their fundamental absurdity, all the Proustian characters are tinged with quixoticism, a very special quixoticism, which Proust defines at the close of the novel. The brutal discovery that the narrator then makes about the real nature of time gives the whole comedy a new and deeper significance, explaining both its function in the novel as a whole and the esthetic laws which determine the form of the novel.

Until the end of the story, the narrator distinguishes only what he can grasp intellectually of the human comedy. He sees only meaningless bonds between people, constantly changing, woven by chance associations, by the habits and the needs which motivate individuals and which they struggle to express. He sees the subjective world of other people as one in which heterogenous and sometimes hostile elements come into play, elements which they have inherited or acquired and which tend to find their own equilibrium, to fall into place as chance events may allow. Under all this agitation the narrator discerns a world common to all, itself rather inexplicable, in which he can isolate an individual's behavior, relate it to a set of motives, and explain it in general terms. A world of feeling juxtaposed with a world of action gives each person's behaviour its proper value; but feelings are perpetually changing and everyone tries to fashion for himself a life which conforms to his own successive wishes. He remains blind to everything else. The narrator sees the observable comedy of actions and behavior and, beyond its variations in form, its monotony, and its basic similarity, all the contrived mechanisms which betray the illusory aspect of any activity. Each person is the central character in a series of short plays, basically the same, but played in different costumes, for which his life is the stage and on which other people appear only in supporting rôles. The human world loses all its mystery for him, and he now believes that in it there are only rather complex automatons, who can easily be taken apart and put together again.

Then, after a long absence, the narrator arrives at the Guermantes reception and literally *sees* in all those friends whom he thinks he knows so well a principle which operates in them all, a principle of a more general application than any others; it gives to the human comedy a unique meaning. Instead of the friends or enemies of old, the narrator enters a crowded theater on the stage of which he sees actors all busy acting their parts in a curious play. It is a "puppet show imbued with the unsubstantial colors of the years, controlled by time, of which the players are an embodiment. Time, though usually undiscernible, becomes visible when its magic lantern is turned upon the bodies it constantly seeks, and inevitably finds." [32] Proust's characters have only one time, are "that time," and while they continue to the end to play their games and construct their illusory worlds with an unconscious and quixotic concentration, time drags them toward death, of which they remain unaware because, oriented entirely toward the past, they enter the void of death in reverse. While the characters have been busily engaged, time has fashioned them relentlessly. Under their successive faces and under the changes time has wrought on their bodies, the narrator recognizes that each of these beings has reached his last stop before death.

Time is the revealer of destiny; it contains each individual's fate. Time is what reveals the startling person whom the young Charlus held in embryo, the person who slowly and surely got rid of all the other possibilities, of all the other ways of life which the young prince might have adopted. As he looks at the cruel and grotesque spectacle of these changed faces, the narrator suddenly sees the unique and irreplaceable character of each of these individuals, that particularity of which he had lost sight in his steady association with them and in his constant analysis of their personalities.

The face of M. d'Argencourt is no longer the face of an enemy; in it he recognizes the "symbolic face of life." [33] The whole world, in the Shakespearean manner, appears to him to be a scene in which each man plays several parts. All these people have made their entrances and exits intermittently, playing rôles which seemed incomprehensible as the narrator temporarily focussed his attention upon them. The narrator also has played his parts, those of a child, an adolescent, a young man about town, a lover; as he played them, a multitude of beings intermittently appeared in him. All these successive and intermittent beings are now merged into a single one, the one who exists, who contains them all, the man who has now become a writer.

The intellect bases its generalizations only on the present. But life is in no hurry; in time it shapes all men. All these masked faces are simply the necessary props for the comedy superficially played by the Proustian characters; but for each person there is one real life which keeps the comedy going. These people are alive; nothing can explain their existence, which is going to cease and which is a fugitive but unique form of life. Placed always at the center of his own life, like the sleeper in a dream, each man forgets it and its transitory character. Engrossed in the everyday business of life, of greeting each other, sneering, gossiping, they let themselves be transported into death. There the unique creation they represent—an individual life developing in time—is finally lost, as finally as the character and personality of Swann are lost in the memory of his own daughter.

It is this comprehension which gives meaning to Proust's human comedy, raises it above the ridiculous and endows it with poetic qualities. Proust's vision is infinitely less cruel, more hopeful and kindly than Flaubert's, for example, for the narrator places himself among the other puppets and yet, by the same standards he applies to them, simply because he exists, he too is infinitely more than a puppet. Proust's viewpoint lends humor to the human world which he describes and softens the ferocity of his outlook. Human life is reintegrated with the mystery against which it struggles so violently—like Tante Léonie, who protects herself against life by an edifice of habits. Much has been said about Proustian psychology; Proust does apply psychological analysis to his characters but for him such analysis is by definition limited. The Proustian character is essentially unknowable and only art restores him in the entirety which analysis, relied upon exclusively, would destroy.

This is why Proust presents successive, disconnected images of his characters: in their manner of speaking, simply of being, he recognizes a certain style which is their style of life, which bears the mark of their time span and their individuality. It matters little then that our judgment mocks the human being as a mechanical robot and derides the Verdurins, Odette, Swann as shallow egotists. They present one of the facets of life, and carry its mystery within them. They are just as deeply involved in life as any hero anxious to make an impression upon his era and busy with the great problems of his time, for by the same right as his they are among the multiple incarnations of life in time; but they are the people who happen to have played a part in the narrator's life, who have crossed his line of vision and coincided with his own "time." Life is there, within them, unrecognized, in a form that it will never again take. At the Guermantes reception, the narrator discovers the cosmic dimension of time which has been lacking in his vision of others and of himself, just as he discovers the hidden dimension of his own inner world. His discovery gives Proust's work a fundamental perspective which somewhat mitigates the too violent deformation that Proust's homosexual obsession imposes upon it. Charlus at the threshold of death is an old man among other old men, and not just a homosexual. He has had to submit, like them to the action of time and he too will soon be "lost" in death.

Actually, and this is a last irony, the human comedy, as Proust sees it, will always be played according to the same mechanisms. It is the individual for whom the curtain falls with death who disappears forever and is irreplaceable. Yet, paradoxically, he never stops acting out his life as though his actions were eternal and his comedy unique. He never knows what Proust calls "real life." It is the individual also who places the stamp of time on everything. The Allée in the Bois without Odette tells us nothing of the reality of time. Time is objectified only in the story of man and preserved only in his creations. Man is all-essential to the Proustian world, to the slow development of the working of time on the successive faces of each character who, like the face of a clock on which the hands move, marks its passage. For the narrator the movement of the hands is for a long time imperceptible; because time works within him continuously and smoothly he does not realize it is working in him. But with each new appearance of the people he knows, the physical change they have undergone in the interval marks the action of time upon them, and a new lap in their journey toward death. As he observes the individuals whose story he is telling, the narrator discovers the rôle that time plays as creator and destroyer of the life of man.

Had the narrator not so discovered the nature of time, he would only partially have understood the essential revelations of involuntary memory. The human comedy in its overall aspect provides him with a proving ground for all the experiences he has to undergo before he can grasp this meaning. He understands it only after he has himself known that obsession with another human being which is called love, and after he has fully measured the equivocal nature of love. The human comedy implicit in the experience of love becomes a drama for him, but a drama which time reduces to the proportions of an anecdote.

EQUIVOCAL LOVE

LOVE is an important theme in *A la Recherche du Temps perdu*, both by virtue of the space devoted to the successive loves of Swann and the narrator, of Saint-Loup and Charlus, and because of the rôle it plays in the reflections and behavior of Proust's characters. The narrator's constant preoccupation with his desire and hope for love is the most influential factor in all his dreams as a child, adolescent, and young man. He dwells upon the image of almost every woman he knows, provided that she is at once nearby and faraway, visible yet unknown. Gilberte Swann, Mademoiselle de Stermaria, the flock of young girls at Balbec, Madame de Guermantes, a peasant girl glimpsed on the road—he desires them all. This longing for love is at first nebulous, associated in his mind with the novels and poetry he reads, and is imbued with a timeless and mysterious quality. He always associates the word "love" with the idea of "vague and superhuman" bliss. For a long time it remains a dream for him, even when he focusses his attention upon Gilberte who is real. Nevertheless, the narrator's existence is oriented by his phantasy of love; if judged without reference to its influence, some of his actions would remain completely incomprehensible—his rovings in the Champs Elysées, his haunting of the streets in Swann's neighborhood and of the Guermantes' town house, his walks along the promenade in Balbec are just as strange as Charlus' behaviour if they are considered apart from the obsession with the possibility of love which motivates them. In one sense it can be said that the most consistent motivating force in the narrator's rather easy-going life is his desire to realize the dream of happiness promised by the word "love." For a long time he is "in search" of something he thinks love will give him.

In the first part of the novel, *Un Amour de Swann,* the harmonious development of this theme, although it perfectly counterbalances the chapter on Combray, can be considered as a separate story. Like *Tristan et Iseult, La Princesse de Clèves,* or *Adolphe,* it can be read as a sort of monograph, a "tale," developed in a single movement, stylized and pure. It could take its place among the great French love stories which go back to the Middle Ages and in this connotation would present, through Swann, a new psychological view of love: the story, complete in itself, of the variations of this particular kind of love as an isolated phenomenon. It would, however, be contrary to the spirit in which *A la Recherche du Temps perdu* is conceived that Proust should have inserted into the novel an episode separable from the whole. *Un Amour de Swann* is placed between the end of Combray and the prelude to the *Jeunes filles en fleurs.* Swann plays an important rôle in all three parts; his prestige in the child's eyes adumbrates his entrance on the stage, while at the same time his story gives the narrator's tale a dimension in time, opening up a perspective on a past which reaches further back than the narrator's. In addition, Swann's story serves as a background for the narrator's dreams of love and for his first experiment in love with Gilberte, and it enriches them. The narrator dreams of a sentimental, idealized, rather tame love which is markedly different from the emotions experienced by Swann. This divergence is one of the essential elements in Proust's orchestration of the theme; it is to be found in all his accounts of various liasons.

The narrator's preconceived notions of love, which are centered in a set of images, are never borne out by reality; in his association with Gilberte, these images are never realized but he finds himself flooded by emotions through which Gilberte becomes his personification of love. The world in which

Swann's love takes place lies between these two, and the realization of that love, both pathetic and trivial, already foreshadows the ambiguity of the word "love" and the inevitable failure of the search for happiness through love. This search is basically the quest for something else which Swann is never able to discern. The enigma propounded to him by Vinteuil's musical phrase in relation to his love for Odette remains unsolved, but the relationship between love, happiness, suffering, and art is established. We are at the very heart of the relationships which give meaning not only to the narrator's experience, but to the structure of *A la Recherche du Temps perdu* itself. It is only through the experience of characters other than the child that Proust is able to present the love theme with all its overtones at the very beginning of his novel. The child experiences love in the form of images: the image of the "lady in pink," or of Montjouvain, so distressingly different from the dream inspired by his reading. It is Swann's experience that gives depth to these images. All the other attempts at love, either episodic or carefully developed, are merely variations of Swann's love.

Each of these "romances" is, like Swann's, circumscribed by time. Each begins, develops, and ends. For a certain length of time romance absorbs the whole existence of the characters, and even transforms them, but they later resume the normal rhythm of an existence scarcely marked by the experience except for minor outward manifestations, habits acquired while the "romance" lasted. The deterioration of Swann's social life after his marriage with Odette, or Saint-Loup's calculated mannerisms, for example, are the traces left by a love which has run its course. Every love story leaves in its wake only a few images, some material facts, and the knowledge that it once was real. The actual experience of love is obliterated little by little until it is almost entirely forgotten.

All these Proustian "romances" follow each other closely and are all eventually lost in the passage of time. When we first catch a glimpse of Swann, the elegant, cultivated, amiable man of the world who holds himself aloof from any profound emotion, his love is far behind him and has long ago lost any significance for him. If he thinks about it at all, it is with a faint feeling of surprise at having "lost" in this way so many years of his life. No matter how painful and all-absorbing a love affair may temporarily appear to those who experience it, it is never in *A la Recherche du Temps perdu* more than an episode, and derives its significance precisely from that fact. This is never the case in the classical love story, although Proust seems deliberately to use the terminology of that kind of story when he describes the emotions of his characters. And they also allude to the "romance" [1] they are living. All of them, with the possible exception of Swann, want more or less consciously to play their part in a great romantic novel. And that is in fact what they do, but not as they imagine it, not according to the tenets of the classical tale in which love per se, happy or unhappy, has intrinsic significance for the individual.

Among these love stories, those of Charlus and Saint-Loup are described objectively. Swann's is presented as it was actually lived by him, but the narrator evokes it from the past just as he evokes his own loves from a past more or less remote, in order to evaluate and analyze them. He merely regards his own loves with a greater degree of subjectivity. The story of Saint-Loup's love for Rachel, and of Charlus' love for Morel are episodes within the novel as a whole, and appear and disappear according to Saint-Loup's and Charlus' position in the narrator's field of vision. On the other hand, Swann's and the narrator's loves have their clearly allotted place in the novel. Swann and Odette, Gilberte and the narrator, Albertine and the narrator, are at first mingled with a great number of other characters though they are somewhat more carefully delineated; then, rather slowly, each couple is detached from the group and moves into the foreground as the other characters recede. The couple play their love scene, supplemented by a few minor figures. The converse movement then takes place, and each of the two partners resumes his autonomy, but not simultaneously. The image of the woman disappears first, leaving the man who loves her, alone, in the foreground of the story; then he too "returns" to his social milieu as Swann returns to the Saint-Euvertes or the narrator to Mme Swann's salon.

Un Amour de Swann, the whole beginning of the *Jeunes filles en fleurs, La Prisonnière,* and *Albertine disparue* thus create, within the very heart of the complex and crowded Proustian world in which the whole human comedy is played, smaller more stable worlds which attempt, without ever succeeding, to achieve autonomy by eliminating everything that has no direct bearing upon them. By this very fact they are doomed to eventual failure, since they are constructed on the most shifting soil imaginable, that of the Proustian personality. To love Odette, Gilberte, and Albertine is to assert a belief in the physical existence of a human individuality which coincides with a particular human body. And even human bodies, which seem to guarantee that individuals exist are portrayed by Proust as frighteningly ubiquitous in time and space; their variations reveal only in part those which the individuals who possess them can undergo.

The particular climate of love in *A la Recherche du Temps perdu* can only be understood in its relation to the Proustian social milieu. This milieu determines the amorous behavior of Proust's characters, but it does not have the same general value as Proust's analysis of their social reactions. Though lives lived only on the worldly plane of opulent restaurants and gala receptions ornamented by countless lackeys may seem to us highly artificial, the social mechanisms of these lives which Proust describes have a general significance; they transcend the limited milieu in which he depicts them. The "little clique," for example, formed about a dominant personality is just as common today, even though it sets as its goal something other than the conquest of the Faubourg St. Germain—no longer so glittering a prize. With its passwords, customs, and language, its cohesion maintained by a mixture of prestige and blackmail, these cliques can still be

observed advancing methodically toward a definite goal, pro-
ceeding, like Mme Verdurin, by successively assimilating and
rejecting chosen individuals. Proust did not foresee the First
World War, and obviously could not include it as a factor in
his novel as it stood in 1913; but when he later included the
war in his novel, the society he depicted could easily take the
war in its stride. He was able with a very few touches to show
how comfortably it could adapt war to its own purposes.
When Mme Verdurin, in a period of strict rationing, uses the
eminent Doctor Cottard to intrigue with the civil administra-
tion so that she may have the breakfast croissants without
which she cannot survive, she remains typically a Verdurin;
at the same time she adapts easily to a later society unforeseen by Proust, even including its concentration camps. When,
ensconced comfortably in bed, she enjoys simultaneously, and
equally ingenuously, her indispensable croissants and the
sinking of the Lusitania, she becomes almost a symbol of the
total egoism of certain permanent social attitudes—like the
Duchesse de Guermantes, for whom a question of evening
slippers takes precedence over a question of life and death.
The Second World War brought about in the upper strata of
society the same sort of kaleidoscopic change which Proust
described first with the Dreyfus affair and then more omi-
nously with the First World War: the phenomenon was simply more abrupt and violent, but essentially the same. This is
not so true of Proust's description of love.

The Proustian world of security, leisure and luxury is
interested in love only as another means to an immediate
gratification of a sensory pleasure which has no deep emotional significance. Eroticism is a worldly pastime just like
other amusements, a little more absorbing perhaps because
it has, like hunting, a mobile prey. In the countless liaisons
which precede and follow his love for Odette, Swann seeks
no real affinity with a woman, no heartfelt joy, hope or intoxication; nor does he offer any feeling of tenderness shaded
with friendship, respect or intellectual companionship, or of
overwhelming passion. All of Proust's characters are normally

vagabonds in love, ready to pursue any name or shadow; their prototype is M. de Charlus, for whom the world offers an exciting array of delivery boys, waiters, street-car conductors, soldiers, all of them indiscriminately objects of pursuit and sources of possible pleasure. Swann's particular form of sensuality is typical; devoid of sexuality, purely superficial and greedy, always alert, it seeks to gratify itself and makes no attempt to control itself. Swann's impatience in love also is characteristic. Proustian characters are in a terrible hurry to enjoy as rapidly as possible any pleasure in view; strangely obstinate, they do not willingly put up with any obstacles to immediate gratification. And on the whole their quarry—cooks, chambermaids, housewives and their masculine counterparts—do not appear to put up more than a feeble token of resistance to these pressing demands.

Yet the Proustian lover is not a Don Juan or a Marquis de Sade. Nor does he merely have a taste for eroticism, for pleasure given and taken as such. He seems rather to be a sleepwalker, wandering in a phantasmagoria of love, his wallet in hand, amid shadows which allow themselves to be briefly seized in order to make off with a few of his ever-replenished supply of bank notes. The atmosphere in which these adventures take place is reminiscent of a rather dreary vaudeville. The Proustian lover pursues his dream of love among people generally inferior to him, hard bargainers of pleasure, real black market dealers, who, like Rachel and Morel, are past masters at the art of raising the ante. He binds people to himself solely by his money; it does not occur to him to attach them by other means. With neither prestige nor personal appeal, he counts only upon a feeling of gratitude mixed with cupidity in his attempt to hold on to the person who attracts him. The operations behind the scenes of this tawdry vaudeville are clandestine, teeming with the meaning glances, casual encounters, signals, passwords, deals, furtive meetings, and gratuities which invariably play a part in the extortion game. Society men and women slip into houses of prostitution to mingle indiscriminately with lesser patrons of a somewhat criminal nature. There is a veritable ballet of secret sensual pleasure in *A la Recherche du Temps perdu.* Pleasure tends to be furtive even in a couple's intimacy. It is only when Albertine is asleep that the narrator experiences that pleasure which he so minutely describes; he enjoys it alone, without his partner's knowledge.

At his very first meeting with Gilberte when he sees her from a distance behind the wrought iron gate of Tansonville, there is between the narrator and the little girl the hint of a gesture, an attempt at communication which precedes any speech. The narrator discovers very much later that this gesture had been an invitation to pleasure and that already at that time Gilberte, as soon as she was left alone, "ran" to have fun in the dungeons of Roussainville with "all sorts of girls and boys who took advantage of the darkness"; among them the young peasant Théodore, the future protégé of Legrandin,[2] has already distinguished himself. When he relates this, the narrator makes quite a curious comment for a mature and detached man: "I had an involuntary start of desire and regret as I thought of the subterranean passages of Roussainville. Yet I was happy to be able to say to myself that that happiness toward which all my energies were then expended, that happiness which nothing could restore to me again, had existed elsewhere than in my thoughts, had in reality been so near to me, at that very Roussainville about which I so often spoke."[3] This is a far cry from the narrator's "green paradise of childhood loves," and the word "happiness" is markedly significant as applied to the meetings in the dungeons of Roussainville. All the Proustian characters, when they are "left alone," like Gilberte, "run" toward this kind of gratuitous and superficial depravation which constitutes their "happiness." Albertine takes advantage of the narrator's shortest absence, and Jupien cannot for an instant "leave alone" the baron even when Charlus is half-blind and paralyzed; Saint-Loup, Legrandin, Andrée, to say nothing of Morel or people like Léa, behave in the same way. Jupien's establishment is but a replica of Roussainville's dungeons.

Beginning most markedly in *Sodome et Gomorrhe,* Proust introduces into his story a number of singular anecdotes dealing with the homosexual relations of both men and women. These are fairly unpleasant, in doubtful taste and of limited literary value; it is very seldom that he succeeds in giving them the general significance of the Baron de Charlus' adventures or of the scene of sapphism which the narrator observes at Montjouvain. The anecdote about Nissim Bernard, about the "tomato," and others of the same ilk or even more unlikely, are quite clumsily inserted into the text of the novel. Illicit and homosexual relations advance into the foreground, and the Proustian world comes to depict not a general social order but a very particular species of mankind. The reader senses distinctly and rather uneasily, Proust's abnormal and all-pervasive obsession, at once cerebral and violent. This obsession finally reduces the activity of his characters to "doing it," as the narrator puts it, everywhere, to haunting bathing establishments, brothels, beaches, and hotels. It is in this way that poor Albertine's ghost ends up after her death, and that the charming Saint-Loup as well as the old snob Legrandin appear at the close of the novel. All the most important Proustian characters finally turn toward us the closed and equivocal countenance with which Albertine confronts the narrator's anxious scrutiny. Undoubtedly true in certain limited cases, this pattern of behavior loses its creditability in Proust's unwarranted generalization.

It would seem that only from a sickroom could so aberrant an obsession be projected upon active human beings. If the social set and the period in which Proust lived partially explain the form that love takes in his novel, his life as a sick man shut up in a room explains it even more clearly. A whole area of human activity remained a mystery to him, subject only to speculation. The reader discerns in *A la Recherche du Temps perdu* a hot-house atmosphere in which there is an astonishing proliferation of social gossip. And here too Proust seems to live on his own account the experiences he attributes to the narrator. The narrator imagines his loves with Gilberte

and Mme de Guermantes; he creates clear images, quite simple and rather static, which spring from his reading and
which accord with his idea of love. Proust, cloistered within
his one room, seems in the same way to foist upon his fictional
world an idea of love which springs from a re-imagined experience, an experience which is echoed by his characters. We
think back on Tante Léonie, isolated and suspicious in her
sickroom, living a drama her solitude has conjured up and
into which she drags Françoise and Eulalie. It happens that
Proust's experience is that of homosexuality, coupled with a
very special sensuality. His sensations seem to have been, at
least at times, hypertrophied and strongly resistant to oblivion—his erotic sensations as well as the others.

One also feels in certain passages of *A la Recherche du
Temps perdu* that Proust enjoyed enormously the cerebral
excitement of dealing with the theme of homosexuality, especially if he could do so indirectly, as in the prelude to *Sodome
et Gomorrhe* or through Charlus. The narrator is so dazzled
by the café waiters and busboys that in order to describe them
—and this Proust sometimes does also through a third irrelevant party—he uses the lines of Racine's choruses which
permit him to celebrate innocently their "youthful beauty";
he also has a singular mania for comparing Théodore, his
chauffeur, and these same busboys to the angels of Gothic
cathedrals, and his tone is a little too tinged with emotion and
lyricism to be attributed solely to preciosity. These preoccupations do not correspond to those of the narrator, who is not
a homosexual, but reveal Proust behind him; they are reminiscent of Charlus. A feeling of guilt, of sacrilege even, is
associated with the enjoyment of these "pleasures of love."

Amorous relations in Proust's work, whatever they may
be, are tainted with the same sort of scandal which in Combray emanated from Uncle Adolphe's liaison with the "lady
in pink." They are always accompanied by the whisperings
which Mlle Vinteuil and her friend promulgate and are often
associated with the idea of sacrilege. The narrator himself
once made a present of a few of the pieces of furniture which

he inherited from Tante Léonie to the madam of the bordello which "Rachel as to the Lord" frequents, and where he comes to enjoy "samples of happiness." He later admits his sense of guilt: "as soon as I saw them again in the house where these women used them, all the virtues which once breathed in my aunt's room in Combray appeared to me tortured by the cruel contact to which I had delivered them without any protection." [4] This equivocal sentiment, in which are mingled feelings of enjoyment and of culpability, is certainly closely related to Proust's homosexuality, and also to his idea of "happiness" in love, as his narrator sincerely and unconsciously defines it in relation to Gilberte. It would seem that Proust believes that to give oneself up to sexual pleasure is to break a taboo; in homosexuality the taboo is no different, simply stronger; the pleasure in each case is increased by the initial guilt.

The feeling of guilt associated with love is so strong in Proust that it unconsciously also determines the behavior of his characters when they are in love. As soon as Swann, Saint-Loup and the narrator have obtained certain favors from Odette, Rachel and Albertine, they act as though they ought to make up by a myriad of attentions for sins committed against the young women. They seem to think that these women granted them an immense privilege; that by granting it, Odette, Rachel, and Albertine have been somehow degraded, and might at any moment notice this situation which Swann, Saint-Loup and the narrator conceal from them feverishly by heaping kindnesses upon them. The young men beg, weep, give presents, express feelings of infinite gratitude. And yet how many times does the expression "to do wrong" recur in their speech to designate relations that are exactly the same as the ones they have with their partners. This explains the aura of suspicion which surrounds love in the Proustian world. Never, at any moment, does the possibility of faithfulness shared and desired, at least temporarily, enter into the picture. Faithfulness is, in fact, impossible since the act of love in which the Proustian lovers indulge makes them enter the suspect, outlawed world of pleasure, which flouts the virtues of Combray. This is truer still of everything that touches homosexuality.

A great deal has been said of the transposition of homosexual experience which Proust made through the girls he describes. This transposition was no doubt necessary if he was to give a more generally applicable picture of love than homosexuality permits. But it seems to have another function. When the narrator anxiously questions Albertine, deploring her "vice," condemning the "wrong" she is doing, we feel that what is in question is more than the transposition of a certain type of jealousy; it is as though Proust's personality were being split. The dialogue which takes place between Albertine and the narrator could very easily be Proust's own, guilty in his own eyes, obsessed by, and captive also of certain pleasures. We are confronted by a type of sensual experience which bears the ineradicable mark of a quite special personality.

It is on this terrain that love in *A la Recherche du Temps perdu* attempts to erect its world. The Proustian lover must deal with the mobile equivocal, ubiquitous Proustian beings. Avid for pleasure, they attach themselves to no one; and indifferent to everything that is not for their immediate gratification, they are pitiless toward those who love them, changeable and capricious. But it must not be forgotten that the Proustian lover is of exactly the same species himself until he tries to escape from himself through love. He then undergoes a transformation and becomes a creature put upon by everyone, and lost in the phantasmagoria of eroticism. All around him the ballet continues, gleeful, ferocious, pointless. Only the lover pays and remains empty-handed. For if Odette sells herself dearly though easily, Rachel gives herself to everyone for a moderate price, and Albertine, it would seem, gives herself to anyone just for the pleasure of it; but they refuse to give themselves to their lovers whom they betray unhesitatingly. These young women have no trace of that inherent uneasy conscience which Proust gives their lovers.

In their eyes a lover is a kind of mentor, an obstacle to pleasure whose maneuvers must be foiled and whose lot it is to be betrayed. The Proustian couple consists of "the loved," a creature laden with gifts but who is forever tracked, beset on all sides by her "lover," a pitiless inquisitor. What do these "creatures of flight" want from each other in their enigmatic loves? And what do these loves themselves mean, loves to which Proust gives so prominent a place and to which he seems to introduce his characters only to entangle them in a more and more hallucinated labyrinth of suspicion, lies, and humiliation? There is no love in *A la Recherche du Temps perdu* that recognizes itself as happy, and this further narrows its scope. The barometer of Proustian loves fluctuates between boredom and suspicion, and the impression which they leave is one of sadness.

Seen from the outside, Saint-Loup's love for Rachel, Charlus' love for Morel is incomprehensible. There is no way of explaining objectively the value which these special creatures have acquired in their lovers' eyes. The choice Saint-Loup and Charlus make does not hinge upon any communicable criterion. The meaning that Rachel and Morel have is conferred upon them by Saint-Loup and Charlus. To see a person and to see a person whom one loves are two entirely different processes, as the narrator observes when he is invited by Saint-Loup to meet Rachel. But Saint-Loup and Charlus believe that the conferred value emanates directly from Rachel and Morel and act as though it were recognized by everyone. This initial confusion renders their behavior incomprehensible. They pass through fluctuations of emotions which nothing seems to justify, drifting into alien social groups; they live in a state of tension and emotionalism which appears abnormal to others.

This state is betrayed in semi-comic, semi-heroic scenes, created by the slightest gestures or words which have any bearing on their love, and justified by specious reasoning, scenes of jealousy by Saint-Loup, indirect threats of blackmail by Charlus. Both men take the most irrational steps, make the most extravagant gestures and greatest sacrifices for the sole purpose of arranging those moments of tranquility and peace they need so that the presence of the one they love may assure them happiness. To achieve this they give up the privileges for which they most care. But when Morel is actually present, Charlus dissembles, becomes mannered and grotesque, and, with Rachel, Saint-Loup is nervous, suspicious and unpleasantly aggressive. Both are finally abandoned after ups and downs, banal and ridiculous, after ruptures and reconciliations. Love, insofar as happiness is concerned, seems to have brought them nothing save expenses, rebuffs, disappointments, and suffering. They certainly seem to have wasted all the time they devote to it. Furthermore, it attacks in them what is most deeply themselves. Rachel underrates the aristocrat in Saint-Loup, and Mme Verdurin uses the baron's love to humiliate him in his pride, which had seemed impregnable and which had served him as a rampart. In this way love corrodes the personalities of Saint-Loup and of the baron and makes them vulnerable; it throws them into disequilibrium with their milieu and with themselves and plunges them into a perpetual state of inferiority and restlessness.

One need only examine the actions of the two men to realize that the baron and Saint-Loup are subconsciously guided by an ulterior motive which explains their odd conduct. It is founded on the subconscious suspicion which they harbor that there is in fact a great gap between reality and their concept of it. This suspicion leads them to set up their own system of relationships with life; their values differ from the usual ones and make Charlus and Saint-Loup sensitive to certain things and blind to what they do not wish to see. Their lives are organized according to a hierarchy which is incompatible with any other and which they accept unquestioningly. From time to time they make a quick sortie into the everyday world, as does Saint-Loup in his brief visit in Mme de Villeparisis' salon; but on the whole they remain within the boundaries of their world and obey the demands it makes upon them. They are the prisoners of love, in the fashion of medieval allegories. They live, like men half mad, in a state of suppressed struggle with the world around them, and in particular with the person who is for them its center, Rachel or Morel. Each is like a man asleep but about to wake up, who struggles obscurely and with an almost visceral obstinacy against awakening, feverishly transforming into dreams the indications of activity which come to him from the outside world. Charlus and Saint-Loup want to reduce, or even suppress, the disparity which they suspect exists between reality and their concept of it by forcing Morel and Rachel to enter the world which they have fashioned for themselves. The effort they make to mold reality to their image of it forces them into countless false situations, gives rise to outbursts of temper and despair, and causes them to behave oddly and incongruously. It explains the persistence with which they pursue the objects of their love and their efforts to have some effect, any effect, upon him or her; for the person they love threatens, more than any other, the world in which they want to continue to live, since it is around this person that they have built that world. And yet this person does not cease to move in an objective world which asserts its independent existence merely through his or her presence. And so the loved one becomes enemy number one. It is not surprising that Charlus ends up by wanting to kill Morel, and we understand why love in Proust's world almost always ends in attempted violence. Charlus and Saint-Loup appear to us, as they do to the narrator, caught up in a senseless and fantastic adventure, as mad as any Don Quixote who views the humblest objects, sheep or windmills, as fabulous armed creatures whom he must attack and vanquish.

And yet we easily follow Swann's adventure as it takes its inevitable course, though in its general outline it traces the same arabesques: the incomprehensible choice of Odette, the incoherent, illogical, often ridiculous conduct of Swann, his enormous material and social sacrifices, his change to another social milieu, the odious scenes and suspicions, the wordless struggle and painful tension, the final defeat. Swann's marriage to Odette is not the consummation of their love; it consecrates, quite ironically, the death of that love. It is not the Swann who loved Odette who finally marries her, but another Swann who is amicably indifferent to her.

The development of Swann's love seems comprehensible and consistent because Proust introduces us to an inner atmosphere of love. Swann's joys and sufferings are only secondary movements which accompany the eternal theme of love, somewhat as the rains of thunderstorms temporarily obscure the good summer weather in Combray. The observer who sees Saint-Loup and Charlus only objectively is unaware that they too move in an inner atmosphere of love, which creates its own consistency, qualifies everything it touches and fuses gestures and words within its ambience. It is an entirely subjective experience, a mode of existence which Proust creates in *Un Amour de Swann* and in which Swann lives without being clearly conscious of it. He feels everything in relation to this inner atmosphere, without perceiving its exact nature. The story of Swann is that of the gradual change which takes place in the climate of his love, a change which is forced upon him and against which he struggles blindly. It is thus that the whole "happy" stage of his love escapes him, insofar as it is happy, though it is restored to us by Proust through the charm which emanates from the beginning of the story: visits from Odette, meetings at the Verdurins, Odette's ridiculous and touching drawing room, the ritual of the musical phrase, the mad chase through Paris in search of Odette, the return in a carriage and the ritual of the orchids. The charm is indeed that of love, for it alights upon this rather silly and commonplace mondaine and bestows upon her an aura of poetry and mystery.

By slow degrees, the atmosphere of love becomes the painful and smothering atmosphere of suffering. Swann's love is a perpetually changing sentiment to which he adapts his gestures and his actions, albeit clumsily and too late. Certain incidents make him conscious that a change has already taken place; he realizes that something in his love has died, and he

tries to bring it back to life. He mistakenly thinks that the
change in his relations with Odette has been brought about
from the outside by these incidents themselves. His love
passes through periods of apparent equilibrium which a
chance event will destroy, setting into motion a whirlwind
of emotions until a new threshold and a new equilibrium are
reached. The curve of this evolution is quite clear, though
Swann unconsciously fights it. First, we are present at
Odette's appearance in Swann's life; it is quite commonplace.
Then, without either encouragement or opposition from
Swann, Odette appears more and more often in his life. These
visits come closer and closer together and Swann, without
even wanting to see Odette, becomes more and more used to
her presence. Swann does not try to explain to himself
Odette's ubiquitousness in his life, nor does Proust explain
it. Does it correspond to Odette's will to conquer Swann, or
is it the peculiar attraction that Swann has for her? Be that
as it may, it sets a certain pattern which we find again in the
narrator's life; when his imagination seizes upon an image,
Gilberte's or the Duchesse de Guermantes'; the image recurs
until it preoccupies his mind and gradually absorbs his whole
thought. Odette's maneuver creates one of the prerequisites
of the birth of love. It reproduces that "mental mania, which,
in love, favors the exclusive rebirth of the image of a certain
person." [5]

In this first stage of Swann's relationship with Odette,
a network of habits is bit by bit created for him; its only purpose is to allow him to see Odette. These habits carry Swann
into Odette's world. His relationship with Odette gradually
includes her "set," which for him exists only in relation to
her and which he judges only within this reference. Swann
tries vaguely to explain this state of things and to justify the
large place Odette now occupies in his life. He builds up,
more or less consciously, a whole network of ties which connect Odette's image to his own esthetic aspirations. In looks,
she reminds him of a Botticelli; the Verdurin's pianist by
chance provides him with Vinteuil's musical phrase which

keeps his sentiment alive. The little Vinteuil phrase, now that he has found it again, is a source of keen pleasure to him the first evening he spends at the Verdurins'. Later it becomes associated with Odette's presence. But it has a past and carries along in its wake a whole fragment of Swann's inner life into which in this way Odette is incorporated. The power to awaken emotion in Swann, latent in the Vinteuil phrase, antedated Odette; it had once been strong enough to turn Swann temporarily away from his superficial life and to transform him into another Swann, the Swann who devoted himself to a study of Vermeer. In brief, it had set Swann in motion; this motion is prolonged, then lost in love. The little phrase had appealed to his sensitivity and because of this had wrenched his mind from the indifference into which it had settled. The phrase was a stranger, the bearer of joy, and he incarnates this stranger in Odette; she is idealized and penetrates into the depths which the little phrase had opened up. So Swann's love is born by chance from the juxtaposition of an image, Odette's, with a musical phrase and with an emotion, an arbitrary, unforeseeable meeting which consequently seems to Swann preordained.

The narrator's love for Gilberte is also born of the juxtaposition of the name Gilberte with the names of Swann, Bergotte and everything the narrator associates with them, and with the enchantment which he felt as a child before a hedge of flowering hawthorn. In the same way, the elements which make the narrator fall in love with the Duchesse de Guermantes or Albertine can be analyzed. In a Proustian love these three different elements are always present: a human being, an esthetic fact, a deep emotion. Each time, the woman's image enters a pre-existing zone of emotion at the source of which is an esthetic sensation on which she capitalizes; but she is able to benefit from it only because the process is involuntary and accidental, working through subjective and chance associations. Swann transfers to Odette the "disturbing mystery" which the phrase of the sonata held for him; he also sees in her the source of the renewal of his youth. Henceforth Odette stands apart from other people, reflecting the prestige of Vinteuil's phrase. Her face ceases to be the sum of "signs that can be practically used for the identification of a particular person who, until then, had represented a bundle of pleasures to be pursued, of annoyances to be avoided or of courtesies to be returned"; [6] it becomes that of a unique and irreplaceable woman. From that moment Swann lives blindly, groping his way through darkness. His love inevitably moves on toward its climax, which reveals his basic mistake. One day he misses Odette's usual presence; he is greatly upset and rushes off like a mad man to find her. The break in his habits makes him suddenly realize that he can be deprived of the source of emotion which has again given meaning to his life. Everything that keeps Odette away from him deprives him of an essential part of himself. His love is nurtured by this woman's presence, which is henceforth indispensable to him.

The possession of Odette inaugurates a period of peace during which he seems to reach a threshold of tranquility. It is at this point that we discern the shaky foundation upon which his love rests. The possession of Odette had appeared to him an end in itself. But the threat of boredom and dissatisfaction pierces through the temporary satisfaction that it brings him. Swann struggles zealously against this threat in order to preserve his love. His goal now changes: he must know what Odette is doing at all times; for only jealousy enables him to create for himself the atmosphere of "disturbing mystery" which his love needs in order to survive. Then, through a confused mass of errors and lies, he discovers the mystery of Odette, which is not what he visualized at all, not the mystery that promised happiness. With an ever-increasing suffering, he discovers the reality of Odette. It innundates the image, the idol which he had created, and which was docile to him because he was its creator. Jealousy gives him a glimpse of a truth which does not derive from love but from life in general, and which seems to depreciate love. He discovers the multiplicity of this woman whom he calls Odette and her face now reveals to him that "the human face is really

like that of the god of an oriental theogony, a whole cluster of
faces juxtaposed on different levels which cannot all be seen
at the same time." [7] He gradually realizes how futile it is to
demand accounts from a creature as diverse as Odette and to
allot a special place to her in his own life. He dimly perceives
around her a vast mysterious matrix, irreducible and infinite,
in no wise ideal, which is the network of Odette's numerous
relationships, peculiar to her; they innundate the present,
stretch into the past and are projected into the future. His
suspicion is directed against all the people whom she sees and
he tries to isolate her without ever succeeding in doing so.
To attempt to know even the external factors of Odette's life
is an enterprise which can never be completed. He can never
possess her completely and it becomes impossible to love her.

The oscillations of jealousy in *Un Amour de Swann* have
often been analyzed. Love moves through them toward another threshold. Swann gives up the idea of knowing Odette,
and tries only to plug up the openings through which suffering seeps; but he does not really want to stop suffering for it
would be a sign that his love was dead. In fact, his love is
already dead without his knowing it. This last phase is
Swann's inner struggle to preserve in his suffering the living
reality of a sentiment threatened by the corroding force of
his own indifference. The whole story of Swann's love, which
he himself never grasps in its totality or in its cycles, is his
effort to preserve the myth he created to prevent time from
turning it into an insignificant and banal liason. Each successive stage in Swann's love is in reality a step toward its
end. It is only because of a myth that Odette touches Swann
in the beginning; in order to be able to believe that he loves
her, he first makes her enter the realm of the conventional
love story. She is the incarnation of his own emotion, the
meaning of which he wants to find through her. Odette, a
living woman, is simply a pretext for this indirect narcissism.
She does not exist for him as herself. And because she is an
autonomous living being she resists the rôle assigned to her.
What Swann finally discovers is that there is a real person

named Odette, and that she escapes him in the very search
by which he attempts to grasp her. In this sense *Du Côté de
chez Swann* is a penetrating critique of that perennial source
of error in love—subjectivity.

At the same time, love reveals to Swann that he has
within him a capacity for feeling, a wealth of emotional life
of which he is usually unaware because he normally lives on
the surface, carefully insulated against this emotional zone.
The Swann who struggles against the proof of his failure in
love asserts by that very failure his belief that love was to
bring him something besides Odette, was to fill another need,
that of his sensitivity. Proust places the story of Swann's love
in a kind of parenthesis, between the two musicales where the
little Vinteuil phrase is played. The first time, the phrase
touches Swann's heart and awakens in him a renewed taste
for love. The second time it re-animates, in all its reality, the
suffering through which he has unconsciously lived, makes
him realize its extent and brings back to him from oblivion
the full memory of his essay at love. But at the same time the
musical phrase again poses the riddle of its own existence, a
riddle which is now compounded with that of Swann's love.
For an instant Swann is at the threshold of a spiritual discovery for which his love has prepared the way because it has
liberated his emotional power. But because of his lack of intellectual persistence he can never understand the real nature
of his experience, nor the nature of the faculty which had
temporarily substituted for his everyday world an hallucinated world in which he recognized neither others nor himself. His love is twice "lost" to him, and with that love he
loses also what Vinteuil's phrase has suggested to him. "It is
one of those powers of jealousy," the narrator says much
later, "to show us that feelings and the reality of facts are
unknown and open to countless suppositions. We think we
know exactly how things stand, what people think about them,
for the simple reason that we don't care. But as soon as we
wish to know something, as a jealous person does, things become a dizzying kaleidoscope in which we see nothing." [8]

Proust's object when he tells the story of Swann's love for Odette is not merely to relate a love story but to show how, because of love, Swann sets forth into an unknown world in which "he no longer distinguishes anything" and which causes the narrow and reassuring setting of his daily life to collapse. Swann proceeds no further in the knowledge of the "terra incognita" into which his love led him; but his adventure is a prelude to the narrator's, and each acquires its full meaning only in relation to the other.

The narrator seems to take up in his life, and to develop separately, each of the variations on love through which Swann had passed. Proust proceeds here as though, having introduced the whole theme at the beginning of his novel, he were taking it up in fragments. These fragments, from Combray to the return from Venice, reproduce with a more powerful orchestration and mingled with other themes, the simple linear theme of Swann's love. From the creation of the conventional love-myth around the image of woman, the narrator passes to the incarnation of his myth in the person of Gilberte. He then goes through all the inner fluctuations which accompany this phase of love; he experiences the surprising alchemy which the world undergoes as love brings about its usual transmutation of values which makes everything related to it poetic. He comes to know the obsession with a single image, Gilberte's, which dominates his whole life, changing its orientation—as far as the life of a small boy whom grown-ups carefully protect can be changed. He comes to know all the disorientations and disappointments that arise from the constant rectification which fact imposes upon dreams and memories, and the state of disequilibrium that results from it. But through an effort of his own free will, he ends his love by forcing it to undergo a phenomenon of decrystallization. He puts aside Gilberte's image; he refuses to give in to his need to see her; he disassociates her from the routines of his life. He proves that this love was an unconscious creation of his own imagination and will for which Gilberte was only a pretext. His experience suggests that love is nurtured by the presence of a human being who really has nothing to do with it. Its goal is not Gilberte, but suffering, even though it labels this happiness.

Against the gay and picturesque holiday setting of the seashore, the narrator's love for Albertine goes through the same first stages; Proust merely amplifies them. By the play of his imagination, the narrator creates about the girls a whole graceful "oceanic mythology"; by the play of associations he attributes to them all the beauty of the Balbec ocean and sun. Youth gives to "those beautiful brown and blond bodies" a brilliance concealing "the mediocre contents with which daily existence had filled them"; and desire flits from one to the other without settling on any one. The whole account of the first summer in Balbec is filled with a kind of ecstasy; the narrator speaks of "indescribable moments," of "keen intellectual joys," of "waves of happiness." The words pleasure, joy, happiness recur on almost every page. From the train which takes him to Balbec the narrator sees a peasant girl leave her house at dawn "and on a path illumined by the slanting rays of the rising sun, come to the station carrying a jug of milk." As he watches her he feels "that desire to live which is reborn in us every time we again become conscious of beauty and happiness." [9] The leit-motiv of the summer in Balbec is thus introduced. A new consciousness of beauty and happiness had been restored to Swann by Vinteuil's phrase; the narrator acquires it through his youth, his imagination, and his feeling of bewilderment in new sourroundings. It is a subjective state of mind which filters everything he sees, and lends its particular quality to the evenings spent with Saint-Loup in Rivebelle, to his relationship with Elstir, and especially to the games and pastimes shared with the little group of young girls.

The narrator's desire for love during this period is only one of the forms of the "multiplicity of oneself that constitutes happiness" [10] and it prepares him for "the unknown possibilities of happiness in life." [11] The narrator's desire is not focussed upon anyone; no woman's face comes to obsess him.

In this prelude to life, the stay in Balbec where a reality rich in joys mingles with the narrator's rêveries, love is only one among many themes. Proust develops what could be called variations on the prelude to love, variations which, for the most part, take up in a major key those which he had developed in a minor key in the more simple line of the prelude to Swann's love for Odette. The narrator afterwards continues to dream of love. He is charmed by other women, Mme de Guermantes, Mlle de Stermaria; his love is colored by the places which serve as its setting and by the associations of subjective images from which it benefits: Mme de Guermantes, Paris and the Faubourg St. Germain; Mlle de Stermaria, l'Ile du Bois and Brittany. But all the narrator grasps of the actual present is a setting; his dream of love always projects him into the future where he thinks it may come true.

For this reason the long prelude which precedes any realization of love opens up in the novel an inner perspective; images, sensations, and ideas, stirred up by his emotions, undergo a strange alchemy on several levels. They are arbitrarily but coherently organized; however, their coherence is only momentary. The dream of love is projected into the future, but the emotions which it arouses are constantly related to the past. Nothing reveals better than love the narrator's inattention to everyday reality. But dreams, as well as emotions, need to be buttressed by facts. The narrator's love focusses only upon women who really exist and whom he sees over and over again. At every moment the inner world of dreams, memories, and ideas strives, through the intermediary of feelings, to rejoin that of outer reality; but it never succeeds in doing so since these two worlds do not coincide in time. Unfailingly, through action and retroaction, love destroys itself in time. Proust establishes this mechanism of love as a constant in all the couples he describes, who are subjected to it and whose loves disintegrate, are "lost" in time.

When Proust again takes up the theme of love in the second part of *Sodome et Gomorrhe,* Gilberte and Albertine, like Mme de Guermantes, have become ordinary acquaint-

ances for the narrator. They have finally disengaged themselves from the fictitious and imaginary world in which he
had enclosed them. The theme of love which has until then
been dominant, repeating with variations the modalities of
Swann's love, has given way to the theme of the human comedy, also present since Combray. The young man's desire for
the unknown is now focussed upon the society of the Faubourg, rather than on any individual person; it has been
liberated from its symbiosis with a preconceived concept of
love.

The narrator's love for Albertine still contains some very
small portion of the dreams and memories of Balbec. Yet love
is now primarily a sensual desire, and the assurance of sensual
pleasure. The desire to see Albertine becomes the habit of
seeing Albertine. Gradually the narrator's affair with her
drags through various stages of love into boredom, and like
all the others, draws to its end. Sensual pleasure brings nothing beyond its repetition. It is then that a dramatic incident
occurs which plummets us along with the narrator into a
veritable hell, a highly civilized hell, of course, replete with
"niceties," feline in their perversities. This hell is presided
over by a grim and calculating jealousy of an intensity which
Swann hardly approached. Love is no longer in question in
La Prisonnière and *Albertine disparue;* Proust is now concerned with a "deluge of reality" which brings with it hideous
suffering. "It was," the narrator tell us, "an unknown country
upon the shores of which I had just landed, a new phase of
unsuspected suffering which opened up. No day would ever
again be new to me, would ever again awaken in me the wish
for an unknown pleasure." [12] The cycle of happiness born of
the sunny days and walks of Combray is ended. This is the
cycle of pain, the theme of torment which, although always
present, has been subordinated until now, and which reappears in *Sodome et Gomorrhe* when the narrator evokes his
grandmother's death. This theme gradually comes to dominate the whole end of the book to such an extent that when
the narrator finally rediscovers his lost joy it appears to the

reader a very fragile counterbalance to so somber a reality.

Until then, love in Proust's novel is primarily a game which has its rules, its pleasures, and its torments, through which it erects its own universe on the margin of reality, a universe which the contact of reality in time destroys. The narrator compares this game, quite accurately, with fishing:

There must be interposed between us and the fish—which if we saw it for the first time cooked and served on a table would not appear worth the endless trouble, craft and stratagem necessary to catch it—the ripples beneath which waver, without our quite knowing our intentions toward them, the burnished gleam of flesh, the indefiniteness of some form in the fluidity of a transparent and flowing azure.[13]

"Without our quite knowing our intentions toward them," Odette, Gilberte, the Duchesse, the "jeunes filles en fleurs" are indeed only shadow-pretexts. The whole equivocal game of Proustian love, as well as the esthetics of its specific presentation, are summed up in that sentence. The fish as a goal and the fish as a pretext absorbs all the attention of the fisherman as long as it is only a reflection, but loses its value as soon as it is nothing but a fish; it merely gives interest to the ripples of the water. Love is a diversion with the single selfish aim of artificially generating a flood of emotions, and these give the prosaic fish its moment of absolute value. By this long circuitous inner route, we come back to the mobile phantasmagoria of love; the figures traced by Swann and the narrator are only variations, seen in slow motion, of the ballet as a whole. The fish matters little provided that it is not at the other end of the line and that between it and the fisherman is an element which conceals it. That is why Charlus scrutinizes so closely creatures whose true nature is at first concealed for him by their sex. Love, therefore, is not an attraction toward someone, but a desire for the unknown which, because it focusses on ephemeral human beings, "wanders." The Proustian lover is really a wanderer, a man who has lost his way. He continually lives in the future, ready for the moment

when he will catch his prey, only to start the chase all over
again as soon as he has caught it.

But love, according to Proust, is equivocal in still another sense. He uses the word to describe another feeling—
the love which binds the narrator to his mother, and especially
to his grandmother. These two women surround the narrator
with a love that is tender and austere, humble and demanding,
tinged with sadness, and which is a necessary background for
his joys. They protect him and he responds with an almost
sacred veneration which he expresses in terms of religious
devotion. But this veneration also is tinged with guilt, a guilt
born of the daily relations which are established among them.
The child, his mother and grandmother are engaged in a
perennial drama, the same drama enacted that night in Combray when, in order to end his torments the child forced his
mother to yield to his will. His filial love manifests itself
principally through gestures of impatience, little acts of
tyranny and emotional blackmail, succeeded by bursts of
despair and emotion. Yet the child knows that there is a great
fund of devotion and a capacity for sacrifice in his filial love.
This emotional conflict between fact and desire results in an
uneasy conscience. It is in the narrator's great love for his
mother and grandmother, abnormal in its intensity but passionate and pure, that Proust reveals the whole ambiguity and
essential impossibility of love.

The narrator's filial love is timeless. It has no beginning
for the child because he has been immersed in it from the
time of his birth. He does not believe that it can ever come to
an end. It is permanent and absolute for him, kept alive by
the presence of beings whom he unconsciously believes to be
unchangeable. He recognizes his love for his mother and
grandmother only when something is lacking in the familiar
and customary aspect of their lives, and he reacts to this lack
with a whole gamut of emotions or actions which spring from
disappointment; paradoxically, ill-humor is the "variation"
of love which appears most often in his life, and it creates a
feeling of guilt in the narrator. Love, for him, is a belief in

the absolute and permanent presence of the two women, a belief doomed to disaster since it is based on a relation with others, and therefore relative. This is the source of all the ambiguities of love and of all the suffering which it prepares, which the narrator discovers only after his grandmother's death.

This ambiguity in the nature of love makes the narrator blind to everything with which it is relative, like, for example, the relative position of his grandmother in time. He notices that she ages only after some change has taken place in their habitual relationship; once when he comes in unexpectedly after a short absence he takes her unawares:

. . . I, for whom my grandmother was a part of myself, I who had never beheld her except in my heart, unchanged through time and memory, suddenly, in our drawing-room . . . for the first time and only for an instant . . . saw on the sofa, under a lamp, a common, red-faced, fat old woman who was sick and weary and whom I did not know.[14]

The blindness inherent in love explains all its dramas: the refusal to accept change, the angry reaction to modification of its ritual, the cruelty which makes one blame a person for the continual transformations time imposes. When the narrator's grandmother dies, he does not immediately feel the heartbreak which he thought was inevitable. One year later, in Balbec, by a chance action, he learns simultaneously, and with deep anguish, the reality of his love for his grandmother and the reality of death. The love between them had been an unconscious communion transcending any rationalization. In Balbec he physically feels his grandmother's absence because the gesture of unbuttoning his boot recreates her presence and what it had meant to him. He realizes that he had loved a unique being who had existed outside himself, and that no one will ever be able to fill that vacuum. His grandmother is "lost," carried off by time, which simultaneously carries away a whole part of her grandson's inner life. The basic drama of even the purest love is that love moves inevitably toward oblivion, for love is a sentiment between individuals who are all subject to the same laws of time. It cannot escape the movement of time, yet it can live only in the illusion of permanence. Love makes no allowance for death; that is why it is a source of error and anguish. It demands from a transitory being an impossible permanence, and from what is relative an absolute perfection. In short, it always finds fault with the flesh. It builds upon misunderstandings and hence leads to all kinds of deceit.

The narrator relates a very minor incident which clearly illustrates the ambiguity which love involves, simply because it is a two-way relationship between two changeable beings who think of it as though it were absolute. The narrator's grandmother wants Saint-Loup to take a snapshot of her. She wants the snapshot for her grandson because she has had the first attack of the illness which will finally kill her. She hides the fact from him to spare him any suffering, just as later she will hide under her hat the slight deformity in her face. Her grandson is irritated by this outburst of unaccustomed vanity and upset by the change in routine which his grandmother seems to bring arbitrarily into their relationship; he takes pleasure in destroying all his grandmother's joy. He wants his love for her to be permanent and unchanged and so he blindly interferes with his grandmother's project because he sees in it the beginnings of a change in her; because she conceals from him the real cause of this apparent change, the young man interprets it as the sign of an inner deterioration of his grandmother's character. Yet, without its ambiguity, love would make life intolerable; because he loves his grandmother, the idea that she is approaching death would be unbearable to him and so the narrator and his grandmother must keep up the pretenses which their fears, giving rise in turn to misunderstandings, make necessary. The theme of the evening torment in Combray reappears. The child's uneasiness in his mother's absence made him demand her actual presence, betraying the unconscious fear that the absence might be final. This fundamental torment, born of love, comes to its full realization in Balbec. There the narrator measures the real import of the final absence of a beloved person. He realizes that love can end only in suffering, or in a refusal to accept reality. Suffering is in itself a signal, a protest against the dissolution of love in time. So love in Proust's novel is indeed a search for life and for the unknown; but it finds death around the corner and it leads to the unknown only through the light that suffering throws on the known. Love leaves unexplained the mysterious joy experienced by the young narrator, the joy with which he equivocally had endowed love.

The subjectivity of love as Proust presents it has been much emphasized. Yet what particularly characterizes Proustian love is that it demands some external being on whom it can be bestowed. To be sure, it is only through Swann or the narrator that we know the women they love. That is why Odette and Albertine seem mysterious. But they cause suffering only because they are real and exist outside Swann or the narrator; they show how erroneous subjective idealism is. Love is a powerful, active agent through which the narrator discovers the ineluctability of objective reality. He is thus able to distinguish it from the easy-going dream world in which his feelings and intellect operate so effortlessly. Love directs the narrator's attention to the discordance of the two worlds, the world of inner consciousness and the world of objective reality in which men move about; consequently it prepares the synthesis which will in the end lead to the narrator's revelation. In the meantime, it gives to the spectacle of the human comedy a rich and mobile foundation which is open to all the hypotheses of analysis, to all the speculations of thought, and yet escapes abstraction. Swann, who forgets his love, remains marked with its slightly melancholy poetry, a poetry which springs from the awakening of his sensitivity and the final failure to which, quite involuntarily, he is subjected.

Love, as conceived by Proust, leads, by two different roads which never seem to meet, to direct contact with a

reality actually experienced—that of the objective and irreducible existence of others, who carry with them the double
mystery of their autonomy in time and their disappearance in
time. They exist, they are elusive, and they die. In this way
the frivolous world of *A la Recherche du Temps perdu,* in
which so many loves are born and die, opens out upon the
mystery of the existence of human beings. Love is not a
"romance"; it only leads to the threshold of that adventure
which begins at the point where love itself fails, the adventure
which human beings live by themselves, in solitude.

With *La Prisonnière* and *Albertine disparue* we enter a
world of suffering in which love is no longer the primary
question. For here Proust describes the narrator's persistent
refusal to accept the fact that an individual is essentially an
unknown quantity, and his consequent refusal to accept what
human relations tend to mask, loneliness.

THE CLOSED DOOR

W HEN we pass from *Sodome et Gomorrhe* to *La Prison-nière* we leave one world and enter another. The Combray cycle does not reappear until the end of *Albertine disparue*. Albertine is dead by then, and with time the memory of her has died too. "My mother," writes the narrator, "had taken me to spend a few days in Venice, and there I delighted in impressions much like those I had so often felt in Combray, but transposed into an entirely different and richer dimension." Combray then reappears in Venice:

When at ten o'clock in the morning my shutters were thrown open, I saw ablaze in the sunlight, not the black marble into which the slates of St-Hilaire used to turn, but the Golden Angel on the Campanile of St-Mark's . . . I was reminded of the shops of Combray . . . But on the second morning what I saw when I woke up were the impressions of my first morning stroll in Venice, Venice whose daily life was no less real than that of Combray, where as in Combray on Sunday mornings one had the delight of emerging upon a festive street.[1]

Sundays in Venice, in the spring, are superimposed upon the Sundays in Combray and carry along in their wake Mme Sazerat, Mme de Villeparisis, M. de Norpois; and then two letters received by the narrator recall all the people belonging to Swann's way and the Guermantes. Gilberte has married Saint-Loup and, on Charlus' side, Jupien's niece has married the young Marquis de Cambremer. Tansonville has joined Guermantes and Balbec has met Paris. The social cycles which began in Combray are closed, the Swann cycle as well as the

Charlus cycle. Everything in *Sodome et Gomorrhe* had already forecast this meeting. When M. de Charlus appears at La Raspelière after his "conjunction" with Jupien, we see the social spheres draw near each other; the slow rising of Odette's salon paves the way for the Saint-Loup-Gilberte union, and "that crossing of two generations and two societies"[2] which the narrator witnesses.

In Venice an amusing and distressing scene takes place between the narrator and his mother; it recalls the bedtime scene in Combray:

When I heard, on the very day upon which we were to start for Paris, that Mme Putbus, and consequently her maid, had just arrived in Venice, I asked my mother to put off our departure for a few days; her air of not taking my request into consideration, of not even listening to it seriously, reawakened in my nerves, excited by the Venetian springtime, that old desire to rebel against an imaginary plot woven against me by my parents . . . that fighting spirit, that desire which drove me in the past to enforce my wishes upon the people whom I loved best in the world, though I was prepared to conform to their wishes after I had succeeded in making them yield.[3]

This time the narrator does not win out as he had in Combray. He tries at first to impose upon his mother the decision to remain in Venice. She refuses and he decides to remain there alone: "And when the hour came at which, accompanied by all my luggage, she set off for the station, I ordered a drink to be brought out to me on the terrace overlooking the canal, and settled down there, watching the sunset, while from a boat that had stopped in front of the hotel a musician sang 'O Sole Mio.' "[4]

In Combray the decision to disobey his mother had stilled the child's anguish. In Venice, this decision is followed by an anxiety that mounts in crescendo as the hour of the train's departure approaches. To the accompaniment of "O Sole Mio," his unhappiness strips Venice of its poetry; it becomes commonplace, cramped, unfriendly and distant. Suddenly the young man jumps up and rushes to rejoin his mother just before the train leaves. The moral cycle begun in Combray, it seems, is also closed. Instead of forcing his mother to give in to his whims, this time he gives way to her. The virtues of Combray at last begin to exert an influence on him.

It is toward Combray, to Tansonville, where he stays with Gilberte, that the narrator "returns." The world he had sought to know is now explored; he knows its limits, for he has reached them. His childhood dream is spent. The two "extra-terrestrial" directions of Méséglise and Guermantes, united socially, close in geographically one upon the other:

> I repeated every evening, in the opposite direction, the walks which we used to take in Combray, in the afternoon when we went toward Méséglise . . . The walks that we took thus together were very often those that I used to take as a child . . . And it distressed me to find how little I relived my early years. I thought the Vivonne a meager ugly rivulet beneath its towpath.[5]

The source of the Vivonne is only "a kind of square washbasin in which bubbles rose," and it is now "easy to go to Guermantes by way of Méséglise." [6] Combray has lost its dimension of mystery and beauty. The door to the past is closed.

However, other perspectives have opened for the narrator. Complex and mobile depths now appear behind the flat magic-lantern images that once were the inhabitants of Tansonville or Guermantes. Instead of an image, each name evokes a network of actions and reactions, of causes and consequences, of relationships in perpetual flux. The simple categories according to which the intellectual and moral world of Combray was organized are irremediably confused; the people one knows are also those whom "one does not know." All the narrator's experiences and all his meditations have only brought him into collision with the unknowable. He discerns a certain permanence in the mechanisms of human behavior, which are always the same. What are Saint-Loup, Gilberte, and Morel if not a variation of the Charlus, Swann, and Odette combination? But the narrator discerns nothing beyond that; on the intellectual side too the world is closed and offers nothing further to his investigation.

Nor does there seem to remain anything to discover in himself. He knows so well the rules of his own sensitivity that he can automatically create love in himself. He knows by heart the only lesson he has learned from his repeated experiences: that love is merely a mirror one holds out to a woman without ever seeing in it anything but one's own image; and, too, that human destiny condemns everything to disappear with time into oblivion and into death, the final obliteration.

The horizon is closed on all sides. There remains nothing for the narrator to do but to wait behind the walls of a sanatorium for death to put an end to a "lost" life. He feels as though he has outlived himself, for living merely means prolonging his existence without opening up any new horizons. The setting for the final dramatic moment of his life is now complete; he is ready for the return to Combray, this time through memory and the magic words "François le Champi."

Yet between *Sodome et Gomorrhe* and the trip to Venice at the end of *Albertine disparue* which leads to the narrator's return to Combray, stretch the two strange and often arid volumes which trace the evolution of the narrator's troubled love for Albertine. His plan for a trip to Venice, constantly put off, reappears at more or less regular intervals in *La Prisonnière* and *Albertine disparue*, as if to bridge the gap between *Sodome* and the Venice episode. But in Balbec a sudden change of tone introduces the episode which adumbrates *La Prisonnière;* and we move from *Albertine disparue* on to Venice through a break in the story, but with no transition.

There are three distinct cycles in *A la Recherche du Temps perdu:* the Swann cycle, the Charlus cycle, and the Albertine cycle. It is true that Proust, through his narrator, links Albertine to Swann: "It was he who had made me want to go to Balbec . . . without which I shouldn't have known

Albertine." [7] Throughout his story he introduces markers which connect Albertine to everything that has gone before; through Mlle Vinteuil and the theme of homosexuality, she is even connected with Combray. But, as the proofs of the 1913 edition reveal, Proust added this cycle to his book after the publication of *Du Côté de chez Swann* and had not originally planned for it. Swann is, as the narrator says, the "pedestal" [8] which supports the novel. He introduces us to all the groups whom the narrator explores and to most of the themes of the novel: the Guermantes, the Verdurins, and indirectly through his friendship with Charlus, the homosexual set. It is he who speaks to the narrator of Balbec and Venice, of Bergotte and La Berma; he knows Elstir and is moved by Vinteuil's Sonata. His love for Odette is a prelude to the narrator's loves. But although Swann does indeed announce all the themes of *A la Recherche du Temps perdu*, he does not prepare us at all for Albertine.

Albertine appears at about the same time as M. de Charlus, but her story never has any point of contact with the baron's. The young girl, silent and passive, merely accompanies the narrator during his visits to La Raspelière, whither Charlus follows Morel. Charlus' adventures are developed on an entirely different level. Albertine has no connection either with the Swanns or the Guermantes. For a while she appears in Balbec as one of the "jeunes filles en fleurs." Then she reappears in a minor rôle in the second part of the *Côté de Guermantes*. During the narrator's second stay in Balbec, the theme of Gomorrha begins to cast its shadow on her, but the narrator's love for her still develops along the normal lines of Proustian loves, through the fluctuations of jealousy toward habit and boredom.

As soon as the narrator decides he will never be separated from Albertine, we change worlds. If the Guermantes are still in the picture, it is only in a subordinate rôle. The Verdurins reappear but they too are only incidental to the story of Albertine. Never, after Balbec, do Albertine and the narrator appear together in a salon. Gradually they are surrounded by a shadowy world, hinted at rather than described, in which Andrée, the chauffeur, Bloch's cousin Léa, Aimé, the headwaiter of the Balbec hotel, play curious parts. This world has ramifications in the sphere of Charlus' hidden life and in the sordid squabbles between Morel and Jupien's niece; it is a world of shady servants and pimps, characterized by a certain depravity to which the rest of the novel has not accustomed us. It is through Morel that the cycle of Albertine touches the Charlus cycle.

Until *La Prisonnière*, love, as Proust evokes it, is surrounded with worldliness and poetry at its birth, and has a certain dignity in its sadness when the lover feels the being to whom he is attached elude him. Even in jealousy, love retains in some measure an atmosphere of courtesy. Swann's jealousy, however painful and unpleasant, is shrouded in melancholy and is dignified by the unreal and leisurely atmosphere in which his story takes place. His very suffering is imbued with the charm which emanates from the first picture we have of Swann in Combray, elegant, mysterious, and peacefully married to Odette. The narrator's love for Gilberte, with its exchanges of childish fetishes, marbles, books, letters, its chocolate cakes, its games of prisoner's base, its joys and sorrows, is all imbued with the innocence of childhood, with solid family security and with the glamour emanating from Odette Swann. The sunlight of Balbec and all the joys of life on the beach set the tone of the narrator's first love for Albertine, while his slow accession to the Guermantes' world dominates its second phase.

The world of *La Prisonnière* and of *Albertine disparue*, after a few pages of prelude, is completely lacking in such graces, in any poetic background; nothing redeems its harshness. The beautiful poetic passages which *La Prisonnière* contains, and there are many, seem like separate selections which fit in rather badly with the remainder of the story. Proust seems not to have had sufficient time in this part of his work to make the transformations which might have blended it into a harmonious whole. A moralizing tone, which is not in keeping with the situation presented, sometimes dominates the narrative, creating a strange atmosphere of uneasiness. The narrator, in Venice, has forgotten this period of his life. The reader has not, and this part of the book never quite gives the impression of complete mastery which makes a character like Charlus come to life and gives him a sane reality.

The story told by Proust in this last part of his work seems to be related to a particular incident in his own life, the love he had for his secretary, young Agostinelli, and his grief at the young man's death in an airplane accident. In any event, it has its roots in a somewhat dark side of Proust's personality, revealed by his habit of actually having "prisoners" in his house, jealously guarded, and hidden from his friends. The episode does not seem to have benefited from the filtering of memories in time, which Proust himself considers necessary to art. The tale is still laden with all the raw material of life and the artistic transposition remains imperfect. In any case, the life described is very curious.

The narrator is cloistered in a room from which he rarely emerges; Albertine lives in the same apartment and goes out all the time, accompanied by a chauffeur, a friend of Morel and of Andrée. The narrator authorizes these outings and receives reports from the chauffeur and from Andrée on any meetings which Albertine may have had. Albertine is never alone. On these terms, the narrator showers expensive presents upon her, and at the same time acts the rôle of accuser, avidly questioning her about her slightest gestures and words, present or past. He seems to have only one object, to catch her in the wrong. Through the slow development of these two parts of the novel, what breaks through at times and gives a new dimension to the story, is neither dream nor memory, nor love, nor even homosexual love, but the shadow of impending madness. It threatens to shut upon the narrator a door too heavy to be easily reopened. The narrator escapes from his creator, and betrays him. At no time does Proust seem to take measure of all the strangeness of the world into which he thrusts us, and which at times is more reminiscent of a psychiatric case history than of literature.

After Swann, after Charlus, the narrator now moves into the foreground. He occupies it almost alone from his bed in the bedroom which he seldom leaves. Until now he has played the apparently modest but all-powerful rôle of the magician who comments on the shadows he evokes, his own as well as others. He has revealed himself primarily through the states of mind which gave their own color to each part of his story: the quiet luminous reveries of Combray, the lively sunlit dreams of Balbec, the amused detachment mingled with curiosity of Guermantes, the Cervantes-like vision of Sodome. He has communicated his states of mind to the reader, who always adopts his point of view. This is no longer true in *La Prisonnière* and *Albertine disparue*. The reader's point of view diverges from the narrator's. The reader must make an effort which the previous part of the novel does not demand in order to accept the bizarre situation as a real premise, even within the framework of fiction. Perhaps one should say especially within the framework of fiction. The strange and far too peculiar reality which gleams through the story challenges even literature. The reader cannot easily enter Albertine's world.

The story unfolds against a background of rather curious facts. A young woman, of her own free will, goes to live with the narrator and is thereby condemned to his ugly accusations. She is surrounded by a network of spies and subjected to incessant interrogation. Her slightest words are used against her, her slightest plans crossed. Her relations with the narrator are those of suspect and inquisitor. But no trial ever takes place; the spies are counteragents and all the plots made by the narrator are turned against him to betray him in fictitious trips, mythical outings, spurious explanations, lying servants. The narrator is a victim of his own inquisition and in this double rôle becomes odious. The masochism he caters to in preparing the setting for his own suffering and the latent sadism which drives him to pursue and track down Albertine, even beyond death, make the reader uneasy and doubtful as to the purpose of such a game.

A rather obscure psychological drama serves as background for these facts. The themes of homosexuality, of jealousy, of guilt and expiation, are strangely and apparently arbitrarily mingled. A direct and unexpected moral concern appears and throws a sinister light even upon the moving story of Swann. The narrator tells us that when he listened to Swann's story, he "had dangerously allowed to widen in him the noxious path, destined to be painful, of knowledge." [9] The very tone tends, at times, to become solemn and oratorical, vibrating with an emotion which has slipped into the story from the outside and which is not created by it. The last pages of *Sodome et Gomorrhe* are heavily charged with such an emotion. The words torture, fatal, terrible, punishment, grief, suffering, pile up for ten or more pages. The "deluge of reality" which, according to the narrator, "submerges" him, is "enormous" compared with the "timid and insignificant suppositions that had foreshadowed it." [10] The intensity of the tone is surprising and seems out of proportion to the cause— the suspicion that Albertine is a lesbian—even if we take into account the explosive force of the memory of Montjouvain. It is this memory surging from the past which sets off the drama. Proust clearly indicates his intention to explore the jealousy connected with homosexuality.

The narrator wants to break off with Albertine because a word which she says by chance about Mlle Vinteuil brings to his memory the image of Montjouvain: "kept alive deep within me . . . to torture me, to punish me, who knows, perhaps for having let my grandmother die." [11] Nothing in the story which precedes explains by what "crossroad" the image of Montjouvain is connected in the narrator's world with the idea of punishment. This association of ideas is all the more surprising because it is linked with a feeling of guilt about his dead grandmother, a "victim," it would seem, of her grandson. However, the association is sustained. The narrator sees the image of Montjouvain springing up "like Orestes from the depths of the night where it had seemed forever buried, striking like an avenger in order to cast him into a life deservedly terrible and new." [12] Deservedly? Nothing in the narrator's life explains this qualification. His laziness seems a negligible shortcoming to cause such a "rain of brimstone and fire." Nothing explains his punishment, unless it be the intimate drama that Proust himself lived, and into which he did not want to drag his narrator but which here escapes his control.

In Proust there is always a connection between the idea of carnal love and sacrilege. The sacrilege relates to his beloved mother. He often uses the words "pleasure" and "vice" interchangeably. The connection may be attributed to his own position as a homosexual, the adored son of an austere mother of strict morality whom he loved and to whom he was very close in thought and feeling. This theme of culpability appears in one of Proust's first stories in *Les Plaisirs et les Jours*, "The confession of a young girl." Coming unexpectedly upon her daughter in the throes of sexual pleasure in the arms of a young man, the mother falls and dies; there remains nothing for the stricken girl to do but to commit suicide. The Montjouvain situation follows a similar pattern, but adds to it the theme of homosexuality. Mlle Vinteuil's sapphism slowly kills her father. After his death, before she gives herself up to the pleasure which makes her feel guilty, Mlle Vinteuil persuades her friend to spit on the photograph of her father whom, nonetheless, she loves. Her feelings of guilt are disclosed by this sadistic gesture. The narrator himself follows this pattern. If his mother, he tells us, had discovered Albertine's friendship for Mlle Vinteuil "It would have been an unsurmountable obstacle . . . not only to a marriage . . . but even to her spending a few days in the house." [13] Why, then, since it is Albertine who is suspected of sapphism, and since it is Mlle Vinteuil who practices it, this curious retrospective self-accusation of the narrator when he accuses himself of having killed his grandmother? Why this offer to expiate a grave sin precisely by the compensating suffering which Albertine's special vice causes him?

The relationship between Albertine and the narrator is not only that between a lover and the woman of whom he is jealous. In order to preserve his narrator from the too special tendency of Sodom, perhaps to put him at a greater distance from himself, Proust has until now, though not without some difficulty, kept him outside the realm of homosexuality. That he should once, through an open window, come upon a scene of sapphism, is acceptable to us; that once, hidden under a stairway, he should by chance witness from beginning to end the consummation of the Charlus-Jupien union we are also willing to accept; that still by chance he should discover Jupien's house of ill-fame adds up to a lot of chances; but when he obstinately sets about to make love to a little bourgeoise and by chance again she evokes the maze of homosexuality which he himself has never explored, credulity falters. If we see behind Albertine the silhouette of Agostinelli or other prisoners, we also seem to see a part of Proust himself which he can, through the narrator, harshly rebuke.

The shadow of the narrator's mother also plays its part in this portion of the novel. She and Albertine are never together in the apartment; their simultaneous presence seems to be incompatible. The narrator's mother vainly opposes the young couple's intimacy. Yet the narrator, with a lack of filial respect reminiscent of Mlle Vinteuil's, constantly compares the peace induced by his erotic games with Albertine with the peace which his mother's presence used to bestow upon him at night. On the other hand, when he speaks to Albertine about her "vice" and the "wrong" she does, he uses, he tells us, the same high moral tone his mother uses when she upbraids him. The problem which Albertine's way of life poses for the narrator is, indeed, exactly the same as that posed for Mme Proust by the son who loved her deeply, yet concealed from her a whole portion of his existence which she must, however, have suspected.

There are moments in *La Prisonnière* when the feverish agitations of the narrator's mind do not apparently concern jealousy but rather what could easily be the state of perpetual moral struggle in which Proust found himself caught. This is the only explanation for the high moral tone of certain conversations which the narrator has with his companion, and the judgments he passes on her. It also explains why he is so quick to point out Albertine as the guilty one, condemned in advance and pilloried with such righteous indignation. Besides her use as a pretext for jealousy, Albertine seems also useful as a scapegoat.

"I preferred," the narrator says, "to have life remain at the high level of my intuitions, in particular the intuition which I had had that first day on the beach, when I thought that those girls *embodied the frenzy of pleasure, were vice incarnate,* and again on the evening when I had seen Albertine's teacher leading the passionate girl home to the little villa, as one thrusts into its cage a wild animal which nothing in the future, despite appearances, will ever succeed in taming, even if my intuitions did not agree with what Bloch had told me when he had made the world seem so fair to me, making me thrill at every encounter during my walks by showing me the universality of desire." [14]

Albertine disappears in death, laden with all the sins of the flesh. "Perhaps," says the narrator about Bergotte, "it is only in really vicious lives that the problem of morality can be posed with all the force of indignation." [15] There is much indignation in *La Prisonnière*. Homosexuality appears there as a heavy moral responsibility which makes any chance of happiness quite problematical.

The very title, *La Prisonnière*, is ambiguous. The narrator explains: he learns by chance from Albertine, that the friend who brought her up is Mlle Vinteuil; "But the words: 'That friend is Mlle Vinteuil' had been the 'Open Sesame' which I myself would have been unable to find and which had let Albertine into the depths of my broken heart. And I could have searched a hundred years without finding the means of opening the door that had closed on her." [16]

So Albertine is a prisoner in the narrator's heart. She is also prisoner of an image, that of Montjouvain, and of a story, Swann's. A prisoner also, according to the narrator, of her taste for pleasure and her weakness for women. She is an actual prisoner too, since she lives with a man who sets spies on her and subjects her to his slightest whim. "She was startled to learn," when she settled down in Paris at the narrator's, "that she was in a strange world that had customs unknown to her, regulated by a code that could not be infringed." [17]

But is it not rather the narrator who is prisoner? Prisoner of his temperament which keeps him locked up in a room; prisoner of the images which obsess him; prisoner of roving desires for passersby—milkmaids and others—which his imagination forces Albertine to satisfy for him; prisoner of the network of spying and lies which he builds up; and, finally, prisoner of all that phantasmagoria which keeps him furthest from what he wants to be—an author. Albertine is, after all, only the instrument he uses to build an imaginary life which diverts his thoughts from work. It is not Albertine, but the narrator's mind—his will, his very life—that is imprisoned; it will be set free only by Albertine's death. The whole relation between Albertine and the narrator has the same ambivalence as their tormentor-victim relationship.

In that sense, *La Prisonnière* and *Albertine disparue* have a very special importance in the novel. The narrator has until now moved toward life, toward joys outside himself which tempted him like veritable Armida's gardens. Nothing has led him to expect the dark dungeon he is now in; he has had only the faintest intimations that it might exist. And his unexpected captivity sometimes seems all too lengthy to the reader.

However, once these reservations have been made, once we have accepted the conventions which Proust imposes, we gradually succumb to the tone peculiar to this part of the novel. It is marked by a long meditative soliloquy which connects it with the opening pages of the novel in which Combray is first evoked. The theme of the room, of sleep and awakening, re-emerges. The narrator leaves the realm of the imaginary in order to "climb once more the abrupt slope of introspection" [18] in an effort to understand the test he is undergoing. Except for the long "interpolated" passages in which Morel, Charlus, and the Verdurins are discussed, the narrator's attention is focussed almost entirely on the "changing moods" of his "inner climate." What prevails over his shifting moods and the febrility of his analyses is the muted tone of meditation; everything appears to be subdued by its passage from an inner distance. The "game of hide-and-seek" which the narrator and Albertine play is symbolic rather than real and, although described at length, it is only the means whereby Proust throws light upon a more general underlying drama: that of solitude and of loneliness.

The fluctuations and chronic fits of jealousy develop in slow motion, but they only repeat, amplify and clarify the rhythm of the malady that Swann knew so well. While jealousy seems always to trample the same threshing floor, beating blindly over the same ground, the narrator progresses toward a knowledge of a different kind. He is torn between two opposite poles, for he begins to realize the two-sided nature of his solitude. At the same time, he seeks to be rid of his loneliness, at any price:

The bonds which unite another person with ourselves exist only in our youth. As memory grows fainter they become flaccid; notwithstanding the illusion by which we would fain be cheated and with which we would cheat other people because of love, friendship, politeness, deference, or duty, *we exist alone.* Man is a creature who cannot emerge from himself; and when he asserts otherwise, he lies.[19]

This is the truth toward which, in spite of himself, the narrator progresses. It remains when the particular experience which made it his is completely forgotten.

Every man is a prisoner, shut up in himself as the narrator is shut up in his room; but it is not a state he accepts any more readily than the narrator, who, it becomes apparent, uses jealousy to struggle every inch of the way against whatever separates him from Albertine:

. . . it was just as well, I told myself, that by incessantly asking myself what she could be doing, thinking, wanting, at every moment . . . I should keep that door open, that communicating door which love had opened in me, and that I should feel another person's life flood through open sluices into the reservoir which must not become stagnant.[20]

The story henceforth assumes its general import, which far surpasses the narrator's particular and somewhat bizarre story. Furthermore, it takes its place in the body of the novel, for what the author discovers during his liason with Albertine is that she is only the human pretext for an intellectual activity experienced in relation to her. Instead of being simply a creature from whom some tenderness may be expected, Albertine is the enigma that any human being presents to the intellect. Through her the narrator realizes his own limitations, realizes that he cannot break through them, and at the same time learns that the life of any other creature is impenetrable. In thus defining the problem of solitude, though without clarifying it, *La Prisonnière* and *Albertine disparue* give the novel its moral dimension. The "communicating door" opened by love is closed to the narrator; nothing remains for him but to turn toward another door, the door Vinteuil's Septet opens in him and which the Sonata had for an instant opened in Swann.

The two themes, solitude and the uneasy obsession about Albertine, alternate quite regularly in *La Prisonnière*. The calm opening pages of this volume are in striking contrast with the harassed tone of the last pages of *Sodome et Gomorrhe*, a contrast which is characteristic of the whole story, although the theme of anxiety gradually predominates over that of calm:

At daybreak, my face still turned to the wall, and before I had seen above the big inner curtains the shade of the first streaks of light, I could already tell what sort of day it was. The first sounds from the street had given me the information—whether they came to my ears dulled and distorted by the moisture of the atmosphere or quivering like arrows in the resonant and empty area of a spacious, crisply frozen, pure morning; as soon as I heard the clatter of the first streetcar, I could tell whether it was sodden with rain or setting forth into the blue. And perhaps these sounds had themselves been forestalled by some swifter and more pervasive emanation which, stealing into my slumber, diffused it in a melancholy that seemed to forecast snow, or gave utterance (through the lips of a little person who occasionally reappeared there) to so many hymns to the glory of the sun that, having first of all begun to smile in my sleep, having prepared my eyes, behind their shut lids, to be dazzled, I awoke finally amid deafening peals of music.[21]

In this peaceful description the narrator creates the atmosphere of a daily life which seems at first anchored in "domestic peace" because of the presence of Albertine in an adjacent room. His waking up, Albertine's visit, her outing, her return, her presence in the evening, and the peace of the night are brought bit by bit into the harmony.

But two opposing elements soon stand out. The morning awakenings, the street cries, the atmospheric changes bring with them happy peace; Albertine's presence destroys it. "It was especially from my room that I was aware, during this period, of life outside of me." [22] But the narrator perceives this outside life only when Albertine is not around him; ". . . as soon as she had left for her outing I was revived, if only for a few moments, by the virtues of solitude." As soon as Albertine appears, either in person or in the narrator's thought, this atmosphere is dispelled. The exchange, peaceful as breathing, that had been made in solitude between the narrator's inner and outer worlds gives way to an uneasy restlessness. His attention is scattered; his thoughts rush around in a series of abrupt, blind sallies. "She was capable," he tells us of Albertine, "of causing me suffering, but not joy." [23] What he expects from her above all is peace of mind, a peace which will free his spirit so that nothing will interfere with his perceptions. In a singular contradiction, he asks Albertine to make solitude possible for him by assuring him complete peace of mind. But in order to achieve this peace of mind he cannot countenance the slightest mystery about her, he must know everything about her:

The image that I sought . . . was no longer that of an Albertine who led a life about which I knew nothing, it was that of an Albertine who was not the reflection of a far-away world, but who wanted nothing except to be with me, to be just like me, an Albertine who was the reflection of what was mine and not of the unknown.[24]

The narrator conceives his own life as being at the center of Albertine's universe, and everything in her life as depending upon it. What he wants from her is perfect unison with himself. The narrator's jealousy is focussed on what remains unknown in Albertine—all the people she knows, all her actions, all her desires beyond himself. He tells us that "we feel love for a person of whose actions we are jealous." [25] Because of his jealousy he plans to scrutinize Albertine's actions; he starts an investigation, the results of which pose problems that go beyond jealousy and are of another nature. From this point of view, *La Prisonnière* and *Albertine disparue* could be entitled "In Search of the Unknown Albertine."

In *La Prisonnière*, the investigation is made through Albertine herself, and secondarily through the testimonies of the chauffeur or Andrée. Albertine's death changes the nature of the investigation but not that of the results obtained. The narrator discovers that Albertine's life is dispersed in space, goes back in time, is tied to countless people. It is impossible to encompass her life. Before disappearing, Albertine, like the Jacques Godeau in Jules Romain's *Mort de Quelqu'un,* had filled an indefinable space which has depth in the memories of other people and also exists on the surface of time. Gradually the narrator realizes that there is an unsuspected permanence

and a continuity in Albertine that cannot be grasped—in the
very Albertine whom he had wanted to reduce to the proportions of what he himself saw of her when he watched her
sleeping. Their relations, as he had understood them, are
transformed; he realizes that

. . . that long complaint of the soul which thinks that it is living
shut up within itself is a monologue in appearance only, since
the echoes of reality alter its course; such a life is apparently like
a spontaneous essay in subjective psychology, which from a distance furnishes its 'action' to a purely realistic novel of another
reality, another existence, the vicissitudes of which in their
turn inflect the curve and change the direction of the psychological essay.[26]

All the information that the narrator obtains about Albertine's life is fragmentary, contradictory, and enigmatic; it
resists any coherent reconstruction. He also gives it different
interpretations, depending upon his mood. If, in order to satisfy his love, Albertine must not be a lesbian, the information
he finds supports this hypothesis; if, when he has become indifferent, Albertine's guilt is no longer of great importance
to him, the information he comes upon seems to reveal her
guilt. We are reminded of his outings in Balbec with Mme
de Villeparisis: "Before getting into the carriage," he says,
"I had already composed the seascape which I was going to
look for." [27] Furthermore, the nature of the information
which reaches him matters little; it actually has no intrinsic
interest. What slowly becomes apparent as the information on
Albertine accumulates is the complete absurdity of such an
enterprise. The results of the narrator's quest for information
seem dubious to the reader because never, as long as Albertine is alive, does he attempt to obtain her co-operation and
confidence; after she is dead it is too late. Besides, Albertine
is in some ways deception personified. However, what Albertine's confidence could have contributed he eventually discovers in his meditations about himself and about his own
life; deception seems to him inherent in the life of even the
most highly ethical human being. "I ought to have reflected"

he thinks "that there are two worlds, one covering the other, one consisting of the things that the best, the most sincere people say, and behind it the world of the same people's actions." [28] So, in the last analysis, Albertine is in that respect like anyone and everyone.

The narrator's investigation of Albertine constantly brings to light surprising and unexpected fragments of life which disconcert him. Albertine's present life, which he tries carefully to circumvent, escapes him on all sides—in outer space, in inner space and in time—dragging along the past and overflowing into the future. "Behind each of her words" he feels "a lie; behind each house to which she says she is going, another house; behind each action, each person, another action, another person." [29] As for the past, "her admissions, insofar as they concerned the past, left large blanks which I had to try to fill in completely, but before I could fill them in I had to learn about her life." [30] His attempt "to learn about her life" from the outside, and to reconstruct it on the basis of evidence, only succeeds in increasing his confusion and in accumulating a mass of tangled contradictions which seem to the narrator to hide what he considers most important. His quest accomplishes nothing but the total destruction of his peace of mind; he is sure that only a life lived in complete blindness is possible with Albertine. "The only result of my exploration of one sector of the great zone that extended round me had been to banish further from me that unknowable entity which another person's life, when we seek to form a definite idea of it, invariably is to us." [31]

In order to imagine effectively the "real life" of a person we must break through our habits, or through the indifference which our superb egocentricity creates in our relation to that person. Love accepts mystery and thrives on the unknown: ordinary jealousy is for the narrator a less powerful instigator of anxious curiosity than homosexuality. The image of Montjouvain suddenly places Albertine in a world which is by definition closed to the young man; he will never be able to enter it, reduce it to a known quantity. And so his anxiety can never be stilled, nor his struggle with the unknown come to an end, except in oblivion. Only Albertine's absence and her death bring forgetfulness. Her objective reality is the core of his obsession; it is because Albertine is "another" that their relationship incurs so much drama. There is a real, logical link connecting the image of Montjouvain with the pitiless investigation which it occasions; but it takes the narrator much further than he expected. The obscure world Albertine contains within her is unknowable at any given moment, even to herself; and this is true too of the whole movement of her life in the past, a movement which no one, including herself, could adequately retrace.

Her death poses another problem for the narrator. It confirms her disappearance, but changes nothing in the hypothetical character of everything that the narrator, and with him the reader, can learn about her. From the moment of her death she follows, though more slowly, the road of the narrator's grandmother, the road which leads to forgetfulness. And so Albertine, who despite all the narrator's efforts has remained a stranger to him, disappears completely from his memory. Her death is a fact, final and absolute, from which nothing can be learned. It is only her life, transitory and relative, but in which she was a unique individual, that is of any importance. It is this unique quality of her life which all the narrator's jealous concentration cannot penetrate. Albertine, alive and irreducible, with "her dark and unrelenting will," alone has value in the young man's eyes. Her death again brings up the problem of the value of transitory life—a problem already raised by the grandmother's death. Proust places beside it Bergotte's death and the survival of the work which he leaves, and also the survival of Vinteuil in his Septet. The elements are all gathered here, ready for the discovery and the synthesis that the narrator will make at the Guermantes matinée, when he will at last realize that death is not accidental, and that it is drawing near for him too. The theme of solitude leads straight to that of death.

The narrator's impassioned investigation of Albertine al-

ternates with moments of private communion with himself.
Shut up in his room, he gradually becomes more conscious of
the inner reaches of time; he is made aware of them by certain moments of the past which spring to life and impinge
upon the present. For the first time he notices "correspondences" which certain sensations awaken between his inner
and outer worlds:

Françoise came in to light the fire, and to make it draw, threw
upon it a handful of twigs, the scent of which, forgotten for a
year, traced round the fireplace a magic circle within which,
perceiving myself poring over a book, now in Combray, now in
Doncières, I was as joyful, while remaining in my bedroom in
Paris, as if I had been on the point of starting for a walk toward
Méséglise, or of going to join Saint-Loup and his friends on the
training-ground . . . The scent in the frosty air of the twigs of
brushwood was like a fragment of the past, an invisible floe
broken off from the ice of a winter of long ago that stole into my
room, often variegated moreover with this perfume or that light,
as though with a sequence of different years, in which I found
myself plunged, overwhelmed, even before I had identified them,
by the eagerness of hopes long since abandoned.[32]

He discovers an "inner violin" which certain sensations, born
of solitude, cause to vibrate; they open up a whole world
within him:

By themselves these modifications (which though they came from
without, were internal) refashioned for me the world outside.
Communicating doors, long barred, swung open in my brain.
The life of certain towns, the gaiety of certain expeditions re-
sumed their place in my consciousness. All athrob in harmony
with the vibrating string, I would have sacrificed my dull life in
the past, and all my life to come, erased with the india-rubber of
habit, for one of these special, unique moments.[33]

Immobile, the narrator discovers within himself gradations of
the "I" superimposed one upon another, starting with the
basic one, a "small inarticulate sun worshipper," and moving
toward "the philosopher." He is quite content to contemplate

them passively. When Albertine has disappeared, he thinks back over the period of their life together:

So, then, my life was entirely altered. What had made it . . . attractive when I was alone was precisely the perpetual resurgence, at the bidding of identical moments, of moments from the past. From the sound of the rain I recaptured the scent of the lilacs in Combray, from the shifting of the sun's rays on the balcony, the pigeons in the Champs-Elysées, from the muffling of all noise in the heat of the morning hours, the cool taste of cherries, the longing for Brittany or Venice from the sound of the wind and the return of Easter.[34]

But he draws no conclusion from these impressions. At first his thoughts are all absorbed in the pursuit of the enigma of Albertine, then he is torn by the anguish her death causes him until he finally forgets her. The objective reality which Albertine represented once more makes the narrator turn away from himself and the contemplative life which he has been leading from his bed. The slow process of forgetfulness brings him the counterpart of these experiences and brings them to him in perfect symmetry. The narrator sees Gilberte, whom he does not recognize, and feels a sensual desire for her:

Under the action of desire, and consequently of the desire for happiness, which Gilberte had aroused in me during these hours in which I had supposed her to be someone else, a certain number of miseries, of painful preoccupations, which only a little while earlier had obsessed my mind, had been released, *carrying with them a whole block of memories*, probably long since crumbled and become precarious, about Albertine.[35]

The narrator never makes the connection between this "suppression" of "a whole part of his association of ideas" with the slow progress of that "invisible floe set loose from a winter of long ago" which a fire had brought back to his mind.

Under the influence of his suffering, his mind lingers over the problem of his various past identities and the moments "lost" in forgetfulness rather than over the complementary problem of his identity in the moments "regained" in solitude:

. . . the memory of all the events that had followed one another in my life . . . in the course of those last months of Albertine's existence had made these months seem to me much longer than a year; and now this oblivion of so many things separated me by gulfs of empty space from quite recent events which they made me think remote because I had had what is called "the time" to forget them. This oblivion, by its fragmentary, irregular interpolation in my memory—like a thick fog at sea which obliterates all the landmarks—confused, destroyed my sense of distances in time, contracted in one place, extended in another, and made me suppose myself now farther away from things, now far closer to them than I really was. And as in the fresh spaces, as yet unexplored, which extended before me, there would be no more trace of my love for Albertine than there had been in the time past which I had just traversed of my love for my grandmother, my life appeared to me to offer a succession of periods in which, after a certain interval, nothing of what had sustained the previous period survived in that which followed; my life appeared as something so devoid of the support of an individual, identical and permanent self, something so useless in the future and so protracted in the past, that death might just as well put an end to its course here or there, without *in the least concluding it.*[36]

The processes of memory, which he has not yet completely understood, make life seem insignificant and absurd, without meaning or direction. This attitude is more important than the suffering from which it springs, for it marks a change in the relationship of the narrator with his life. He has reached the threshold of indifference. Art alone seems still to escape the triteness of life. The resurrection of past "I's" in his moments of solitude, and the apparently unconnected "I's" which succeed one another in time are contradictory elements which he does not attempt to reconcile; they are the two facets of the experience which will open for him the vistas of *Le Temps retrouvé.* In his exploration of solitude the narrator again approaches the mystery of time, but he fails to understand its double aspect. The door closes on the search which had been motivated by his jealousy, leaving him only the conviction of failure. "Truth and life are hard taskmasters; although I did not really know them, all they left me was an impression of sadness which gave way to weariness." [37] With the end of the Albertine episode, the narrator enters the realm of despair. His life turns from the future toward the past, from imagination to recollection, from the world outside to the world within him. In this part of his work, Proust restates, not without some repetition, all the psychological and moral "truths" scattered throughout the whole novel, and bestows upon them the weight of definitive truths; he gives so abstract a character to this analysis that it seems at times almost a treatise on psychology. The narrator puts these concepts in a new perspective, orienting them around memory and its lapses, and explains in this way all the other "intermittences" in his inner life; but the overall impression is one of monotony, in the experiences he describes as well as in the "truths" he formulates.

These truths are not without their esthetic counterpart. The narrator never succeeds in reconstructing Albertine's life, in really knowing her. He never succeeds in seeing this young woman in all her aspects, or in unravelling the tangle of her complex relations in time and space. Albertine breaks up into a thousand fragments because the narrator has no key to the "inner soul which gave cohesion" to "this ephemeral and active whole." [38] What was Albertine's story during her stay at the narrator's, and consequently what was the real story of the narrator's life with her? And the real story of Swann and Odette? This question arises about all the characters in the Proustian world, and in all kinds of ways about the narrator himself.

Proustian characters are unknown quantities and the narrator is obliged finally to accept this fact, which the whole novel illustrates. People enter his field of vision, group themselves as in tableaux vivants, play their parts, then disappear only to reappear later, just as untouched and impenetrable as before. It is curious to see how each character "makes his en-

trance" before the narrator, either in a series of candid cam-
era shots or in slow motion. The narrator may ponder at
length their successive appearances, but even his closest scrutiny never succeeds in explaining their various aspects, or in
finding a connection between the different "snapshots" which
could define their character: Miss Sacripant, Odette de Crécy,
Odette, friend of the Verdurins, the Botticelli-like Odette beloved of Swann, Mme Swann, the mistress of the Duc de Guermantes. How many other Odettes are there between each of
these "photographic proofs" of Odette? And how many
others in that part of her life which never coincides with the
narrator's? Even the narrator's life is neither reconstructed
nor explained in all its continuity. Nothing ever explains his
vocation, for example, which is simply given as a fact, like a
place, Combray, or a person, the Duchesse. There are great
stretches of shadow behind everyone in *A la Recherche du
Temps perdu*—shadow which Proust suggests in the narrator's analysis of character. But the analysis is limited to those
aspects of them which are visible to the narrator. They remain
in great part as unknown to us as Albertine.

The narration in the first person has a definite function
in this respect. In *La Prisonnière* and *Albertine disparue* the
narrator realizes that his investigation always reflects his own
frame of mind, the lapses of his attention, his alternate anxiety and calm. The same holds true for the rest of the novel.
Proust relates the analysis of his characters to the narrator's
particular point of view rather than to the character being
analyzed. He does not impose it upon the character observed,
or even upon the reader: actions, bodies, and words present a
surface which analysis never succeeds in disturbing. The relationship between what the narrator sees and what he thinks
is quite subtle; all his thoughts are tinged with its uncer-
tainty. If he is to "decipher" the symbols that people are, he
must first clearly read the hieroglyphs in himself. As he discovers in the case of Albertine, it is futile to try to reconstruct
the world of others according to his own emotions. The whole
complex rationale which accumulates around Proustian char-

acters becomes, after a certain stage, speculation and hypothesis just as it does in the case of Albertine. The narrator "formulates truths" which are really simple observations of fact, drawn from what he sees of the world and generalized in reference to that world.

There would be a real contradiction in Proust's work if we could logically reconstruct any of his characters and explain their evolution. For his whole novel is proof of his own assertion that what gives men their individuality can only be translated by art, which transcends the intellect. Proustian analysis, with all its keen attention to exact detail, is the means Proust uses to isolate what is unique in an individual; analysis allows him to strip his characters of everything which is explicable, and therefore not particular to them. What remains is their essential being, mysterious and inexplicable. The narrator could perhaps more fully understand and explain the people around him if he were in constant contact with them; but because they appear intermittently, they preserve their autonomy. Despite their continual appearances and disappearances, they give the impression of continuity and, up to a certain point, they can be explained. But what the narrator analyzes is the outward person; no amount of analysis can explain the essence of the inner person. It is simply a matter of vision.

Proust presents his characters as his narrartor sees them —when their paths cross his and a fragment of their lives is spotlighted. We are left with the impression that they are moving independently along their own trajectories, which at intervals automatically cross the narrator's path. Each follows his isolated course, distinct from the narrator's and from that of any other character. All the characters seem "distant" from each other, strangers, though they move in the same world. We catch innumerable glimpses of them; a Proustian character is primarily a series of diverse images which we know are connected and animate, but it is never possible to distinguish exactly how. The same is also true of minor characters like Jupien, Aimé, or even Princesse Sherbatoff.

Proust is infinitely greater as a creator of characters than as a psychologist, simply because his characters resist all psychological theories—even his own. They are remarkable for their resistance to logic, for their sheer impact upon the imagination. Because each character is a complete, closed world in himself, his world determines for him his values, his joys, and his suffering. But only the narrator is able to force open the door to his own world, and then only for himself.

ART, MORALITY, AND HAPPINESS

I have long had the habit of going to bed early. Sometimes, when I had put out my candle, my eyes would close so quickly that I had not even time to say "I'm going to sleep." And half an hour later the thought that it was time to go to sleep would awaken me; I would try to put away the book which I imagined was still in my hands, and to blow out the light; I had been thinking all the time I was asleep, of what I had just been reading, but my thoughts had run into a channel of their own until I myself seemed actually to have become the subject of my book: a church, a quartet, the rivalry between Francis I and Charles V.[1]

"A church, a quartet . . ." They reappear at the end of *Le Temps retrouvé,* the church now a cathedral, the quartet a symphony or "musical phrase." When he seeks a comparison for the novel he wants to undertake, the narrator turns more readily to a church or a piece of music than to literature or even to painting, which is one of his main interests. The church, in *A la Recherche du Temps perdu,* is first of all the Combray church; the musical work in general is Vinteuil's, either a sonata, a septet, or a "short phrase."

The Combray church is minutely described at the very beginning of the novel and the last lines in *Le Temps retrouvé* recall the description indirectly, but in almost the same terms. The Church is both the point of departure and the point of arrival in the narrator's spiritual journey; it is closely associated with the basic psychological and esthetic idea which, when he finally discovers it, permits the narrator to accede to his own vision of the world, and to conceive the means by which he will objectify it in his work. Nothing gives him as accurately as the Church the immediate sensation of "time incarnate," although he only perceives it in its full reality during the Guermantes matinée, when he finally formulates the key idea which dominates his whole experience and gives it unity:

"If only," says the narrator at the end of a long meditation on the work which he is going to undertake, ". . . there were granted me time enough to complete my work, I would not fail to stamp it with the seal of that time the understanding of which was this day so forcibly impressing itself upon me; I would describe therein men—even should that give them the semblance of monstrous creatures—as occupying in time a place far more considerable than the restricted one allotted them in space, a place which on the contrary, extends boundlessly, since, giant-like, they reach far back into the years, touching simultaneously epochs of their lives—with countless intervening days between, so widely separated are they from one another in time." [2]

Proustian characters, who occupy such a restricted place in space and whose singular individuality is made up of different, heterogeneous "periods" juxtaposed in time, are, in the Proustian vision, analogous to the Church of Saint Hilaire. "Simple citizen" of Combray, squeezed in between M. Rapin's pharmacy and Mme Loiseau's house, this building nonetheless occupies ". . . four dimensions of space—the fourth being time"; it "had sailed the centuries with that old nave, where bay after bay, chapel after chapel, seemed to stretch across and hold down and conquer, not merely a few yards of soil, but each successive epoch from which the whole building had emerged triumphant . . ." [3] The narrator realizes in a flash of insight that the Church can be compared to human beings. It also suggests by analogy the completed form of Proust's work. His novel too, volume by volume, crosses "successive periods" and suggests others which, like the worn apse of Saint Hilaire, are lost in the night of time. Thus the Church can also be compared with the work the narrator must undertake, which will tell the story of his life. "It is like an 'optical view,' but an optical view of the years, not a view of a monument but of a person in the distorting perspective of time." [4] So the narrator, reflecting on his book, wants "to build it like a cathedral" and to give it "the form of time" which he had "already vaguely perceived in the Church of Combray." [5]

The Church is in fact the past and the present; its permanent form is achieved through a succession of distinct heterogeneous forms, each stamped with the seal of a period. These forms are nonetheless amalgamated in an individual construction, singular and special. "Certainly every part of the church served to distinguish the whole from any other building by a kind of general feeling which pervaded it; but it was in the steeple that the Church seemed to display a consciousness of itself, to affirm its individual and responsible existence." [6] Through its relationship with the whole of the edifice, each part of the church receives its particular value. The whole Church finds in the steeple a meaning which confirms its distinct and irreplaceable identity, its spiritual unity. The narrator finally sees that he too has a spiritual identity which he must transpose into a book which will be its specific manifestation.

In the Combray Church the passing of time is arrested by the different "styles" which fashioned the edifice. Paradoxically, the church draws its unity from this very succession. The creative power of time, measured by the gigantic scale of the centuries, is manifest in this unpredictable, original creation. The unity of the edifice is a function of its history in time. Though its parts may have been built at different stages, each stage in its history is an "invention" directed by an inner principle which makes this church particularly the Church of Combray. Different from any other church, it nonetheless retains an essence common to all churches. The child could never confuse the stones of Saint Hilaire with those of Mme Loiseau's adjoining house. As the narrator sees it, the Church is an individual incarnation of a constant spiritual principle which has been embodied in diverse temporal forms. Its phys-

ical presence and architecture are for the narrator proof of a
fact to which an important part of his intellectual experience
is linked. The Combray Church provides him with certain of
the basic elements of his esthetic conception. In *A la Recherche du Temps perdu,* esthetic experience is at no time
separable from the whole of the narrator's spiritual experience, or from his very life. Proust steadily reiterates his rejection of estheticism; it is even more clearly expressed when he
speaks of music and of the place it occupies in the lives of
both the narrator and Swann.

The Church seems to convey and sum up a whole part of
the narrator's intellectual experience. Its form suggests that
objective vision of the human world which eventually determines the plan of his book. On the other hand, music is always associated with the narrator's emotional experience and
gives it its meaning. Swann's experience emphasizes this
basic relationship between a musical composition and human
sensitivity. Vinteuil's short phrase directly affects that "inner
lake" [7] in Swann which only it can affect; what the phrase
touches in him is entirely subjective. At first Swann likens its
effect to the emotions of happiness or suffering associated
with his love for Odette. Later at the Sainte-Euverte soirée, he
tries to understand the strange power of that short phrase—
why it can give his inner life so intense a reality. Then he tries
to reach, intellectually, the man who composed that phrase,
Vinteuil:

Swann's thoughts were borne for the first time on a wave of pity
and tenderness toward that Vinteuil, toward that unknown and
sublime brother who also must have suffered so greatly; what
could his life have been? From the depths of what well of sorrow
could he have drawn that god-like strength, that unlimited power
of creation? [8]

Vinteuil's phrase opens the doors which had immured Swann
in his solitude. It is a communion, a communion far more
satisfactory than that of love or friendship, especially of love,
with which it is closely associated.

Swann's intellect penetrates beyond the wholly subjective emotion that the phrase awakens in him, beyond the brotherly surge which brings him close to Vinteuil; he ponders the enigma of the very existence of the musical phrase which touches him so deeply:

But ever since more than a year before, when it had revealed to him many of the riches of his own soul, when the love of music had been born and, for a time at least, had dwelt in him, Swann had regarded musical "motifs" as actual ideas, belonging to another world, to another order, ideas veiled in shadows, unknown, impenetrable by the human mind, but nonetheless perfectly distinct one from another, unequal in value and in significance.[9]

"The idea shrouded in darkness" transmitted by the short phrase reaches him through a series of sounds. These he hears and grasps as composing an independent sonorous structure. Swann can understand this structure, but this does not make the inherent power of the little phrase any clearer:

. . . he had observed that it was to the closeness of the intervals between the five notes which composed it and to ,the constant repetition of two of them that he could attribute the impression of a clear, concentrated sweetness.[10]

This structure, he realizes as he follows the successive notes, makes sense only as a complete organism: nothing can be deducted from it, and nothing can be substituted, as the phrase is played note by note:

But in reality he knew that he was basing this conclusion not upon the phrase itself, but merely upon certain equivalents, substituted, for his mind's convenience, for the mysterious entity of which he had become aware before he knew the Verdurins, at that earlier party when for the first time he had heard the sonata played. He knew . . . that the field open to the musician is not a miserable stave of seven notes, but an immeasurable keyboard, almost all of it still unknown, on which, here and there only, separated by the gross darkness of its unexplored tracts, some few among the millions of keys—keys of tenderness, of passion, of courage, of serenity—which compose it, each one differing from all the rest as one universe differs from another, have been discovered by certain great artists who do us the service, when they awaken in us the emotion corresponding to the theme which they have found, of showing us what richness, what variety lies hidden, unknown to us, in that great black impenetrable night of our soul which discourages exploration, and which we have been content to regard as valueless, as waste and void.[11]

Swann does not look upon the "entity" of this little phrase with its simple and unique notes as a chance creation; rather it refers to an inner reality which it succeeds in communicating. This reality affects the whole gamut of human emotions. Swann, whose sensitivity is at this moment in his life sharpened by suffering, can conclude from the objective reality of that phrase that the inner domain of emotion whence it sprang, and which it expresses, really exists.

Swann does not learn a lesson from his encounter with Vinteuil's sonata. He does not search further for the "personal root" of the impression it made upon him. Thus he becomes one of those "celibates of art" who find a diversion in estheticism and in erudition, in that "escape from life which we haven't the courage to face." [12] He becomes Swann the collector of pictures who, in his evening visits in Combray, accurately supplies all the historical or technical details connected with the paintings he owns. In the last analysis, music has made him live more intensely—but only for a moment. For a long time he does not even distinguish the little phrase from the effect which it produced upon him. Then he tries to free himself from this error, but he does not progress beyond this stage; he ceases to ponder the mystery of the enigmatic relationship between himself and those "five notes." Vinteuil's little phrase could have opened up for Swann the path to understanding, but that path must pass through his own life if it is to lead somewhere. No one in the Proustian world can grasp reality through an intermediary like art. Art derives from life, calls us back to life, but it cannot at any moment be substituted for it. The sonata can give Swann insight into the true nature of the deepest forms of sensitivity; it cannot exempt him from understanding for himself the nature of that sensitivity. This is the basic Proustian moral law, and it peremptorily closes the door to all escape. Swann remains a "celibate" of art because of an intellectual and a moral insufficiency; it is his moral evasion, his lack of persistence, hence of power, which determines his intellectual evasion. But he takes the first step toward an understanding of what goes on inside him, for, because of the music of Vinteuil, he enters, at least temporarily, the "realm of the only reality of the human being, the realm of his own sensitivity." [13]

The narrator, like Swann, hears Vinteuil's music for the first time at Mme Verdurin's. He hears the septet, that "triumphant and complete masterpiece," [14] and almost point by point he relives Swann's experience, then goes beyond it. When he first recognizes the little phrase, he feels the same deep joy Swann felt at the Verdurins. But his enjoyment is enhanced because the familiar phrase appears in one of Vinteuil's unpublished compositions; unpredictable, unforeseen, it evokes the sonata in the very heart of the septet. The narrator is at first content to dwell on his subjective emotions: the septet is at that point only the instrument which awakens his feelings, which are at that time centered on his love for Albertine. But he soon feels the insufficiency of this stage at which Swann, until the Sainte-Euverte soirée, had so willingly stopped. "And yet . . . ," he thinks, "something more mysterious than Albertine's love seemed to be promised at the beginning of the composition, in these first sounds of dawn." [15]

Like Swann at the Sainte-Euverte concert, he then turns toward the composer, the man he knew. The septet proposes to him the enigma of Vinteuil's human personality and this later raises an esthetic problem. "It seemed as though the composer were living reincarnated forever in his music; one felt the joy with which he chose the color of such a tone, matched it with the others." [16] The young man meditates on a double enigma, the enigma of Vinteuil's living presence in the septet —Vinteuil, who had been dead for several years—and the enigma of the inner joy that the composer, despite his sadness, succeeded in transmitting through the septet to anyone who knew how to listen to his music. "That same Vinteuil, whom I had known so timid and sad, had, when he chose a tone and united it with another, a boldness and, in the full sense of the world, a felicity that was indubitable when one of his pieces was heard." [17] The mysterious survival of Vinteuil in his compositions and the equally mysterious revelation of a Vinteuil filled with a joy no one could have guessed, lead the narrator to reflect upon the general problem of artistic creation, of the meaning and value of the work of art.

What, he asks himself, is the relationship between the composition and its composer? What is it that explains the unique accent, recognizable and individual, which gives this "sonorous order" the unmistakable stamp of Vinteuil, and of Vinteuil alone? And why are the "dazzling architectures" [18] of that musical composition both the cause and the messengers of so deep a joy? The narrator then formulates a hypothesis. He catches a glimpse of the mysterious truth that the sonata seems to declare. Vinteuil's work, he thinks, corresponds to "a certain spiritual reality. It must surely at least symbolize such a reality in order to give that impression of profundity and truth." [19] He understands that the septet has its own independent identity, but that that identity is explicable only in relation to a particular spiritual atmosphere, the one in which Vinteuil lived. The narrator places the origin of the music within the composer himself, rather than, as Swann had, in an "other world."

The problem which he then tackles is metaphysical, not esthetic: that of the existence of the soul, which is linked to the problem of its immortality. The tone so unmistakably peculiar to the music created by Vinteuil appears to him "a proof of the irreducibly individual existence of the soul" [20] and thus suggests the possibility that the soul survives the body that harbors it.

The narrator now analyzes his own experience. He connects the joy which the septet gives him with the ecstacy which marks his "joyful sensations," experienced when he was standing before the steeples of Martinville, "before certain trees on a road in Balbec and . . . in drinking a certain cup of tea." [21] He is at the threshold of the discovery which will make of him also a creator. He feels that music reveals and communicates states of deep sensitivity which escape rationalization, and of which music alone makes us aware; he connects those states with those moments of ecstasty during which he feels he is living more intensely and which also elude all analysis. But he does not yet reach the conclusion that these fleeting states are his own particular equivalent of the enigmatic musical phrases which give mystery and beauty to Vinteuil's work, and which so clearly communicate the joy inherent in Vinteuil's inner life. He does not yet recognize in these fleeting impressions the presence of his own individual "soul." His analysis stops there, and deviates. When, far from Vinteuil's music, he thinks back on the septet, "it was the other hypothesis, the materialist hypothesis, the hypothesis of nothingness which presented itself" [22] to him. It seems to him now that Vinteuil's music corresponds only to fleeting and unimportant states of mind which have no bearing on objective reality, states of mind comparable to those he considers accidental and illusory.

Vinteuil's music has aroused in him intense joy, the feeling of communion with "another," and it starts a whole train of thought; music is a subject of reflection and not simply a source of pleasure. Whereas his love for Albertine plunges him deeper and deeper into the maelstrom of emotions, Vinteuil's music delivers him from his emotions and confronts him with an intellectual problem of which at least one of the terms, the septet, escapes all alteration. But no amount of meditation can bring him the solution to his problem: does a work of art correspond to a "spiritual reality," individual and extra-temporal in nature? Or is a work of art mere "nothingness"? Swann's experience, as well as the narrator's, suggests at least this: artistic creation can be understood only in relation to the human being. It seems to proclaim the existence of an individual human soul, and to be a sign that the soul is spiritual in essence. It poses for the intellect an enigma which the intellect is unable to solve: where does a combination of five or seven notes draw its human value? Why are they something besides a mere combination of sounds? Engrossed in his love for Albertine, the narrator is content with a general solution to the problem. He seeks in every work of art to discern an individual presence such as he feels in the septet, much as he had already done in Combray when he isolated Bergotte's "style" from the book he was reading.

In the course of his reflections, he analyzes Vinteuil's septet at some length. Somewhat preciously at times, he transposes it from the realm of sound to that of color, a "transposition of art" in great vogue among the "decadent" group which Proust had frequented as a young man. He also conjures up the "architecture" of the septet as it unfolds in time, that whole invisible structure which exists only as long as the mind of the listener grasps and retains the sequence of its components. He follows the process by which Vinteuil draws "from the silence of the night" an "unknown universe," [23] which is constructed in an orderly progression and which does not seem to depend in any way upon an objective reality.

Here the very words recall the beginning of a *A la Recherche du Temps perdu*—the silence and the night in which the narrator "progressively" builds his universe through memory, independently of present sensory reality. The analogy is maintained and accentuated: the narrator distinguishes "in the heart of that septet" the "different components" which are exposed "in turn, and are combined at the end." The septet is constructed from elements which are apparently simple, which form that "tune of seven notes, but the most completely unknown [elements]," the narrator adds, "the most unlike anything I could have imagined." [24] Whereas the Church describes within a restricted space its immutable duration, evoking by analogy the objective and intellectual vision which organizes the construction of the narrator's novel, the septet builds up progressively an increasingly dense interweaving of themes which meet or are superimposed. It is comparable to the inner development of the narrator which began with the few simple notes contributed by Combray. His is a gradual and invisible development, the momentum of which, like the septet's, is that of "life, a perpetual and happy movement." [25] This movement, like the septet's, finds its full expression only when it reaches the final theme upon which it ends. For the narrator as for the septet, the end consecrates the triumph of the theme of joy over the painful counter-theme which was opposed to it. The septet "recomposes" the inner life where ". . . sounds seem to assume the inflexion of the human being himself, to reproduce that interior extreme point of our sensation, that part of ourselves which gives us the peculiar exhilaration which we recapture from time to time." [26] It corresponds, in the musical order of things, to the waves of grief or joy which intermittently surge up in the narrator, and which he must express in words.

Hence the Church and the septet appear to play a dual rôle in the book; they are comparable to Giotto's symbolic figures, photographs of which Swann had brought the Combray child. "For a long time" he found "no pleasure when he looked at them. But in later years," he adds:

I understood that the arresting strangeness, the special beauty of these frescoes lay in the great part played in each of them by its symbols; while the fact that these were depicted not as symbols, for the thought symbolized was nowhere expressed, but as real things, actually felt or materially handled, added something more precise and more literal to their meaning, something more concrete and more striking to the lesson they imparted.[27]

The Church and the septet are sources "of esthetic joy, of intellectual and emotional experience"; they bear witness against the universal passage of time and pose the problem of the relations between time, life, and a work of art. They have an even more important rôle because of "the great part played in each by the symbol." Each in its way "translates" an aspect of the work which contains it. Both its form and the substance which fashioned it, and from which it cannot be separated, are significant. Through that particular church, and that particular septet, Proust relates his book to all churches and to all musical compositions. He consciously chooses the two artistic fields in which any direct borrowing from the objective world is reduced to a minimum. Man's creative power is most purely manifested in them for it appears to be inherent in his being and spiritual in its essence.

The church and the septet indeed play an important rôle in the novel, but Proust also considers all the other arts. The realm of the creative arts is a familiar one which the narrator explores all his life, especially literature, drama, and painting. Each of these arts is represented by an individual; Bergotte, la Berma and Rachel, and Elstir, just as music is represented by Vinteuil. Art is an everyday matter for the narrator, and artists are ordinary people no different from those with whom he comes in daily contact. The child is raised in a milieu in which reproductions of Giotto's frescoes and the novels of George Sand are as much a part of his life as Tante Léonie's well-prepared meals and the water-lilies of the Vivonne. Art has its natural place in the novel. It is not there to serve as decoration; it is one of the elements of the human puzzle which the narrator confronts right from his childhood. Art is not a domain which he discovers with surprise or dazzlement at some given moment of his existence. He never has the impression of being initiated into it, as he is initiated into the world of the Guermantes or of homosexuality. The social and intellectual atmosphere in which he moves partly explains this familiarity; it is a reflection of the milieu in which Proust himself grew up—the cultivated Parisian upper middle class.

But Proust furthermore wants deliberately to destroy all the intellectual habits which would carefully separate art from life or nature. Just as in a painting of Elstir's the sea penetrates the land everywhere and is united with it, so art penetrates the life of the narrator from all sides and is united with it by organic ties which Proust continually emphasizes. The narrator meets Vinteuil or Elstir as ordinary men outwardly undistinguished from other men. Under Swann's guidance the child learns to see in all forms of art ties that bind it to his life: the kitchen maid looks like a Giotto; the sculptured characters of Saint-André-des-Champs recall the peasant types of Combray, like Françoise or Théodore; the stained glass windows of St. Hilaire call to mind the lords of Guermantes, and so on. In *A la Recherche du Temps perdu* a tight network of comparisons, allusions, and metaphors force art to descend from Olympus, where it has a tendency to remain enthroned, and connects it firmly with the everyday world: the church spire with the brioche, and the narrator's father, "in his white nightshirt under the violet and rose Kashmir shawl in which he had wrapped his head ever since his neuralgia had started," [28] with Benozzo Gozzoli's Abraham.

At no time does art strike the narrator with the force of a revelation. Real hawthorn and apple trees arouse ecstasy in him; the real absence of his grandmother, physically felt in a real action, reveals to him the painful drama of love, of suffering and of death. The revelation that comes to him in *Le Temps retrouvé* is brought about by a madeleine, a pavement, a spoon, a radiator, a book—all of them real also—not by the Giottos, the Gozzolis, the sculptured characters of Saint-André-des-Champs, or even by the church or the septet. Every time he seeks a revelation in art the narrator is disappointed, as he is when he sees la Berma act for the first time.

The work of art is essentially one of the things the narrator thinks about, a source of reflection like the rest of his experience; but it differs from the rest of his experience in that it is never contaminated by his passions and desires. He approaches it in a disinterested manner. It is a source of momentary peace.

Swann draws the narrator's attention to the connection between a work of art, of whatever period, and the everyday world; Elstir draws the narrator's attention to the close connection between the work and the artist. When the young man enters Elstir's studio in Balbec, he experiences a pleasure which is first intellectual:

I felt perfectly happy, for, with the help of all the sketches and studies that surrounded me, I foresaw the possibility of achieving a poetic understanding, rich in delight, of many forms which I had not hitherto isolated from the general spectacle of reality.[29]

The word "poetic" here assumes its original meaning as the narrator's impressions become more precise:

Elstir's studio appeared to me as the laboratory of a sort of new creation of the world in which, from the chaos in all the things we see, he had extracted, by painting them on various rectangles of canvas that were hung everywhere about the room, here a wave of the sea crushing its lilac foam angrily on the sand, there a young man in a white linen suit leaning upon the rail of a vessel. His jacket and the spattering wave had acquired fresh dignity from the fact that they continued to exist, even though they were deprived of those qualities in which they might be supposed to consist, the wave being no longer able to splash nor the jacket to clothe anyone.[30]

The painter is the creator, the "poet," and his creation is a powerful mental act. For Elstir the act does not consist in representing what he actually sees; he abstracts certain elements from what he sees and, the narrator realizes, he makes a conscious and voluntary choice:

But I was able to discern [he says of Elstir's seascapes] that the charm of each of them lay in a sort of metamorphosis of the things represented, analogous to what in poetry we call metaphor, and that, if God the Father had created things by naming them, it was by taking away their names, or giving them other names, that Elstir created them anew.[31]

The young man's reflections bear upon the dual relationship which binds the "seascapes" to the "things," and to Elstir. He notices that what is manifest in the canvases is a certain "vision," but a double vision. When he looks at the sensory world, Elstir sees things directly without intermediaries. His first perception is new; no intellectual abstraction interferes with it, no dull habit, no preconceived notion: "Elstir's canvases were made up of the rare moments when one sees nature poetically, as it is." This direct vision is buttressed by a direct mental apprehension which discerns among the elements seen a simple relationship; it groups them, sees in them a fundamental structure, and thereby gives them their "poetic" value. The narrator compares this interaction to a metaphor. One of the metaphors which recurs most frequently in Elstir's seascapes "was in fact the one which, in comparing the land to the sea, abolished the line of demarcation between them." [32] The narrator makes the distinction in Elstir's work between an exact physical vision and a conscious, deliberate, intellectual vision. The second draws from the first a structural motif which evokes, everywhere, other structural motifs analogous to it. The canvas reveals a general pattern, which it suggests, and which infinitely surpasses it. When Mme Elstir appears, the young man sees that at the root of Elstir's initial visual perceptions is an emotion closely akin to love.

I was sorry to have Mme Elstir arrive . . . not that she stayed for any length of time. I found her most tedious; she might have been beautiful had she been twenty and driving an ox in the Roman Campagna . . . and it was touching, but at the same time surprising, to hear Elstir, whenever he opened his mouth, repeat with a respectful gentleness, as if merely uttering the words moved him to tenderness and veneration: "My beautiful Gabrielle." [33]

One might be tempted to say that this is the only relationship in *A la Recherche du Temps perdu,* except that of the narrator with his mother and his grandmother, in which one feels the accent of genuine love. But that is not what interests the narrator. He seizes upon the problem of the adjective "beautiful" as applied by Elstir to his wife. The emotion expressed by Elstir seems to him to be spiritual in origin. Elstir, he thinks, carries within him a notion of certain combinations of lines, of certain formal relationships. He sees them mysteriously incarnated in Mme Elstir, and this explains his adoration for her. It is a form of the "deep, exacting adoration" that he has for the "ideal type" [34] which he carries within him. Elstir is dedicated to this "ideal type." The narrator does not probe any further. He does not explain the origin of that "ideal type" which, he says, affirms "the law, the formula of Elstir's subconscious." [35] Through the "spiritual pleasure, the impetus to work" [36] caused by the presence of certain phenomena, the artist recognizes the material which his subconscious can use to give expression to this "ideal type."

The narrator can distinguish in Elstir's painting an emotion born of sensations which differ from all other sensations. They give Elstir a pleasure which is not merely sensuous, a pleasure which awakens his sensitivity and conveys a message to his mind because the initial sensation corresponds to an unconscious need of his spirit. Only then are Elstir's intellect and will aroused. Elstir's problem is to emphasize, first the visual character of this correspondence, then its essence, the law that governs it; otherwise the sensation disappears. From the moment that this mental effort begins, the initial sensation becomes a vision and Elstir conceives what his canvas will be; the technique he uses derives naturally and rationally from the quality peculiar to that vision. It is the one moment in the entire process of creation when logic plays a part. Elstir needs the sensory world. A few simple visual sensations reveal to him the "formula of the subconscious" which he carries within himself; they provide the substance without which the formula would remain unexpressed. Only through the forms and colors he sees can Elstir become aware of this most secret part of himself which, the narrator thinks, expresses Elstir's basic harmony with the world. Curiously enough, it seems that for Proust the unconscious is spiritual rather than organic in nature; it seeks a form in which to be incarnated.

What is the source of Elstir's power to move the narrator, to convey to him a pure "intellectual joy," free of the murky element which enters into all his contacts with other men, but which does not alter his relations with Elstir? It seems that Elstir appeals to the narrator because he "recognizes," after a slight initial shock, the newness and the truth of Elstir's vision, and its spiritual significance. A canvas by Elstir satisfies simultaneously his visual sense and his mental sensitivity; it frees him from himself, from his individual and fleeting preoccupations; it withdraws him from the flux of time because the painting is timeless.

His contact with Elstir increases the narrator's understanding of art; but his greatest gain is a peace of mind and body, together with an intellectual stimulation which awakes him to disinterested thought. He is led to formulate the basic intellectual problem posed by his experience of life, that of the relationship between the objective, sensory world and his subjective, invisible world. Elstir's canvases play a rôle in his life similar to that of all his other experiences, but comparable to those which take place in solitude and which escape the direct grasp of the intellect: the play of sensations, of sleep, of dreams, of illness, of intoxication. These experiences are all connected with the enigmatic life of his body, that body which the narrator tells us "is the greatest threat to the mind." [37]

All these experiences presuppose that the narrator's normal awareness of his body is temporarily suspended. Here the narrator reflects the particular case of Proust, who was ill and often confined to his room. He never knows the joy and satisfaction which a strong, healthy person experiences in a sports contest or in a struggle against the elements. Nature never strikes the narrator, any more than it does Elstir, as a force to be mastered, against which man measures himself. For him nature is a "tableau"; he sees the sea from his window—not while swimming or from the bridge of a vessel. "Human and thinking life," the narrator observes, "(which we should consider less the miraculous perfecting of animal and physical

life than an imperfection as rudimentary as the common existence of protozoas or polyps . . .) on the level of spiritual
existence is such that the body encloses the mind in a fortress . . ." [38] All the narrator's adventures are attempts to de-
liver his mind from that fortress; art is the only path which
leads him to this deliverance. The sensory world and the
world of the mind are fused in Proust's universe somewhat
as they are in certain medieval allegories. The senses are
breaches in the fortress of the body. Through them the physical world comes into contact with the spirit, albeit through
all the errors which the body, to which they belong, suggests
to the mind. But whereas in these medieval allegories the
outer world is generally the source of temptation and the
cause of a fall, in the Proustian world it is a means to possible salvation and to the liberation of the spirit. The body is
indeed, in *A la Recherche du Temps perdu*, the active center
of all disappointments and suffering; it is the mocking enemy,
protean and two-faced, which jeers at the spirit, which im-
mures men in their solitude, isolates them from the sensory
world, and finally delivers them over to death. But the body
is also the key to all mysteries, for it differentiates human
beings and subjects them to the surprising experience of individual life. Proust's novel contains a curious and tragic "debate between the body and the soul," which Proust never
succeeds in resolving. This debate is supported by a rather
extensive knowledge of the scientific and philosophical speculations current in Proust's time. Proust's attempt to resolve
this debate is sufficient to give even the most controversial
passages in his book a certain importance. This debate is the
source of what could be called the metaphysical mystery story
contained in *A la Recherche du Temps perdu*.

During the evenings spent with Saint-Loup at Rivebelle,
the narrator realizes how intensely he can feel present reality
when he is in a state of physical well-being, artificially induced by wine. His state of intoxication fills him with an
"inherent subjective happiness." [39] His happiness imparts to
the women of Rivebelle, to the waltzes played by the café

band, to the activity of the restaurant, an absolute value which is certainly not intrinsic:

But if already before this point on my arrival at Rivebelle, I had flung irretrievably away from me those crutches of reason and self-control which help our infirmity to follow the right road, if I now found myself the victim of a sort of moral ataxy, the alcohol that I had drunk, by unduly straining my nerves, gave to the minutes as they came a quality, a charm which did not have the result of leaving me more ready, or indeed more resolute to defend myself against them; for while it made me prefer them a thousand times to anything else in my life, my exaltation made me isolate them from everything else. I was confined to the present, as heroes are, or drunkards. Eclipsed for the moment, my past no longer projected before me that shadow of itself which we call our future; placing the goal of my life no longer in the realization of the dreams of that past, but in the felicity of the present moment, I could see nothing now of what lay beyond it.[40]

Intoxication, through the modifications which it brings about in the body, the moral paralysis and the euphoria which it causes, does indeed produce an intense subjective vision of the world. But this vision is limited to the present; it originates in a sensation which has no valid relation with the world other than mere co-existence in space. Intoxication temporarily favors a precarious synthesis between the sensory world perceived by the narrator and his emotional state. It is an illusory synthesis, for it has no guarantee other than a physical state just as transitory and artificial as the variations of atmospheric pressure. But the state of euphoria temporarily does away with all tension and frees the narrator from the laws of time. For a few hours he has neither past nor future; he is free from all the emotional, intellectual, and moral problems which the past and the future impose and he is happy. The narrator's joy is not comparable to Elstir's, it does not come from the mysterious coincidence between an exigency of the mind and an external phenomenon. The mind alone has the ability to create, and, in the case of intoxication, it is passive and docile to the body.

The process initiated by intoxication is exactly the opposite of the dream process. In their dreams, the narrator and Swann create objective images steeped in an emotion which seems to emanate from the outer world, but which is really only a pale reflection of subjective physical or emotional states. Since they are completely cut off from the tangible reality of the moment, Proustian dreams sometimes synthesize states of mind and images which until then had not coincided in the memory because they had been experienced at different times. Dreams make no temporal distinction between the past and the present; everything that goes into their making is contemporaneous. But they work only with events or images taken from the past:

It was perhaps also because of the preposterous game they played with time that dreams had fascinated me. Had I not often seen in one night, even in one minute of one night, dim remote periods of my life, so far in the past that I could scarcely distinguish any longer the feelings I had had at that time, come rushing down upon me full tilt, blinding me with their brightness . . . in order to apprise me of everything that they held in store for me . . .[41]

Dreams combine the emotions and memories of the subjective world with images of the objective world, regardless of their place in time. This synthesis, like the one achieved by intoxication, is linked to a physical state, sleep; it is only temporary and is wiped out when the dreamer—Swann or the narrator—wakes up; it is essentially impermanent. The restoration of the past experienced in dreams does not come within the reach of the dreamer's intellect; it is wiped out with the sensation or emotion from which the dream originated. The dreamer's mind is passive, as it is under the influence of alcohol, and subject to the suggestions of sensitivity. When the narrator has had a little too much to drink, he thinks that what he observes around him is the cause of the abnormal intensity of his sensations, which is in fact due only to his intoxication; in dreams, feelings and sensations create images to which the dreamer attributes an objective reality. In both cases, the synthesis lasts only a few moments and remains specific to the individual. It has no general value, and is not communicated. In both cases, neither the narrator's mind nor his will controls his body; he is in a state of simple receptiveness and submits passively to the fantastic games which, while they last, obtrude upon the consciousness and eject all notion of relativity. In the narrator's experience, love tends to produce the same synthesis as intoxication; all the sensations which come from the outside world seem to group themselves in the fashion of a dream.

The narrator diverts himself by setting up, with an isolated sensation as a starter, fictitious worlds which are always pale reflections of the real sensory world. He needs only to close his eyes and listen to the sounds of a fire crackling in his room to fill the room with active bustling people. Whenever he is alone and unpreoccupied, he can change the natural order of the world and "make the rain sing in the middle of the room" and the water boiling for his tea "rain into the courtyard." [42] These are purely exercises in virtuosity. Though they are characterized by the same disconcerting gratuitousness as intoxication and dreams, these mental games are signs of the mind's creative activity, and of its freedom with respect to objective fact.

The narrator is sometimes aware that his contact with the objective world goes deeper than the interchange which takes place in intoxication, dreams, or the play of his sensations. Certain aspects of the world "shock" him, bring him to a halt, and arouse in him "a very special pleasure," a real intoxication and an intensification of vision comparable in part to that produced by drink. But this visual intensity differs from the one created by liquor in that it seems to be imposed upon the narrator from the outside. It fixes him in a shaft of light; his own physiology remains normal. One day, for example, while the narrator is taking a walk with Mme Villeparisis, he sees before him a veritable apparition:

But as soon as I had arrived on the road I was met by a dazzling sight. There, where in August with my grandmother I had seen only the leaves and what looked like evenly spaced apple trees, the apple trees were now in full bloom, clothed in unheard-of luxuriance. Their feet in mud and dressed as for a ball, they were careless of spoiling the most beautiful pink satin ever seen, which glistened in the sun; the distant horizon of the sea provided the background of a Japanese print. When I raised my head to look at the sky between the flowers which made its blue seem clearer, almost violent, they seemed to stand aside in order to show up the depth of that paradise. Under this azure a slight chilly breeze made the rosy bouquets tremble. The rays of the sun were rapidly succeeded by those of the rain; they barred the entire horizon, enclosing the row of apple trees in their gray netting. But the apple trees remained erect under the downpour in their pink flowering beauty, in the wind which had become freezing: it was a spring day.[43]

The ecstasy and dazzlement he experiences greatly resemble the communion of love, a love immune from intellectual distortion because it is free from all anxiety. The narrator later calls such impressions "joyful"; numerous during his childhood, they become rarer as he grows older, and finally completely cease. He objectively notes this disappearance in *Le Temps retrouvé* while he is in the train which brings him back to Paris and the Guermantes reception; it is a source of deep sadness for him. There are also other impressions of a different kind which give him a very special pleasure. They appear later in his life, and become more frequent as the "joyful sensations" become fewer.

At the beginning of *La Prisonnière*, lying in a dark room, his mind alert, the narrator indulges passively in a game which affords him a good deal of pleasure. Docile, free from all personal preoccupations, he loses himself in the sensations which come to him from outside and simply follows the repercussions that they have within him. In short, he receives a sensation, isolates it and follows its path within himself. This sensation with all its associated harmonies generates a physical state of well-being which turns into a mental state. The narrator's mind then seizes upon a general theme; he remembers, for example, the sunny or misty mornings of the past. He orchestrates a whole symphony around the central theme and recaptures fragments of his past:

If I had not gone out with Albertine on her long drive, my mind could stray all the further afield. Because I had refused to savor with my senses this particular morning, I enjoyed in imagination all the similar mornings, past or possible, or more precisely a certain type of morning of which all those of the same kind were but the intermittent apparition and which I had at once recognized; for the keen air blew the book open of its own accord at the right page, and I found clearly set out before my eyes, so that I might follow it from my bed, the gospel for the day. This ideal morning filled my mind full of a permanent reality, identical with all similar mornings, and filled me with a cheerfulness which my physical ill-health did not diminish . . . The activity with which I was overflowing and which I kept constantly charged as I lay in bed, made me spring from side to side, with a leaping heart, like a machine which, prevented from moving in space, rotates on its own axis.[44]

As in dreams, the narrator's consciousness is more or less suspended and he forgets the passing of time; but the real sequence of time is not destroyed as it is in dreams. The narrator does not confuse the present mornings with the past ones. Stimulated by the pleasure which a sensation gives him, he first recognizes an entity, "a sunny morning," upon which his mind dwells until he can isolate the deep organic tie which binds this notion, "a sunny morning," to him. He finds that it appeals to that "small inarticulate sun worshipper" [45] within him who is made happy by the faintest ray of sun. This inner alchemy produces a happiness which gives the young man a sense of power. But he is selfishly content to enjoy the experience and does not think of putting it to use. It becomes exacting only when the particular sensation elicited by the present sensory world touches a deep-rooted part of the narrator's past and evokes it with the particular special intensity that characterizes the "joyful sensations." The narrator then experiences something closely akin to what he saw in Elstir's canvases: a new, direct vision organized in harmony with the "law of the subconscious" which, for the narrator, seems to be the law of involuntary memory. Just as this law explained the perspective peculiar to Elstir's painting, it explains the relations between time and human life perceived by the narrator.

This analogy is not enough to give the narrator complete insight; his power simply takes the form of joy and remains unused. Elstir could have set him on the right path. Elstir, a solitary and dogged worker, just like Vinteuil, gives him an example of a man who is dedicated to the realization of his work and who has gradually sacrificed everything to it. There is no artistic creation without conscious will—will to discover the material "half sheathed in the object, half buried in us," [46] will to conceive the work and to execute it.

The truth which emerges from his study of Elstir's canvases is not an easy one for the narrator to grasp: the mind has the power to create, but it is only under the compulsion of the will that its power becomes effective. To be an artist, like Elstir, is a moral enterprise, not only in a general way, but in daily life. The artist is the repository of a truth which he must transmit; and in order to transmit it, he must submit to a harsh discipline. Art is ascesis. At the Guermantes reception, the narrator realizes that he must be willing to do more than just enjoy the happiness given him by involuntary memory if it is to lead him to the mental vision which will organize his work. He must be ready to settle down to work seriously and to sacrifice everything to his work in order that it may be completed. When he sees death incarnated in that gathering of masks at the Guermantes reception, his vocation as a writer at last becomes clear. The direct apprehension of death gives him a sense of the value of his life, and of the duty which devolves upon him to transmit it. He is somewhat in the position of the servant in the parable who has been content to bury his talent in the ground and who finds he must account for his actions to his master. He now joins the ranks of Bergotte, Vinteuil and Elstir, all of whom are haunted by the thought of the emptiness and meaninglessness of life, a thought which is closely associated with their will to create. The work of art seems to be an exorcism of this obsession. The clues which lead to the solution of the metaphysical mystery story in *A la Recherche du Temps perdu* are found in the narrator's inner life, in the happiness and joy which he experiences. In his outer life too, the artists with whom he associates bring him peace and real joy; they also give the narrator's experience as an "artist" an outside corroboration, and therefore a general human significance.

If it can be said that there is a social and metaphysical mystery tale in *A la Recherche du Temps perdu*, it can also be said that it contains a moral detective story, a medieval morality play. Which will triumph in the narrator's soul—the virtues of Combray or the vices of the world?

It is not by chance that the novel opens and closes with the episode of *François le Champi*. One evening, in Combray, the child gives in to temptation. He follows the path of self-indulgence instead of following the path of moral discipline which his mother and grandmother have tried to make him take. He has a good pretext, his nervousness. The pretext remains good for the rest of his life. Because he is ill he breaks down his grandmother's opposition to his taste for alcohol, his mother's to his affair with Albertine, and the opposition of the two women to his laziness and frivolity. From that Combray evening, he says, dates "the decline of my will, my health." [47] It is only at the Guermantes' reception that he "recovers" his will, and with it the virtues of Combray.

The story which the narrator tells us goes, in short, from the moral fall of that particular evening in Combray to the moral redemption which will be consecrated by the work, the conception of which ends the narrator's story. It is not the realization of the narrator's book which interests Proust, but how it becomes possible. The narrator's determination to become a writer is strengthened, at the end of the story, by a peculiar obsession with expiation and salvation through his future work. Although he speaks of this obsession in a language tinged with mysticism, it does not seem really mystic in essence. Rather, it betrays a personal and rather questionable concern in which esthetics and morals mingle somewhat strangely. The narrator accuses himself of having let his grandmother and Albertine die; it would seem that he associates their deaths with a lack of love in himself:

My grandmother whom I had so indifferently seen go through her last agony and die close beside me! Oh, might I in expiation —my work completed, wounded beyond relief and abandoned by all—suffer for long and weary hours before I died! In addition, I felt infinite pity even for those less dear, even for those to whom I was completely indifferent, for all those human destinies the suffering, and even the absurdities, of which I had used intellectually for my own purposes in an endeavor to understand them.[48]

Despite this pity, the narrator clearly has the feeling that his work will serve as the justification for all his failings, and that it will redeem his indifference. This lack of human love is perhaps after all, despite the narrator's sensitivity, what is most noticeable in Proust's creation. There is undeniably in *A la Recherche du Temps perdu* a certain lack of human generosity and a certain cold cruelty which do not exclude a sort of indulgence; but if Proust is indulgent, it is because he delights in pointing out vanity, complacency, cruelty, and especially irresponsibility and the sham to which it reduces all apparent virtue. The narrator's destructive indulgence is also not unrelated to a certain false humility, under cover of which he makes a detailed criticism of others and destroys in them any appearance of superiority. He never leaves intact any superiority—aristocratic, intellectual, emotional, or moral. In this respect he does not differ from Legrandin or Bloch, whom he judges so severely.

The narrator's vision is extraordinarily rich and precise, his intelligence singularly keen. But between the two there is no zone of human sympathy, of broad and charitable understanding, in which the trusting world of selfless, simple, and sincere friendship and love could blossom. The narrator singles out only one act of real kindness which he has heard about; he notes it for no particular reason except, it would seem, because it was performed by Françoise's millionaire cousins. Proust seems conscious of this lack of "the milk of human kindness" in his work. He blames it on the artistic vocation, which forces the man to sacrifice individuals to the general truth which the artist will draw from them. But his generalization is questionable. The narrator conceives his book as an artist, to be sure, but at the same time he appears to us as devoid of certain human traits the existence of which he denies simply because he himself is without them. His book does not take their place, and this basic lack automatically limits its scope. Proust generalizes and esthetically justifies an individual lack peculiar to him, and not to the artist in general.

The narrator discovers that Vinteuil and Elstir hope to win by their artistic production the respect and admiration which life in society has not secured for them. It would appear that art is something of a makeshift, a compensation. We also feel in the narrator a need for self-justification which goes hand-in-hand with his depreciation of the position, the sentiments and the motives of others. He strips them of the values which they are most anxious to keep in order to impose upon them the one single value which is his, that of the artist. In this way he proves irrefutably, but by means of a vicious circle, his superiority over them. He proves it for good; neither Swann, Robert de Saint-Loup, nor the Guermantes can refute it. *A la Recherche du Temps perdu* is a sort of "Last Judgment"; Proust is both accuser and judge, and let us only hope that he weighs his characters less impartially than God the Father. He does not admit that there are several roads that lead to heaven; he only admits one, his. And Bergotte, Vinteuil, Elstir, and the narrator, all of whom Proust has created, support his position.

The narrator doggedly persists in destroying the moral

fabric of all the characters in the book, except those of his mother and grandmother. He suggests that most people are inferior to him because they are less "nice." They are all vicious, but it is not their vices which the narrator condemns. Those he simply describes. He shows people as being sometimes good, sometimes bad, never in the light of moral principles but simply in their attitudes toward each other. Being good consists in giving pleasure, being bad in causing suffering. The Proustian characters do one or the other, indifferently. Therefore their goodness has no value since, like their badness, it is the effect of chance, of whim. What the narrator does condemn them for is their lack of lucidity. And there again he has an indisputable superiority. Only an artist is a consciously sentient being, therefore only an artist is a moral being, except for the narrator's mother and grandmother who are devoted to him. The narrator, when he discovers his vocation, accedes to the morality of the artist, the only one which he actually recognizes and which Proust has provided him in the good examples of Vinteuil and Elstir.

It would seem that the narrator's basic reasoning is as follows: he did not live up to the human ideal set for him by his grandmother and mother, and thereby caused them great suffering which precipitated his grandmother's death. But in this he was less guilty than one might think because even at that time he was still better than the people around him, who were far more selfish and insensitive than he. Furthermore, he has an excuse which they do not have: his vocation as an artist, the realization of which frees him from all other obligations and redeems the suffering he has caused, in his eyes a capital sin. Proust does not seem to have completely solved the dilemma of his own life. He gives Bergotte a rather questionable private life, while Elstir's, on the other hand, is most austere. It would seem that, after all, purely human moral values do not necessarily have any connection with genius. The narrator notes a link between immorality and genius, but the episode of François le Champi seems to deny implicitly that such a link can exist. The narrator seems unable to separate his vocation from "repentance and inner perfection." Proust seems never to have rid himself of the notion of "vice" and of guilt in human relationships. This may explain why he has no affection for the characters he creates, and pricks them full of pinholes as though he would avenge himself through them. It is also perhaps the reason why human beings are not really a source of joy for him. The "truths" and the "laws" which Proust draws from the human spectacle do not add up to a completely satisfying human wisdom, or to any system of human ethics. In order to give his characters substance and the dimensions required by the novel, he was obliged—and therein lies his great originality—to see them as monuments, viewed in the perspective of time, a view which is essentially intellectual and none too humane.

But genuine wisdom and a high moral tone do mark all the meditations which bear upon the artistic calling as such. Happiness, art, and morality are linked together in an extraordinary affirmation of faith. The individual, whether Elstir, Bergotte, Vinteuil, or the narrator, has value only because of the treasure which he bears. His duty, under penalty of sinking into despair, is to transmit this treasure to mankind. In each of its stages, the work of communication is difficult and demands heavy sacrifices from the artist, transforming his life into an ascesis in which suffering plays a large part. His sacrifices are recompensed by the self discovery which the artist makes; it is a source of joy comprising both pleasure and pain. It enables him to grasp consciously what is best in him, to attain his own particular form of harmony with life. The artist then enters that magical zone of calm in which men create, and in which they communicate across time to each other, by means of their work, what they know of life. Because a work of art is a manifestation of a harmony between man and the sensory world in which he lives, all works of art are related to one another, and communicate to all men, reminding them that they all mysteriously participate in a common spiritual and physical life. It is not because of preciosity or estheticism that the narrator always connects what he sees with works of art he knows, and what he feels with music that he hears; by way of the apple trees he finds the Japanese prints. It would be a mistake to take pleasure in the apple trees only because they appear in Japanese prints, to confuse these two worlds of nature and art, which mutually support each other. *A la Recherche du Temps perdu* is the story of the dedication of the narrator's life to art; only it must be an art created by him, hence subordinate to his life. And "excuses cut no figure in art, intentions are not counted . . . art is what is most real, the most austere school of life and the real Last Judgment." [49] Only realization and success count in art.

The narrator's particular harmony with life is always described as contained in impressions like those made upon him by the Balbec apple trees. In this Proust reveals his own love for nature, a love which he apparently could not give human beings. For Proust, nature is completely passive: it can pass directly from the state of mere physical vision to the state of unconscious spiritual possession; it can be "regained" later by involuntary memory without passing through the distortion of intellectual, emotional, and moral reactions. In this way nature retains a purity which nothing can impair. Proust seems to have found in nature that intimate relation with reality which is a source of happiness; but it is not because nature reflects his passions, comforts him in his sufferings, or because he loses himself in it. Nature, as he describes it, is a stylized terrestial paradise; human beings are only there in spirit, through art. This paradise is free of evil, and in it reign the beauty, purity, calm and innocence to which, in his overheated room, Proust seems to have aspired. Banished from it are these three enemies of human happiness, intelligence, death, and time, which only art can exorcise.

9

PROUST THE NOVELIST

A REAL novel," according to the critic Thibaudet, "is like
an autobiography of what might have been possible." [1]
A real novel, Proust could well answer, is the gradual unfolding in time, through a narrative, of a conscious vision of life
the formation of which is the only real autobiography of an
author. No other novelist has so intimately linked within a
single book the story of the origination of a work and its
realization; no other novelist has so specifically delineated
the spiritual genesis of a vocation. Proust is unmistakably
the contemporary of such writers as Gide, Valéry, and Joyce.
His work plainly reflects the intellectual climate of the early
twentieth century in its attempt to illuminate and comprehend
the details of the creative process. In this respect Proust is
more explicit than any other writer. His narrator, drawn out
of Proust's own personality, attains in the experience of life
which Proust arranges for him a general understanding of the
relation between life and art; he applies it to himself as an
individual, to his future work. This understanding emerges
gradually from the narrative, but the conception as a whole
is transmitted to us all at once, and in the most minute detail,
at the end of the novel in *Le Temps retrouvé*. Never has a
novel been so clearly explained. Its complexity and richness,
however, tend to blur the relationship between the genesis of
the narrator's novel (a novel which is never written), the
theory of the novel which he expounds, and the book which
Proust himself has written. The relationship is far from simple, and that is why Proust, justifiably and with a clear con-

science, can attack those authors who present their theories side by side with the novels which illustrate them; his case is different.

In *L'Etranger*, one of the stories in *Les Plaisirs et les Jours*, the young Proust inscribed a quotation from Emerson: "Every man also is a god disguised who acts the fool." Though in the Proustian world only men "act the fool," everything reflects "the god disguised." Hawthorn, apple blossoms, or buttercups appear suddenly, in sumptuous garb, to pose the enigma of their identity, just as do Odette, Swann, or Vinteuil's little phrase. For Proust maintains as the one essential condition of any work of art that the artist must have kept alive within himself a sense of the mystery implicit in all life. The artist is by definition the man who has not allowed "the heavy curtain of habit" to fall between himself and life; nor the veil, no less heavy despite its apparent transparency, of intellectual generalization. Proust believes that the process of creation begins precisely at the point where abstract thought stops. It does not reinforce intelligence. It explains nothing. The artist simply observes and transcribes. And the authenticity of this transcription is guaranteed only by the sincerity with which the artist has entered into contact with life and has felt its mystery. Artists see the god no matter what disguise he may assume. That is to say, they grasp not only the particular aspects of a landscape, an emotion, or a human being, but also perceive in them something more universal than they which can, like the god, don other disguises. Proust qualifies this vision as "poetic." If the artist seeks to produce a work of art, it is because he has no other way of showing us the god.

A work of art thus derives all its poetic value from the fact that it persistently suggests the existence of a mysterious presence behind everything we perceive. This is particularly true in *A la Recherche du Temps perdu*. Every person or object in it is a "sign," an "undecipherable hieroglyphic." Proust does not explain the nature of the mysterious presence behind them, for the very explanation would destroy it. On the poetic level, he says, it is akin to the essence of things, their ideal "archetypes"; on the intellectual level it is apparent in "laws," the operation of which can be observed but which themselves remain inexplicable; on the emotional level it is manifested in the "joyful sensations." The formal structure of a work of art points to that presence. Proust's narrator proposes the hypothesis that these formal artistic structures correspond to the mysterious, human, presence of an "individual soul" different in substance from the body. The soul, spiritual in its essence, would not be subject to the limitations of matter, and consequently time, and would be eternal. But Proust, like his narrator, is careful not to commit himself on the subject. He presents only the secular mystery of the work of art, the structure of which, according to him, suggests that there exists a deep and happy harmony between the life of the individual man, the life of men through the ages, and the existence of the world. He does not go beyond this suggestion. His world is close to being symbolic, and sometimes even allegorical; but nothing in it, except occasionally and by chance, is symbol or allegory because Proust never defines precisely the relation that exists between the tangible world and the "other world," except as art reveals it. He throws about each object and individual a whole network of possible relations, thereby suggesting that everything is a "gateway to the unknown," an unknown that remains unattainable. Curiously enough, critics who have studied Proust's novel have insisted on his talent for analysis, not on the poetic vision which he makes the very condition of art. Yet poetic vision pervades his entire work, orients it both as a whole and in detail, and unifies it. The aura of poetry clearly distinguishes *A la Recherche du Temps perdu* from the realistic novels, as well as from the novels of psychological analysis. There is not one detail in the book which does not derive significance from its relation to some aspect of the whole work, an aspect which in turn is tied up with Proust's poetic vision. Composition and style are simply the means whereby Proust constructs a novel organically bound to the general vision from which it originated.

However meticulous, however precious Proustian descriptions may occasionally appear to the reader, they are never gratuitous, never included merely for decorative effect. Nor are they composed simply to create an appearance of reality. Apple trees in bloom bear in their wake the sea and all the seasons, Japanese prints and women's clothes, spring loves and their atmospheric variations. The magic lantern, the kaleidescope, the plates decorated with scenes of the Arabian nights come out of Combray and take as long a journey through the novel as the scent of the madeleine, bearing with them a quantity of associations. We think of the long, minutely detailed description of Tante Léonie's lime-blossom tea, one of the most precious that the novel contains, with the notable exception of the descriptive variations Albertine executes on the theme of ice cream:

The drying of the stems had twisted them into a fantastic trellis in the intervals of which the pale flowers opened, as though a painter had arranged them in the most decorative poses. The leaves, having altered or lost their own appearance, assumed instead those of the most incongruous things imaginable, as though the transparent wings of flies or the blank sides of labels or the petals of roses had been collected and pounded together, or interwoven as birds weave their nests. A thousand trifling little details—the charming prodigality of the chemist—details which would have been eliminated from a manufactured preparation, gave me, like a book in which one is astonished to find the name of a person whom one knows, the pleasure of finding that these were indeed real lime-blossoms, like those I had seen in the Avenue de la Gare, different not because they were imitations, but because these were the very same blossoms grown old. And as each new character is merely a metamorphosis of an older one, in these little gray balls I recognized green buds plucked before their time. But it was especially the rosy, moon-like, tender glow which lit up the blossoms like little golden roses among the frail forest of stems from which they hung . . . that showed me that these petals which flowered within the chemist's package were the ones which before had embalmed spring evenings. Their color was still that of rosy candle-light, but half extinguished and deadened in the diminished life, a twilight of flowers, which was now theirs. My aunt was presently ready to dip a little madeleine in the boiling infusion, in which she relished the savour of dead or faded blossoms, and she would hold out a piece of the madeleine to me when it was soft enough.[2]

What do the dried-out lime blossoms foreshadow if not the final vision of the Guermantes reception, and the twilight of those gods disguised as fools into which the Proustian characters are metamorphosed by time? They evoke also the evolution of everything in time: the dried-out lime-blossoms recall the "dried-out and naked images"[3] of Saint Mark in Venice, the death of all things in the dessication of memory, leaving only the arid heart which, for example, so cuts Swann off from life. The description also by analogy calls to mind the process of involuntary memory. It unites the image of the lime trees with the thousands of little twigs in the pharmacist's bag, just as involuntary memory evokes the slim Gilberte of Tansonville at the side of the fat Paris lady. This juxtaposition of two phases in the life of the "tilleul" is tied to the main theme of the whole novel, for it suggests the enigma which the narrator encounters—that of a unity apparent beneath a metamorphosis, the always recognizable unity of the lime-blossoms; in short, it raises the question of essence.

Proust certainly runs his risks, and it is interesting to see how close he comes to allegory in this instance without quite falling into it. Even the lime infusion does not turn into a symbol. Proust draws no moral from the story, nor does he formulate the relations that bind it to the novel as a whole. It is solely the words themselves which suggest these bonds. When the narrator rediscovers Combray in the taste of a madeleine, it is in a madeleine soaked in tea. The slight qualification suffices to keep the lime-blossom tea autonomous; so far it represents nothing except itself, yet, by analogy it brings to mind at the same time the major themes of the novel. The rôle of the Proustian "comme" is always essential to his descriptions. By the abundant use he makes of it, Proust is able to evoke around and inside his world all possible ramifications without ever committing his novel to any one; its integrity is intact. Everything in his world is interrelated and reverberates from the realm of sensitivity to the intellectual, emotional, or moral realm, but the correspondences are never really defined.

When Proust defines the will, he describes it as the "faithful servant, persevering and inflexible, of our successive personalities" which "hidden in the shadows, overlooked, tirelessly faithful," works "continually and without heeding our ego to see to it that we never lack what is necessary to us." [4] The description recalls the major theme of the novel, the theme of an artistic vocation: without the narrator's realizing it, and while he believes "he is wasting his time," he patiently accumulates in his subconscious the materials he needs, those from which he will construct his opus. The "faithful servant" also recalls Françoise, by a "crosspath" the humble virtues of Combray, and behind them their incarnation in the statues of the church of Saint-André-des-Champs. The correspondence is not accidental: "It is true that something within me knew," says the narrator, "the part played by beliefs: it was my will. But the will knows it in vain if intelligence and sensitivity continue not to know it." [5] Françoise lives by certain obscure and well-defined beliefs with which she refutes all the gibes and arguments of the narrator. But Françoise is not at all confined within this particular relationship; she overflows it with all the authority of her "dazzling, stiff, and fragile bonnet" [6] and the other thousand aspects of her personality. Proust continually suggests to us similar parallels. He compares to neurasthenics the water-lily on the Vivonne which, carried by the current, always pursues the same ill-fated course, and Tante Léonie springs to mind; she pops up again in Albertine's lover, like her, shut up in a room, and whose mind oscillates like the water-lily to a strong inner current of jealousy. And when Proust describes the im-

pressions which listening to Vinteuil's sonata produces, all the
words bring us back to the walks of Combray:

> As, in a stretch of country which we suppose to be strange to us
> and which as a matter of fact we have only approached from a
> new angle, we find ourselves, after turning out of one road,
> emerging suddenly upon another every inch of which is familiar
> but which we have not been in the habit of entering from that
> end, we say to ourselves immediately: "Why, this is the piece of
> land that leads to the garden gate of my friends the X's; I shall
> be there in a minute," and there, indeed, is their daughter at the
> gate, come out to greet us as we pass; so, all of a sudden, in
> the midst of all this unknown music, I found myself right in the
> heart of Vinteuil's sonata.[7]

> Since the next day was Sunday, with no need to be up and stir-
> ring before high mass, my father would, if it were a warm moon-
> light night, take us for a long walk. In his thirst for personal
> distinction, he would lead us round by the Calvary, for my
> mother's utter incapacity for taking her bearings, or even for
> knowing what road she might be on, made her regard this as a
> triumph of strategic genius . . .
> Suddenly my father would bring us to a standstill and ask
> my mother "Where are we?" Exhausted by the walk, but still
> proud of her husband, she would lovingly confess that she had
> not the least idea. He would shrug his shoulders and laugh. And
> then, as though he had slipped it out of his waistcoat pocket along
> with his latchkey, he would point out to us, right in front of us,
> the back gate of our own garden; it had come, hand-in-hand with
> the familiar corner of the Rue du Saint-Esprit, to await us, to
> greet us at the end of our wanderings over unknown paths.[8]

The reader has many occasions during the course of the
novel to admire the "strategic genius" of Proust. Over and
over, at the end of long detours, the familiar world of Combray suddenly appears, until we come back to it entirely at
the Guermantes reception when the narrator reads the words
"François le Champi." We are also in close touch with the
narrator's own life, for it is when—like his mother during the
walks—he thinks himself far away from Combray that, tast-

ing the madeleine, he sees the door of memory spring open and suddenly finds himself in the heart of Combray, the "smallest nooks" of which are familiar to him. A point of view crystallizes out of all these connections, one which is independent of the sonata, of the walk, and of what they evoke in common. It connects us once again with the ideas organized around Proust's key words "known" and "unknown"; for everything in the Proustian world is, like Swann, at once partly known and unknown.

A multitude of these examples can be cited. No study of Proust's style can rise above the level of a mere examination of detail unless it is related to the vision which organizes the whole novel, for everything continually refers to it. Proust himself, as usual, gives us fair warning; his narrator asserts that "style, for the writer as well as for the painter, is not a question of technique, but of vision." [9] His own vision is characterized by his extraordinary ability to distinguish the relations between impressions which originate objectively, in nature, men, or art, and the moods of an inner life, emotional intellectual, or moral. This capacity is undoubtedly reinforced by the astonishing memory which struck Proust's intimate friends as so remarkable; apparently every impression awakened in him a thousand latent memories. "What we call reality," says the narrator, "is a certain relation between sensations and memories . . . a unique relation which the writer must rediscover in order to bind together these two different factors forever in his sentence." [10] We may dispute the generality which the narrator gives this assertion, and the dictatorial "must," but not its exactness as far as the Proustian style is concerned. It is no wonder, then, that in Proust's novel it is impossible to isolate the setting, the milieu, or the characters; they are all interrelated, all merged.

However, a style of this sort does not necessarily make a novel, and there are moments when the profusion of interrelations established from one point to another makes the reader lose the general outline of the work from which these connections originate. Proust's habit of turning back and grouping around one of these relationships all the possible extensions and analogies suggested by the whole novel sometimes changes the initial proportions of the text, obscures its sense, and baffles the reader, who begins to wonder just where Proust is taking him. Nonetheless, it is this very profusion which prevents the book from becoming a symbolist or allegorical novel, two extremities toward which it tends. This tendency recalls Proust's literary youth, spent in an atmosphere of symbolism, although rather on the margin of its small cliques and sanctums.

The Proustian style gives the Proustian world its depth, its autonomy, and its unity, as well as its meaning. For it is itself the incarnation of the rationale which presided over the genesis of that world. Because of Proust's concept of style, his novel recalls those geometric figures in which any point leads by various lines to all the others. Almost every page plays to some extent the rôle of the madeleine: a world springs into being. Except in the parts in which, harassed by time, Proust did not complete his text, and in which his attention wavers, his novel is carefully thought out down to the smallest detail. That there are lapses in the course of the execution of such a work is not surprising. It is surprising, on the other hand, to observe the extent to which the Proustian vision subjugates the whole novel so that its broad outlines sustain the weight of the secondary developments which Proust makes them bear. And it is rather astonishing to find that critics have so often praised the subtlety rather than the power of Proust's intelligence. The magnitude of his achievement in the objective, conscious construction of such a novel indisputably manifests this power. For if the experience related in it and the point of view it promulgates are subjective, the structure of the work is conceived objectively and with the greatest mastery.

It is primarily and beyond question a novel. The narrator's work becomes possible only when he grasps, both subjectively and objectively the concrete reality of Time. He recognizes that time is inseparable from human reality, and indeed essential to it; it is from this angle that he will start to work. His own life, and that of those around him, appears to him in the form of a story which unfolds in time and is fashioned by time. The essential characteristic of that protean genre, the novel, is that it tells the story of one or several lives unfolding in time; the narrator is obviously not a poet, a painter, or a musician, but a novelist. Proust's work meets this requirement for a novel because it relates the story of a fictional life which unfolds in time; the narrator himself becomes a novelist because the reality which finally impresses itself upon him and which he wishes to communicate is that of the rôle of time in human life. *A la Recherche du Temps perdu* is constructed in conformity with the same basic idea, that of Time molding an individual life.

The narrator tells how he discovered his vocation, which is to transcribe in a work of art the essence of human experience as he discovers it in himself. The difficulties which he encounters do not arise from literature but from the reality he seeks; for it is this reality which will impose its own form upon his work, and determine its content. His vocation as a novelist exists and can be realized only in terms of this discovery. True, according to Proust, of any work of art, it seems that this relationship with reality is particularly true of the novel. For the novel has no pre-established form and need conform to no such exigencies as a metric system, a stage, a musical notation, or a plane surface. The form of the novel can only be imposed by its substance. Proust's narrator tells the tale of his search for the substance of his work; it is a search through life and not through art. The search ends only with the realization of the enigmatic quality of time— that constructive and destructive Janus, eternal and ephemeral, so essential to the novel. The discovery is not in itself remarkable any more than are the narrator's observations about time, which are common knowledge. Much more interesting is the fact that Proust constructed his novel in relation to these observations, and on so vast a scale. In this respect it is not Proust's thought that is extraordinary, but the scope and the originality it confers upon his novel.

The same is true of the form which Proust gives, for example, to the tale of Swann's love for Odette, or the narrator's for Albertine. To say that love creates its own universe, its seasons, its climate, and its time; to say that it is a subjective phenomenon which clashes with objective reality and leads to disappointment; to say that as love grows it makes the lover blind to everything that does not relate to it—all this is not very new. Far more extraordinary is the story of Swann's love, every sentence of which embraces these points of view and magically individualizes them. The manner in which love gradually isolates Swann and detaches the figure of Odette from the Verdurin milieu; the manner in which Swann weaves a whole dream about her person; the unconscious slipping into disappointment and jealousy; the "decrystallization" of love and finally the complete curve of that love as it is inscribed in time: it is this whole story, and the character of Swann, himself, which is infinitely powerful, rather than the analysis it contains.

Thought is, however, integral and necessary to the novel. Proust thinks that what is real in human experience is hidden from consciousness. His narrator discovers that he is an artist, and is made aware that his rôle is to make this hidden reality visible to men. Hence it is natural that the story of his life is that of a subjective search which unfolds in time. He is one of the knights-errant of art. His adventure is spiritual and hence its meaning emerges only through meditation; it is lived, then thought over as it remains in memory. His reflections, however, do not explain his adventure, which derives from life and ends only when he has succeeded in deciphering the enigma which life proposes to him. The rôle assigned to thought in the novel is actually the rôle which, according to Proust, belongs to the intellect in artistic creation. The artist does not invent; but he reads what life has written within himself, the original and inexplicable data which it offers to his intellect. *A la Recherche du Temps perdu* is an account of the formation of a personal philosophy.

Proust does, however, take advantage of what he conceives to be universal in all human experience, and allows his narrator vast powers of generalization. Upon the basis of the particular world which Proust constructs for him, the narrator generalizes; he wants to give a universal significance to the way in which he has found meaning and balance in his own life. This is in itself a vicious circle which tends to weaken the analytical part of the novel. Not content with making the narrator formulate the "laws" which rule the particular world created in harmony with these laws, Proust claims, through the narrator, that these laws apply to the total experience of man. Many of the aphorisms and "laws" which are sprinkled through the novel are therefore subject to question, and are indeed already dated, as are certain of the psychological and medical explanations he gives. Descriptive analysis is often only the means whereby the narrator's mind gropes toward that truth which the intellect can apprehend and strip of its contingencies, but cannot discover. Proust sometimes, however, substitutes for this individual search an explanatory analysis which imposes its dictates upon the objective world; demonstration is substituted for creation, and the Proustian world momentarily staggers. This is particularly true of *La Prisonnière* and *Albertine disparue*. The tendency is all the more dangerous because Proust's experience of human beings may sometimes seem narrow, special, and limited.

Yet here also the structure of the novel sets up its guard rails. The narrator alone is involved in the decrees of reason, the absolute Proustian judgments which are halfway between condemnation and admonition. The Proustian world is not smothered by them because Proust, however close he may be to the narrator, remains distinct from him. It is not the narrator who has created the characters he judges. His judgments, however general they may be, however solemn, are only those of one fictional character among many others.

When the narrator, prefixing his aphorisms with a "we" or a "one" tries to extend to our lives the conclusions which he has drawn from his, we can perfectly easily take exception to them without shaking the foundations of the Proustian world. The reader may well profit from them, for the stretches of meditative speculation often initiate a whole train of thought in the reader relevant to his own experience. He thus participates directly in the evaluation of the Proustian universe, which is bound to his own by the problems posed to the narrator and the solutions he proposes. But the behavior of Proustian characters throws more light on the novel than do the narrator's rather moralizing and pompous judgments on human nature. Their idiosyncrasies break the vicious circle which sometimes seems to enclose the Proustian world, a circle within which the author, Proust, creates a world according to certain ideas and then makes one of the characters draw from that world the principles according to which it was formed. This would have considerably weakened the power of the novel. And then, too, the very copiousness of the analysis and its often hypothetical character destroy the danger of too systematic an abstraction, of a novel with a psychological or moral thesis.

The stature and the mystery of Proust's characters derive largely from the manner in which he presents them and fills them out in the course of the novel. Plucked by the narrator's memory from the semi-darkness which surrounds him, almost all of them appear first of all simply by name. Then they advance into view, observed objectively, like Swann coming forward in the garden in Combray. Sometimes they are only sketched, sometimes minutely described, like the Duchesse de Guermantes or Charlus. And each sketch or description has a specific meaning within the framework of the novel. The Proust who describes Charlus' costume with such precision can honestly claim that he never gives unnecessary details; everything in the description is significant. So great—too great sometimes—is the force with which Proust emphasizes the meaning of his descriptions that he sometimes seems over-insistent to the reader. Swann coming forward in the shadows of the garden personifies the mystery of all individuals seen from the outside. Charlus is frankly the homosexual in disguise, but what human being is there who is not, like him, in disguise? Side by side with the first sketches of the characters the narrator places others, many others, drawn from different moments of the past. They only very occasionally include allusions to the "future"; almost always the surprise of future rôles is kept in reserve. Proust describes simultaneously the Swann of the Combray garden and the Swann of the Jockey Club, and then evokes the Swann in love with Odette; but he keeps in reserve the Hebrew prophet of the soirée at the Princesse de Guermantes. He sketches Charlus seated next to Odette, and his elegant youth; but he does not permit the reader to foresee the Charlus of the second stay in Balbec, or the one who frequents Jupien's house.

Although the basic autonomy of the characters emerges from these multiple descriptions, they elude us just as they elude the rationalization of the narrator who describes them. All Proust's characters, even when they are secondary, are introduced to us in this way: ephemeral from the very moment of their appearance, they remain elusive, like their future. They resemble those genii in fairy tales who change shape every time they are on the point of being captured; their stories are those of their metamorphoses. They appear intermittently, and each time the narrator minutely analyzes their motives, throwing upon them the spotlight of his impersonal view. He sees them clearly, but from the outside, so that their actions, their gestures, and their words are judged from his own point of view, and in a restricted, strangely lit segment of their lives—in the course of a dinner or a reception, for example. Between each of these spotlighted segments stretch great zones of shadow, the obscurity of their inner lives. Each of their appearances presents anew the problem of their personalities. From the landmarks which Proust gives us, we may discern the general curve of their lives: Odette's life is that of a successful demimondaine; Charlus' life, that of a homosexual more and more obsessed. But nothing ever foretells the particular form the characters will take at each point of this curve. The reader no more foresees in Odette the old lady mumbling in a corner of the drawing room than he deducts from the existence of the *"dame en rose"* that of Mlle Sacripant or of Odette de Crécy, wife of the old provincial aristocrat, the Comte de Crécy.

Proust allows his characters a dimension of the unknown into which they escape. It is supplied by his concept of time, which allows the past to loom up in the present so that the various revisions which time makes during the course of a single individual life may be viewed simultaneously. The multiplicity of images elicited in the reader's mind by each character flouts any intellectual endeavor to pin any one of them down; the character asserts itself, and at the same time escapes us. Proust's characters challenge the reader's imagination and understanding. Furthermore, the appearance of unexpected versions of one character, like one of the appearances of Mlle Sacripant, gives the reader a slight intellectual shock, a surprise which provokes in him a pleasure akin to laughter.

When we consider all the pain these inexhaustibly various versions of each character cause the other characters in the novel, we realize that Proust's work here fulfills one of the essential functions of literature. For in these images he reconstitutes one aspect of the human drama, the suffering caused by the impenetrability of others and, without sweetening it, renders it acceptable, a natural part of the human condition. He ameliorates it by making it impersonal, and by "representing" it with insight and within a structure satisfying to the mind.

No Proustian character is isolated or unique. Each is bound to other characters who surround him, and who reflect certain aspects of his personality. But these families of characters are as numerous for each individual as are the aspects of his own character, so that none is ever enclosed within a "type." A secondary character like Legrandin, for example, takes his place with the Proustian "snobs," a pale reflection of Swann, of the narrator, of Bloch, and of so many others; through his homosexuality he joins Saint-Loup whom he resembles outwardly, the Baron de Charlus, and, indeed, a whole Proustian population; through his literary vocation he is part of a whole company of would-be artists who are failures, or incomplete artists: Ski, the baron, Swann. Each principal character is thus doubled, tripled, quadrupled by a whole series of secondary Legrandins, as well as many others paler than he. The narrator reminds us of Swann in his worldly career and his loves; he accedes at the end to the family of creators, Elstir, Vinteuil, Bergotte; physically, he resembles Andrée. Charlus is flanked at different moments of his life by doubles whose changing character puts into relief the path which he pursues: young men of the high aristocracy at the Phoenix club; society women in the drawing-rooms of the Faubourg St. Germain; Morel and Jupien; hooligans from the Paris gutters. This play with mirrors gives for each character a series of reflections, each a little distorted, which are variations of his own species. In this way the individual goes beyond his own individuality, and is related to a general type. But he is never merely an example of that type, for he always evokes in addition a multitude of other characteristics. Charlus is not the prototype of the homosexual. He is the Baron de Charlus, a great lord like his brother, the Duc de Guermantes, or like Monsieur, the brother of Louis XIV; he is a scholar and an artist, like Swann. No Proustian character entirely exemplifies one species. He suggests several, and Proust gathers about him other individuals of the various species to which he belongs, who again are never simply doubles. Each character has infinite possibilities; he remains enigmatic and complex by virtue of all the ties which link him, quite humanly, to a great many other people. The Proustian vision is determined here by Proust's marked conviction that in every individual there exists a general humanness which is greater than he, but of which he is a unique specimen.

The situations in which the characters find themselves are also reflected and reverberated throughout the novel, without ever being exactly duplicated: Charlus with Odette, at Swann's at Tansonville; the narrator with Gilberte, at Saint-Loup's at Tansonville; Swann and Odette in the Verdurins' drawing room, Charlus and Morel in the Verdurins' drawing room. The two great social events of the novel, which are like two great thresholds, are the two receptions at the Princesse de Guermantes': the soirée which marks the narrator's arrival at the heart of the Faubourg St. Germain and the concert given by the Princesse de Guermantes which marks his last appearance in that world. But at the second reception the Princesse has changed and, with her, the guests. In the detail of the situations as well as the whole, there are everywhere configurations which recall one another but which are in no case superimposed. They give the reader a pleasure similar to the one he experiences in seeing the characters reappear, the same pleasure the narrator feels in discovering in Vinteuil's septet the little phrase of the sonata.

The accumulation of these situations gives the reader the clear feeling that there is, in the lives of all these characters, some principle which is not subject to their wills and their consciousness, a principle outside themselves which carries them along. It is not they who lead their lives, but life which leads them along the well-trodden human paths. They are predestined, but their predestination is not so much idiosyncratic or linked with what is unique about them, as the result of their human condition as Proust conceives it. They do not feel any limitations in life, which is much vaster than they are; they do not oppose their fates. In the Proustian world there is no conflict between art and nature, any more than there is between man and his "human condition." The human condition is what defines men, and art makes this definition visible. That is why the limitations of the Proustian world matter so little. For this world projects rays from all sides similar to the beams of a searchlight; the beams may be mere slits at the starting point, but they continually broaden out as we watch them. Proust illuminates simultaneously the unique complexity of each human life, like that of the narrator, and the numerous general "laws" which link it with other lives. But these abstract laws never replace Swann or Charlus, for example, never explain them. They only throw between these characters and other individuals innumerable bonds which humanize and extend them. Swann and Charlus, and all the other Proustian characters are not universal types; neither their lives nor their destinies are exemplary. Proust is content simply to link them to the whole human order; the narrator's search through himself and others is thus the search for this human order, which is concealed from the individual by his apparent isolation.

Everything in the Proustian universe converges toward the revelation, beneath all its disguises, of a general human truth. Proust always compares human beings to portraits by great artists which superimpose upon human individuality an esthetic individuality. Proustian characters consequently derive their value, not from themselves, but from that quality of "sign" with which they are thus endowed. It detaches them from the narrow limits of their individual existence and gives them the "poetic" and universal aura which, according to Proust, characterizes the whole domain of art.

A la Recherche du Temps perdu is not, however, a metaphysical novel. Although Proust's outlook on the world unquestionably involves an intellectual depth which rarely finds expression in novels and seems more suitable to the essay, Proust did not write his book in order to illustrate his philosophy. His intellect is simply the means by which he organizes his work and gives it its substance. His ideas are always at the service of Swann, Odette, Charlus, the Verdurins, and the Guermantes, and not vice-versa. Proust makes use of the ideas which he distilled from his own life to give his novel an esthetic structure which permits him, within the limits of literature, to bring a world to life with the maximum truth.

It so happens that in order to do this he used almost all the themes which had begun to preoccupy his contemporaries: the problem of personality in all its facets, and in particular the problem of the subconscious with the associated problem of the relation of morals to social life and sexuality, which had been made so prominent by the works of Charcot and Freud; the problem of time and duration which Bergson had made the order of the day; and closely allied to it, the problem of the nature of man which gave rise to the reaction against materialism; the problem of the creative role of the spirit, and that of the meaning of art, as well as many others which *A la Recherche du Temps perdu* brings up in its wake. But far more remarkable than Proust's intellectual conclusions themselves, from which it is dangerous to deduct a system, for they are marked by fluctuation and contradiction, is the fact that he developed a new and conscious esthetic form for the novel. The novel has no technical limitations other than those imposed upon any written matter: it must consist of words inscribed on the surfaces of successive pages. Proust defines the creative principle which gives its form to the novel: it is an individual grasp of a meaning in life derived from the author's personal experience. For him the novel is not simply a story; it is a story consciously told from a given point of view which determines the very structure of that story. The story, however, pre-exists the point of view. This is, in itself, certainly nothing new. What is new is the complexity of the point of view, and the lucidity with which, without sacrificing that complexity, Proust deliberately constructs a world. The structure of his novel breaks the linear "chain" development of the story. Proust no longer assumes, as did the realistic writer, at least in theory, that his novel is an imitation of reality. His esthetic theory claims for the novel the right to be instead, like music or poetry, a recreation of reality. The world of objects, of commonplace accepted general notions, of simple causalities disintegrates, and in its place slowly rises an edifice free from the servitude of realism. Proust successfully liberated the novel from the traditions inherited from the nineteenth century.

Proust's anxiety to base the esthetics of his novel upon a general human truth, a personal knowledge of life, and his ambition to create a microcosm, the structure of which would be in itself an idea, are both characteristic of his time. We can distinguish in his work the two great temptations of the contemporary novel: to delete the story from the novel to the advantage of metaphysics, making it an essay in concrete metaphysics, and to project a closed and autonomous world so subjective that the reader no longer knows how to penetrate it. These two tendencies are checkmated in Proust because he has an acute sense both of the objective presence of the real and of the "ideal," unique unity of the spirit. This sense permits him to erect his world on concrete foundations, and suggests the sturdy, inventive, and original scaffolding from which the novel derives its unity. It is almost always the secondary aspects of his work which have been imitated: the predominance of psychological analysis; the concern about homosexuality; the contamination of the novel by metaphysics; the poorly dissimulated autobiography. And yet the power of this work arises from Proust's astonishing ability to subordinate everything, story, characters, thought, erudition, and style, to the creation of a world which makes its impact because of its unity. The characters he creates are unlike any other group in fiction. They remain distinct in the imagination, mysterious and recognizable, belonging entirely to the coherent world which surrounds and supports them. This world is certainly strange, yet by virtue of its inner resonances it remains forever open to ours. Its power as a creation can only be measured by the shock the reader receives in his first contact with a work for which nothing prepares him, so unforeseeable is everything in it.

The fictional universe of *A la Recherche du Temps perdu,* created at the beginning of the twentieth century, dominates the literature of our time by its power, its originality, and its beauty. And we may echo of Proust himself what the narrator says apropos of those authors who, "watching themselves at work as though they were both the workman and the judge, reaped from this contemplation a unique and autonomous beauty, superior to the work itself . . ."

1871   Marcel Proust was born in Paris on July 10 in the
        house of his maternal uncle, Louis Weil, at 96 rue
        de la Fontaine, in Auteuil. His father, Dr. Adrien
        Proust, a native of Illiers, in Beauce, had originally
        intended to become a priest but, though he re-
        tained his deep religious interests, dedicated him-
        self instead to the study of medicine. House sur-
        geon, then head of clinic, in 1884 he became in-
        spector of the French Service of Hygiene, and in
        1885 professor of the Faculté de Médecine; he
        took part in several international meetings on sani-
        tation. Proust's mother, Jeanne Weil, of Jewish
        origin, from Lorraine, had a deep influence on her
        son. Intelligent, cultivated, she was scrupulous and
        exacting in all that concerned moral principles.
        The closely knit family, who belonged to the well-
        to-do middle class of Paris, lived at 9, Boulevard
        Malesherbes. Although brought up a Catholic,
        Marcel Proust was always in close touch with his
        mother's family. His childhood was divided be-
        tween the house in the Boulevard Malesherbes, the
        Champs Elysées, where he played, and the house
        of his father's sister, Madame Amiot, in Illiers.
1873   Birth of Robert Proust, Marcel's brother and future
        surgeon.
1880   First attack of asthma.
1882–1889 Rewarding and active years at the Lycée Condor-
        cet: became intimate with Daniel Halévy, Fernand
        Gregh, Jacques Bizet, Robert de Flers, Jacques
        Baignères, Louis de la Salle, etc.; contributed to
        the school magazine, *La Revue Lilas;* singled out

by philosophy professor Darlu whose influence on him was a lasting one; began to frequent society, in particular the salons of Madame Émile Strauss and of Madeleine Lemaire.

1889 Received his baccalaureate. Spent his year as a volunteer in the 76th Infantry Regiment in Orleans, where he struck up a friendship with Robert de Billy and Gaston de Caillavet; went to Madame Arman de Caillavet's salon where he met Anatole France.

1890–1896 Period of great social activity and literary beginnings.

1891–1893 Continued his studies at the École des Sciences Politiques, at the Law School, and at the Sorbonne, where he attended courses given by Bergson. Began to make an appearance in the salons of the Faubourg St. Germain; met Reynaldo Hahn who became one of his intimate friends.

1892–1893 Appearance of first literary essays in *Le Banquet*.

1893 Start of his relationship with Count Robert de Montesquiou, which, with all its ups and downs, lasted until the Count's death in 1921.

1893–1896 Several of his articles and stories published by *La Revue Blanche*.

1895 Trip to St. Moritz, Normandy, and Brittany. Passed competitive examination for attaché to the Bibliothèque Mazarine (but never occupied post).

1895–1899 Period of apparent inactivity: declining health and diminishing social activities; wrote his unfinished novel which was to be posthumously published as *Jean Santeuil*.

1896 Publication of *Les Plaisirs et les Jours*, with preface by Anatole France, illustrations by Madeleine Lemaire, and music by Reynaldo Hahn.

1897 Duel with Jean Lorrain.

1898 Followed the Dreyfus affair with passionate and pro-Dreyfus interest.

1899 Discovered and began to translate Ruskin; became keenly interested in French cathedrals and read works of Émile Male.

1900   Family moved from Boulevard Malesherbes to 45
            rue de Courcelles. Death of Ruskin. Publication of
            "Pèlerinages ruskiniens en France" (*Le Figaro,*
            January 13). Trip to Venice and Padua (May) ac-
            companied by his mother, where he found Reynaldo
            Hahn and Miss Nordlinger, who helped him correct
            the proofs of his translation of *The Bible of Amiens.*
1902   Period of poor health; rarely left his bed.
1903   Death of father, Dr. Adrien Proust, November 26.
1903–1905   Articles by him published in *Le Figaro.*
1904   Publication of *The Bible of Amiens.*
1905   "On Reading" published in *Renaissance Latine*
            June 15. Trip to Evian with Madame Robert Proust,
            who was seriously ill with uremia (August–Septem-
            ber) ; death of Madame Proust in Paris (Septem-
            ber 26).
1905   Entered (December) Dr. Sollies' nursing home but
            remained less than a month. Publication of his
            translation of Ruskin's *Sesame and Lilies.* Began
            the critical study published posthumously as *Contre
            Sainte Beuve.*
1906   Established himself at 102 Boulevard Haussmann
            (with the walls of his room lined with cork) where
            he remained until 1919.
1907   Wrote a large part of *A la Recherche du Temps
            perdu* which he probably began in this year. Pub-
            lished several articles in *Le Figaro.* Stayed at Ca-
            bourg (August) ; trips by automobile to Caen,
            Bayeux, Lixieux, etc., with his chauffeur, Agosti-
            nelli; published "Impressions de route en automo-
            bile" in *Le Figaro,* November 12.
1908   Apparently worked again on the novel to which he
            had been referring over a period of years.
1909   In the autumn, locked himself up in his apartment
            to devote himself entirely to his novel; rarely went
            out and then usually at night to meet his friends,
            preferably at the Ritz.
1912   Agostinelli became Proust's secretary.
1913   Céleste Albaret became Proust's housekeeper. Un-
            successful negotiations with Fasquelle, *La Nouvelle*

Revue Française, and Ollendorf, to publish his book. Publication at author's expense agreed to by Bernard Grasset (March 13) ; publication of *Du Côté de chez Swann* (November).

1914   Agostinelli, enrolled in an aviation school at Antibes under the name of Marcel Swann, was killed in an airplane accident (May 30).

1914–1918   Remained in Paris during First World War. Death of his friends, Bertrand de Fénelon (December 17, 1914), and Gaston de Caillavet (January 13, 1916). Revised his novel.

1918   *A l'Ombre des Jeunes Filles en fleurs* published by Gallimard.

1919   Publication of *Pastiches et Mélanges.* Received the Prix Goncourt. Obliged to leave the Boulevard Haussmann; moved to 44 rue Hamelin, where, until his death, he worked doggedly to finish his novel.

1920   *Le Côté de Guermantes* (I) and (II) and *Sodome et Gomorrhe* (I) published.

1922   *Sodome et Gomorrhe* (II) published. Died November 18.

1923–1927   Posthumous publication of the last volumes of his novel: *La Prisonnière* (1923) ; *Albertine disparue* (1925) ; and *Le Temps retrouvé* (1927). NOTE: In the 1954 edition of *A la Recherche du Temps perdu,* the title *Albertine disparue* is replaced by *La Fugitive,* the title Proust used in his manuscript.

1928   Publication of *Chroniques* (Gallimard, Paris).

1952   Publication of *Jean Santeuil* (Gallimard, Paris), an unfinished novel on which he worked immediately after *Les Plaisirs et les Jours.*

1954   Publication of *Contre Sainte-Beuve* followed by *Nouveaux Mélanges.*
            (Most of the above biographical data has been extracted from the biographies of Proust by Professor Harold Marsh and Monsieur André Maurois.)

NOTES

All quotations are translations from the three-volume edition of *A la Recherche du Temps perdu*, N.R.F., Gallimard, Paris, 1947.

CHAPTER I

1. Vol. III, p. 582
2. *Ibid.*, p. 592
3. André Gide, *Journal*, Bibliothèque de la Pléiade, 1939, p. 692
4. Albert Feuillerat, "Comment Marcel Proust a composé son roman," Yale University Press, New Haven, 1934; Robert Vigneron, "Genèse de Swann," *Revue d'histoire de la philosophie* (Lille), January 15, 1937, pp. 67–115
5. *La Table Ronde*, April 1945, no. 2, pp. 30–31 (Les éditions de la Table Ronde, Paris)
6. *Ibid.*
7. *Ibid.*
8. Vol. I, p. 10
9. Vol. II, p. 239
10. *Ibid.*, p. 367
11. *Ibid.*, p. 514
12. Vol. III, p. 325

CHAPTER II

1. Vol. III, p. 631
2. Vol. I, p. 595
3. *Ibid.*, p. 516
4. Vol. II, p. 34
5. *Ibid.*
6. Vol. I, p. 596
7. *Ibid.*, p. 483
8. The image of the "path," the "road," and the "way" reappears in *A la Recherche du Temps perdu* and is manifestly associated with the very theme of the "Search": "the deadly road of knowledge"; "the subterranean paths of grief"; "the path of Time"; "the narrow road of homosexuality"; "the road of Art"; "the paths of memory"; etc.
9. Vol. III, p. 469
10. *Ibid.*
11. Vol. III, p. 564 (*my italics*)
12. *Ibid.*, pp. 564–65 (*my italics*)
13. *Ibid.*, p. 565
14. *Ibid.*
15. Vol. III, p. 566

16. *Ibid.*, pp. 566–67 (*my italics*)
17. *Ibid.*, p. 567
18. *Ibid.*, p. 569
19. *Ibid.*, pp. 571–72
20. *Ibid.*, p. 572
21. *Ibid.*, p. 313
22. Vol. I, p. 652
23. Vol. II, p. 99
24. *Ibid.*, p. 566 (*my italics*)

CHAPTER III

1. These words recur frequently in *Le Temps Retrouvé*, for example, vol. III, pp. 694, 695
2. Vol. II, p. 49
3. Vol. I, p. 321
4. Vol. III, p. 581
5. *Ibid.*, p. 525
6. *Ibid.*, p. 254
7. *Ibid.*, p. 255
8. *Ibid.*, p. 256
9. *Ibid.*, p. 583
10. Vol. II, p. 38
11. Vol. III, p. 684
12. *Ibid.*, p. 607
13. Vol. I, p. 299

CHAPTER IV

1. Vol. I, p. 398
2. *Ibid.*, pp. 468, 517
3. Vol. III, p. 670
4. Vol. I, pp. 484, 485
5. Vol. III, p. 167
6. Vol. I, p. 470
7. *Ibid.*, p. 342
8. *Ibid.*, p. 445
9. *Ibid.*, p. 294
10. *Ibid.*, p. 442
11. *Ibid.*
12. Vol. I, p. 505
13. *Ibid.*, p. 470
14. *Ibid.*, p. 504
15. *Ibid.*, p. 505
16. Vol. II, p. 387
17. *Ibid.*, p. 390
18. *Ibid.*, p. 493
19. *Ibid.*, p. 392
20. *Ibid.*, p. 393
21. *Ibid.*, p. 394
22. *Ibid.*, p. 450
23. *Ibid.*, p. 406
24. *Ibid.*, p. 407
25. *Ibid.*, p. 408
26. *Ibid.*, p. 606
27. *Ibid.*, p. 611
28. Vol. III, pp. 154–55
29. Vol. II, 412

CHAPTER V

1. Vol. I, p. 14
2. *Ibid.*, p. 179
3. *Ibid.*, p. 205
4. Vol. III, p. 589
5. Vol. I, pp. 44–45
6. *Ibid.*, p. 46
7. *Ibid.*, p. 486
8. *Ibid.*, p. 82
9. *Ibid.*, p. 20
10. Vol. III, p. 680
11. Vol. I, p. 53
12. *Ibid.*, p. 92

13. Vol. II, p. 615
14. Vol. I, p. 198
15. Vol. II, p. 17
16. Vol. III, p. 680
17. *Ibid.*, p. 651
18. *Ibid.*, p. 657
19. Vol. I, p. 388
20. *Ibid.*, p. 520
21. *Ibid.*, p. 521
22. Vol. II, pp. 377–84
23. Vol. I, p. 526
24. *Ibid.*, p. 530
25. *Ibid.*, p. 17
26. Vol. II, p. 479
27. Vol. I, p. 188
28. Vol. II, p. 99
29. *Ibid.*, p. 411
30. *Ibid.*, p. 412
31. *Ibid.*, p. 414
32. Vol. III, p. 612
33. *Ibid.*

CHAPTER VI

1. For example: vol. I, p. 628; "It is with her that I shall have my romance." Vol. III, pp. 654, 679: "The sterile romance" which the narrator builds up about Madame de Guermantes.
2. Vol. III, p. 458
3. *Ibid.*, p. 460
4. Vol. I, p. 403
5. *Ibid.*, p. 568
6. *Ibid.*, p. 232
7. *Ibid.*, p. 630
8. Vol. III, p. 348
9. Vol. I, p. 455
10. *Ibid.*, p. 548
11. *Ibid.*, p. 551
12. Vol. II, p. 754
13. Vol. I, p. 550
14. Vol. II, p. 99

CHAPTER VII

1. Vol. III, pp. 418–19
2. *Ibid.*, p. 649
3. *Ibid.*, pp. 432–33
4. *Ibid.*, p. 433
5. *Ibid.*, pp. 456–57
6. *Ibid.*, p. 458
7. *Ibid.*, p. 606
8. *Ibid.*
9. Vol. II, p. 754
10. *Ibid.*
11. *Ibid.*
12. *Ibid.*
13. Vol. III, p. 13
14. *Ibid.*, p. 408
15. Vol. I, p. 389
16. Vol. II, p. 762
17. Vol. III, p. 14
18. *Ibid.*, p. 313
19. *Ibid.*, p. 303 (*my italics*)
20. *Ibid.*
21. Vol. III, p. 9
22. *Ibid.*
23. Vol. III, p. 22
24. *Ibid.*, p. 54
25. *Ibid.*, p. 44
26. *Ibid.*, p. 336
27. Vol. I, p. 490
28. Vol. III, p. 409
29. *Ibid.*, p. 412
30. *Ibid.*, p. 69

31. *Ibid.*, p. 45
32. *Ibid.*, p. 21
33. *Ibid.* (*my italics*)
34. Vol. III, p. 321
35. *Ibid.*, p. 397 (*my italics*)
36. *Ibid.*, p. 398
37. *Ibid.*, p. 417
38. Vol. I, p. 295

CHAPTER VIII

1. Vol. I, p. 9
2. Vol. III, p. 697
3. Vol. I, p. 49
4. Vol. III, p. 613
5. *Ibid.*, pp. 694, 696
6. Vol. I, p. 51
7. Vol. III, pp. 542, 605
8. Vol. I, p. 247
9. *Ibid.*
10. *Ibid.*
11. *Ibid.*
12. Vol. III, p. 290
13. *Ibid.*, p. 585
14. *Ibid.*, p. 171
15. *Ibid.*, p. 172
16. *Ibid.*
17. Vol. III, p. 173
18. *Ibid.*, p. 253
19. *Ibid.*, p. 254
20. *Ibid.*, p. 174
21. *Ibid.*, p. 177
22. *Ibid.*, p. 258
23. *Ibid.*, p. 170
24. *Ibid.*, pp. 170–71
25. *Ibid.*, p. 173
26. *Ibid.*, p. 253
27. Vol. I, p. 63
28. *Ibid.*, p. 32
29. *Ibid.*, p. 573
30. *Ibid.*, p. 575
31. *Ibid.*
32. Vol. I, p. 576
33. *Ibid.*, p. 586
34. *Ibid.*
35. Vol. I, p. 587
36. *Ibid.*
37. Vol. III, p. 688
38. *Ibid.*, pp. 688, 689
39. Vol. I, p. 561
40. *Ibid.*, p. 563
41. Vol. III, p. 604
42. *Ibid.*, p. 695
43. *Ibid.*, p. 531
44. *Ibid.*, p. 21
45. *Ibid.*, p. 11
46. *Ibid.*, p. 590
47. *Ibid.*, p. 696
48. *Ibid.*, p. 597
49. *Ibid.*, p. 581

CHAPTER IX

1. Albert Thibaudet: *Réflexions sur le roman,* N.R.F. Gallimard, 1938, p. 12.
2. Vol. I, p. 42
3. Vol. III, p. 579
4. Vol. I, p. 599
5. *Ibid.*, p. 591
6. *Ibid.*, p. 83
7. Vol. III, pp. 169–70
8. Vol. I, p. 85
9. Vol. III, p. 593
10. *Ibid.*, p. 588

PROUST'S WORKS

French Editions

Les Plaisirs et les jours. Paris: Calmann-Lévy, 1896; reprinted by Gallimard, 1924.

A la recherche du temps perdu. 3 vols. Paris: La Pléiade, Gallimard, 1954.

    Combray. Edited by Germaine Brée and Carlos Lynes, Jr. New York: Appleton-Century-Crofts, 1952.

    Un Amour de Swann. Edited by William S. Bell. New York: Macmillan, 1965.

Pastiches et mélanges. Paris: Gallimard, 1919.

Chroniques. Paris: Gallimard, 1927.

Jean Santeuil. 3 vols. Paris: Gallimard, 1952.

Contre Sainte-Beuve. Préface de Bernard de Fallois. Paris: Gallimard, 1954.

TRANSLATIONS

Ruskin, John. *La Bible d'Amiens.* Paris: Mercure de France, 1904.

    Sésame et les lys. Paris: Mercure de France, 1906.

LETTERS

Choix de lettres. Edited by Philip Kolb. Paris: Plon, 1965.

Correspondance générale. 6 vols. Paris: Plon, 1930-1936.

Correspondance avec sa mère (1881-1905). Paris: Plon, 1953.

A un ami: Correspondance inédite 1903-1922. Préface de Georges de Lauris. Paris: Amiot-Dumont, 1948.

Correspondance de Marcel Proust avec Jacques Rivière. Annotated by Philip Kolb, Paris: Gallimard, 1956.

Lettres à Reynaldo Hahn. Annotated by Philip Kolb. Paris: Gallimard, 1956.

Lettres à André Gide. Neuchâtel and Paris: Ides et Calendes, 1949.

Lettres à la NRF. Les Cahiers Marcel Proust, VI. Paris: Gallimard, 1932.

Lettres à une amie: Recueil de quarante-et-une lettres inédites adressées à Marie Nordlinger, 1899-1908. Manchester: Editions du Calame, 1942.

Kolb, Philip. *La Correspondance de Marcel Proust: Chronologie et commentaire critique.* Urbana: University of Illinois Press, 1949.

English Translations of Proust

Pleasures and Days and Other Writings. Translated by Louise Varèse, Gerard Hopkins, and Barbara Dupee. Edited and with an introduction by F. W. Dupee. Garden City, N.Y.: Anchor Books, 1957.

Remembrance of Things Past. Translated by C. K. Scott-Moncrieff and Frederick A. Blossom. 2 vols. New York: Random House, 1932.

Marcel Proust: A Selection from His Miscellaneous Writings. Translated by Gerard Hopkins. London: Allan Wingate, 1948.

Jean Santeuil. Translated by Gerard Hopkins. New York: Simon & Schuster, 1956.

Marcel Proust on Art and Literature, 1896-1919. Translated by Sylvia Townsend Warner. New York: Meridian, 1958.

The Maxims of Marcel Proust. Translated by Justin O'Brien. New York: Columbia University Press, 1948.

LETTERS

Letters of Marcel Proust. Selected and translated by Mina Curtiss. Introduction by Harry Levin. New York: Random House, 1949.

Marcel Proust: Letters to His Mother. Translated by George D. Painter. New York: Citadel Press, 1957.

Letters to a Friend. Preface by George de Lauris. Translated by Alexander and Elizabeth Henderson. London: Falcon Press, 1949.

SELECTED PROUST BIBLIOGRAPHY

Books and Articles

Abraham, Pierre. *Proust: Recherches sur la création intellectuelle.* Paris: Rieder, 1930.

Alden, Douglas W. *Marcel Proust and His French Critics.* Los Angeles: Lymanhouse, 1940.

Autret, Jean. *L'Influence de Ruskin sur la vie, les idées et l'œuvre de Marcel Proust.* Geneva: Droz, 1955.

Barker, Richard H. *Marcel Proust: A Bibliography.* New York: Criterion, 1958.

Beckett, Samuel. *Proust.* London: Chatto and Windus, 1931; reprinted by Grove Press, New York, 1957.

Bell, William Steward. *Proust's Nocturnal Muse.* New York: Columbia University Press, 1962.

Bersani, Leo. *Marcel Proust: The Fictions of Life and of Art.* New York: Oxford University Press, 1965.

Bonnet, Henri. *Marcel Proust de 1907 à 1914.* Paris: Nizet, 1959.

Brée, Germaine. *The World of Marcel Proust.* London: Chatto & Windus, 1967.

Cattaui, Georges. *Marcel Proust: Documents iconographiques.* Geneva: Pierre Cailler, 1956.

Marcel Proust. Paris: Juillard, 1952.

Proust perdu et retrouvé. Paris: Plon, 1963.

Chernowitz, Maurice Eugene. *Proust and Painting.* New York: International University Press, 1944.

Cocking, J. M. *Proust.* New Haven: Yale University Press, 1956.

Coleman, Elliot. *The Golden Angel: Papers on Proust.* New York: Coley Taylor, 1954.

Dandieu, Arnaud. *Marcel Proust, sa révélation psychologique.* Paris: Firmin-Didot, 1930.

Deleuze, Gilles. *Marcel Proust et les signes.* Paris: Presses Universitaires de France, 1964.

Ferré, André. *Les Années de collège de Marcel Proust.* Paris: Gallimard, 1959.

Feuillerat, Albert. *Comment Marcel Proust a composé son roman.* New Haven: Yale University Press, 1934.

Fowlie, Wallace. *A Reading of Proust.* Garden City, N.Y.: Anchor Books, 1964.

Girard, René, ed. *Proust: A Collection of Critical Essays.* Englewood Cliffs, N.J.: Prentice-Hall, 1962.

Green, F. C. *The Mind of Proust.* Cambridge: Cambridge University Press, 1949.

Guichard, Léon. *Introduction à la lecture de Proust.* Paris: Nizet, 1956.

Hier, Florence. *La Musique dans l'œuvre de Marcel Proust.* New York: Columbia University Press, 1933.

Hindus, Milton. *The Proustian Vision.* New York: Columbia University Press, 1954.

LeSage, Laurent. *Marcel Proust and His Literary Friends.* Urbana: University of Illinois Press, 1958.

Levin, Harry. *The Gates of Horn: A Study of Five French Realists.* New York: Oxford University Press, 1963. Pp. 372-444.

Louria, Yvette. *La Convergence stylistique chez Proust.* Geneva: Droz, 1957.

Lowery, Bruce. *Marcel Proust et Henry James: Une Confrontation.* Paris: Plon, 1964.

March, Harold. *The Two Worlds of Marcel Proust.* Philadelphia: University of Pennsylvania Press, 1948.

Martin-Chauffier, Louis. "Proust and the Double I." *Partisan Review,* XV (1949), 1011-26.

Maurois, André. *A la recherche de Marcel Proust.* Paris: Hachette, 1949. English translation by Gerard Hopkins, *Proust, Portrait of a Genius.* New York: Harper, 1950.

Miller, Milton L. *Nostalgia: A Psychoanalytical Study of Proust.* Boston: Houghton Mifflin, 1956.

Monnin-Hornung, Juliette. *Proust et la peinture.* Geneva: Droz, 1951.

Moss, Howard. *The Magic Lantern of Marcel Proust.* New York: Macmillan, 1962.

Mouton, Jean. *Le Style de Marcel Proust.* Paris: Editions Corrêa, 1948.

Muller, Marcel. *Les Voix narratives dans "A la recherche du temps perdu."* Geneva: Droz, 1965.

Newman, Pauline. *Marcel Proust et l'existentialisme.* Paris: Nouvelles Editions latines, 1953.

Painter, George D. *Marcel Proust: A Biography.* 2 vols. London: Chatto & Windus, 1959, 1965. Published in the U.S. as *Proust: The Early Years* and *Proust: The Later Years.* Boston: Little, Brown, 1959, 1965.

Peyre, Henri. *The Contemporary French Novel.* New York: Oxford University Press, 1955. Pp. 67-101.

Picon, Gaëton. *Lecture de Proust.* Paris: Mercure de France, 1963.

Pierre-Quint, Léon. *Le Combat de Marcel Proust.* Paris: Le Club français du livre, 1955.

Piroué, Georges. *Par les chemins de Marcel Proust: Essai de critique descriptive.* Neuchâtel: La Baconnière, 1955. English translation by Gerard Hopkins, *Proust's Way: An Essay in Descriptive Criticism.* London: Heinemann, 1957.

Poulet, Georges. *L'Espace proustien.* Paris: Gallimard, 1963.

Remacle, Madeleine. *L'Elément poétique dans "A la recherche du temps perdu" de Marcel Proust.* Brussels: Académie royale de langue et de littérature françaises de Belgique, 1954.

Revel, Jean-François. *Sur Proust.* Paris: Juillard, 1960.

Rogers, B. G. *Proust's Narrative Techniques.* Geneva: Droz, 1965.

Shattuck, Roger. *Proust's Binoculars: A Study of Memory, Time and Recognition in "A la recherche du temps perdu."* New York: Random House, 1963.

Strauss, Walter A. *Proust and Literature: The Novelist as Critic.* Cambridge: Harvard University Press, 1957.

Turnell, Martin. *The Novel in France.* London: Hamish Hamilton, 1950. Pp. 317-406.

Vallée, Claude. *La Féerie de Marcel Proust.* Paris: Fasquelle, 1958.

Vigneron, Robert. "Genèse de Swann," *Revue d'Histoire de la Philosophie* (Lille), January 15, 1937, pp. 67-115. Condensed, undocumented translation of this article in *Partisan Review,* VIII (1941), 460-75.

"Marcel Proust ou l'angoisse créatrice," *Modern Philology,* XLII (1945), 212-30.

"Structure de Swann: Balzac, Wagner et Proust," *French Review,* XIX (1946), 370-84.

Wilson, Edmund. *Axel's Castle: A Study in Imaginative Literature of 1870-1930.* New York: Scribner, 1953. Pp. 132-90.

Periodical Publications Devoted to Proust

Marcel Proust: A World Symposium. Adam Internation Review, no. 260. Edited by Miron Grindea. London, 1957.
Bulletin de la Société des amis de Marcel Proust et des amis de Combray, no. 1 — (Illiers, 1951 —).
Les Cahiers Marcel Proust. I-VIII. Paris: Gallimard, 1927-1935.
    I. *Homage à Marcel Proust.*
    II. *Répertoire des personnages de "A la recherche du temps perdu."*
    III. Selections from *In Search of Time Lost.*
    IV. *Au bal avec Marcel Proust.*
    V. *Autour de soixante lettres de Marcel Proust.*
    VI. *Lettres à la NRF. Bibliographie proustienne.*
    VII. *Répertoire des thèmes de Marcel Proust.*
    VIII. *L'Amitié de Proust.*
L'Esprit Créateur, Vol. V, no. 1 (Spring 1965).
Yale French Studies, no. 34 (Summer 1965).

banality. Her thought is dense and often profound, and she claims the reader's patient attention."— Henri Peyre, *The New York Times*

Erich Hartman

Germaine Brée, who was born in the South of France, was preparing her degree in English at the Sorbonne when a friend suggested that she apply for a scholarship in America. She spent a year at Bryn Mawr and returned to the Sorbonne to pass the Agrégation examinations in 1932. After teaching for several years in Oran, Miss Brée accepted a post at Byrn Mawr and she remained there, except for two war years, until 1953. This book first appeared in French in 1950, and in English translation in 1955.

Joining the French Army in 1943, Miss Brée served first as an ambulance driver and later did liaison work. She was awarded the Bronze Star and the Army Commendation Ribbon by the American Army, besides receiving a citation from the French Army.

In 1953 Miss Brée became chairman of the French Department of New York University and the following year was appointed head of the Romance Language Department of its Graduate School. Since 1960 she has been a member of the Institute for Research in the Humanities at the University of Wisconsin.

Other books by Miss Brée include *Camus,* first published in 1959, and brought out in a revised edition in 1961, following Camus's death; *An Age of Fiction: The French Novel from Gide to Camus,* with Margaret Guiton (1957); and *Gide* (1963).